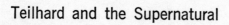

Teilhard and the Supernatural

Teilhard
and the
Supernatural

by
Eulalio R. Baltazar

HELICON
Baltimore—Dublin

Helicon Press, Inc.
1120 N. Calvert Street
Baltimore, Md. 21202

Helicon Limited
20 Upr. Fitzwilliam Street
Dublin 2, Ireland

Library of Congress Catalog Card Number 66-26481

PRINTED IN THE UNITED STATES OF AMERICA BY
GARAMOND/PRIDEMARK PRESS, BALTIMORE, MARYLAND

Preface

The evolution of human thought is by no means always a linear ascent. There are ups and downs. One striking example of retrogression today is the increasing chasm between philosophers and theologians, so that each is less and less familiar with the other discipline. No doubt, the distinction between philosophy and theology introduced by Descartes was a step forward, for it gave to each group their identity. Nevertheless, it was a phase and should not be taken as the normal state of affairs. It was a phase based on the inadequate hellenic assumption that to define is to cut off, that identity lies in separation, not in union. This premise has influenced the development of both philosophy and theology into our own times. Most philosophers and theologians still attempt to work independently of one another until, with increasing frequency, the members of each group are left talking only to themselves. Their advances, if any be made, are of interest only to themselves. It is as if each group had gone into a room and closed the door to the rest of the world. But the truly profound questions, the questions that shake foundations and lead to great advances in human understanding, are provoked most often by the confrontation of disciplines. In science, for example, few great advances are achieved in physics, chemistry, biology, medicine, or nuclear and space efforts without inter-disciplinary exchange of knowledge and insight. And so it is with philosophy and theology. Christian philosophers tend to become sterile when they fail to seek inspiration from the profound truths of revelation which, after all, speak about this world—its beginning, nature and destiny. And theologians cannot solve their problems and arrive at formulations significant for the modern world if they fail to keep in touch with modern philosophy.

If there is to be any progress in Christian renewal, philosophy and theology must again converge, to use a teilhardian phrase. And so in the following pages I have tried to "team up" philosophy and theology in the hope that through this union new formulations relevant for the modern world may be attained. The particular area in which we seek the aid of philosophy is the problem of the supernatural. For today we need a formulation of the supernatural which states unequivocally its immanence to an evolving universe.

Teilhard de Chardin has already presented us with a view of an evolving universe tending towards Christ as its immanent end. But in terms of traditional philosophic and theological categories, such a view is suspect and untenable. For how can the evolutionary process, which is a natural one, attain to Christ-Omega as a supernatural end? A natural process can attain only a natural end by its own natural powers. If it can attain a supernatural end, then the supposedly supernatural end is really natural. But Christians believe that the supernatural is gratuitous, that it is beyond the natural powers of created being or process. To say then that a natural process such as evolution is able to attain to Christ as Omega is to endanger the gratuity of the supernatural. In effect, it ceases to be supernatural; it becomes natural. In theological parlance, it would mean that nature is intrinsically ordained to the supernatural; it is ontologically structured for it and claims it as its due—and all these statements endanger the gratuity and transcendence of the supernatural.

Those who are unschooled in philosophy and theology

may embrace Teilhard's world-view unreservedly, unaware of the formidable theological objection to it. Many who are sympathetic to Teilhard have tried to show the possibility that evolution tends towards Christ as the supernatural end, either from the point of view of science or from that of the Scriptures. But to my mind the solutions proposed so far seem inadequate. In general, all those who defend Teilhard on this question say that Christ as supernatural end of the evolutionary process is a gratuitous gift of God, hence beyond the powers of nature to attain; Christ as supernatural is gratuitous, then it is not really immanent and tionary process is just a preparation for the supernatural fulfillment in Christ which in itself is gratuitous.[1]

We do not deny the truth of these explanations, but what they fail to indicate is the unresolved dilemma: if the supernatural is gratuitous, then it is not really immanent and essential to the intelligibility of the evolutionary process. What is gratuitous to a thing or process is not essential to it, hence not truly constitutive of and immanent to its meaning. In safeguarding the gratuity of the supernatural, they have, inadvertently perhaps, sacrificed its immanence. As a result, they have really failed to show to the secularistic world the essential relevance of Christ and grace. We are

1. Cf., for example, the more important works that are partial to the teilhardian view such as: Henri de Lubac, *Teilhard de Chardin: The Man and His Meaning*, trans. by René Hague (New York: Hawthorn Books, Inc., 1965), pp. 124ff.; Claude Tresmontant, *Pierre Teilhard de Chardin: His Thought*, trans. by Salvator Attanasio (Baltimore: Helicon Press, 1959), pp. 67, 70, 72; Christopher Mooney, "Body of Christ in Teilhard," *Theological Studies*, (December, 1965), pp. 583-84; Peter Schoonenberg, *God's World In The Making* (Pittsburgh: Duquesne University Press, 1964), p. 65; Paul Chauchard, *Man and Cosmos*, trans. George Courtright (New York: Herder and Herder, 1965), pp. 147, 159; J. Edgar Bruns, "Cosmogenesis and Theology," *The World of Teilhard*, ed. Robert T. Francoeur (Baltimore: Helicon Press, 1961), pp. 169-70; Olivier Rabut, *Teilhard de Chardin: A Critical Study* (New York: Sheed & Ward, 1961), p. 180; A. Hulsbosch, O.S.A., *God in Creation and Evolution*, trans. Martin Versfeld (New York: Sheed & Ward, 1965), pp. 27-28, etc.

back where we started, left with the old traditional formulation in which Christ is extrinsic and accidental to the universe. It is precisely this extrinsicism that Teilhard sought to remedy. But it would seem that his defenders, in trying to save Teilhard's orthodoxy, have done so at the expense of his basic insight, that there is only one head and center, or Omega, to the evolutionary process and that is Christ. No doubt, Teilhard believed in the gratuity of the supernatural, but he also believed that Christ is essential to the intelligibility of the universe. The reconciliation of these two elements, however, was not clear in Teilhard's mind. For this reason, some of his critics were justified in accusing him of radically confusing the two orders of natural and supernatural and reducing Christianity to evolutionism of a naturalist type.[2] But, to my mind, the defenders of Teilhard have not successfully reconciled the immanence and the transcendence of the supernatural either.

My purpose in this study is to explore the possibility of this reconciliation in the context of an evolving universe. As with all explorations, many related areas will be left uninvestigated and unanswered, and even the area I intend to explore will not be completely mapped out. I am not, therefore, presenting a treatise on the supernatural in which everything is in order, all questions neatly answered. I am, however, attempting a different approach to the problem of the supernatural by developing a philosophy of process intrinsic to, and derived from, an evolving universe—a philosophy, I believe, that will furnish an adequate framework for the proper understanding and formulation of the problem of the supernatural.

2. This is the objection, for example, of Père Philippe de la Trinité, "Teilhard et Teilhardisme" in *Quadrani de Divinitas*, p. 98. Cf. De Lubac, *op. cit.*, p. 127, to whom I am indebted for this information.

The presentation starts with three chapters on the general problem of the supernatural: 1) its importance in relation to Christian renewal, 2) the history of the problem, and 3) a critique of the scholastic formulation of the relation between nature and supernature. Those readers who are acquainted with the scholastic problem of the supernatural may bypass these three chapters and go directly into the heart of the study: 1) the presentation of a philosophy of process, and 2) the application of the philosophy of process to the problem of the supernatural.

A word may be in order at this point about the ulterior purpose of the work. While the philosophy of process outlined in this study is secondary in importance to the problem of the supernatural, its full value transcends the use made of it here. The philosophy of process is being presented as a feasible framework for theological reformulation in general. This is the larger purpose of the work. For this reason, the unexpressed underlying title of the work could very well be: The Philosophy of Process and Christian Renewal. I could have presented the philosophy of process in and for itself, but most of us are more inclined to accept something if it works. Consequently, I have attempted in this study to show the workability of the philosophy by applying it to a major theological problem.

I believe that theological renewal depends at bottom upon philosophic renewal. I believe, too, that the problem of theological renewal would not have reached such ominous proportions as it has today if theology had not limited itself to one philosophy which in practice it took to be unquestioned, perennial and absolute. If theologians want the Church to influence the modern world, they must reformulate Christian truths in terms of the categories of the modern world. But for several centuries theology has lived in a world of its own shut off from the modern world.

The wider implication, then, of this study is that if there is to be a renewal of theology, its statements must be reformulated in the context of a philosophy valid for an evolving world. Such a philosophy is outlined here.

Eulalio R. Baltazar

Table of Contents

11

PART ONE

The Problem of the Supernatural

CHAPTER I

The Supernatural and Church Renewal

Many problems confront the Church in relating to the modern world—but none so severely as the self-understanding of the Church itself. In a rapidly changing world, the Christian community has found itself more and more in isolation from the concerns and convictions of the wider human community. A solution to the problem has been sought primarily through return to the Scriptures. But this return—however important—will be of little significance if the truths of Scripture are not related to the thought-categories of modern men. The problem is, then, to express in the language of our contemporary world-view the true relation of the Church to the world.

To the practiced eyes of theologians and Christian philosophers, the task of Christian renewal is fundamentally the task of grasping more deeply the relation between nature and supernature. In the course of the long history of Christianity, this problem has been phrased in various ways. Thus it has been seen as the problem of the relation between reason and faith, immanence and transcendence, finite and infinite, natural theology and revelation, man and God, Church and State, Church and the modern world, etc. The emphasis has varied, but basically the problem has remained the same. Today, we are concerned about secularism. The problem of relating the Church to the secularist world is made acute by the triumph of science, which many believe will be able to do away with all religion, given enough time.

From the Christian point of view, secularism is the loss of the sense of the sacred and the belief that nature is self-sufficient, that there is no need for the supernatural. Some Christian thinkers believe that the traditional presentations of Christianity, perhaps unwittingly, give occasion for the secularist position. When a natural order is set up alongside the supernatural, the natural order is made to appear autonomous, self-sufficient. In relation to it, the supernatural is thought of by the uninitiated as something outside, extrinsic, accidental, foreign, superficial, and so forth.

The upholders of the traditional formulations would argue that the distinction between the two orders is valid and true, hence it could not possibly be the cause of secularism. The usual explanation for secularism, often heard from the pulpit, is the gross materialism of modern man. If people were not blinded by the attraction of material things, it is claimed, then they would have a hankering for the things that are above. But the truer reason may well be the failure of Christians to rethink the truths of our faith in terms of modern categories. Materialism may be not so much the cause of secularism as the result of this failure. For when people fail to grasp the meaning and value of a truth, however important it may be in itself, it becomes practically insignificant. If, therefore, they do not grasp the value and relevance of the supernatural, people will look for other values to give meaning to human existence.

The supernatural, to be made meaningful, must be given a place in the modern world; Christianity, to be an effective force, must show the central place and role of Christ. Too often the traditional presentations of Christian faith fail to give meaning to Christ and the supernatural by making them extrinsic to the world. Thus Blondel wrote in 1930:

I share the ideas and the sentiments of Father Teilhard de Chardin in the face of the Christological problem. Before the broader horizons created by science we cannot, without betraying Catholicism, remain satisfied with a feeble and limited Christology, in which Christ appears almost as an accident of history, isolated like a stranger amid the crushing and hostile immensity of the universe.[1]

Apropos of the Blondelian sentiment, it is necessary to comment that those who are dissatisfied with the traditional presentation are not for a moment questioning the feeling of Christians about Christ, namely, that he is central to their lives. What is often forgotten, however, is that the way Christians feel is not necessarily the way treatises on the supernatural and on Christology are presented. Hence, the dissatisfied are not necessarily questioning the feelings and attitudes of Christians; they are questioning the doctrinal presentation of these truths of the faith.

If the Church is to win the confidence of the world, we must remain open to the ways of thought of modern man. The modern man wants all values related to the world, and not just to any world, but to his world—the modern world. Furthermore, any supernatural value must be seen as central, intrinsic, "natural" to this world. If there is to be any spirituality at all, it must be "naturalistic" as opposed to supra-naturalistic, immanent rather than transcendent. Values which are signified by the term supernatural must be shown to have a real relation to the natural tasks of this world.

The failure to respond to the needs of the modern world by the reformulation of Christian truths has driven many to naturalistic humanism and communism. Communism in particular is a powerfully attractive philosophy for modern

1. See his work, *Une énigme historique:* Le "Vinculum substantiale" d' après Leibnitz et l'ébauche d'un réalisme supérieur (Paris, 1930), 105-06. I borrowed this quote from C. Mooney, *op. cit.*, p. 609.

man for it respects the values of earth; it does not tell a man to withdraw from the world but rather to involve himself in it, this being his only purpose. Communism promises a value in the future dependent on man's powers, and not some extratemporal value beyond his powers. Great intellectuals like Nietzsche, Freud, and Sartre have criticized a presentation of Christianity that would make it seem supratemporal, with a God beyond this world.

Faced with the threat of secularism, a great Catholic theologian some twenty years ago made a strenuous attempt to show the intrinsic ordination of nature to the supernatural, in other words, to show that the supernatural is constitutive of nature itself. But Henri de Lubac's efforts were abortive. The problem continued to grow to such great proportions as to warrant the convoking of the Second Vatican Council. Protestants, too, are faced with the problem. The enthusiastic reception accorded to J. A. T. Robinson's *Honest to God* was symptomatic of the widespread need and search for a fresh formulation of the truths of faith that would take into account the knowledge and the experience of the modern world. Paul Tillich's whole life was devoted precisely to showing God's presence in the world as the "ground" of being.

The problem of renewal concerns not only the proper presentation of truths of our faith to non-Christians but also the correct understanding by Christians themselves of these same truths in the context of the modern world. This second problem could very well be the more important one facing the Church, since to reform the world Christians must first reform themselves. In effect, this means reforming our spirituality and our theological understanding.

The modern Christian believes in the value of the supernatural—but he also believes in the values of earth. It is here that tension results. For if the supernatural is supratemporal, should not one forsake the temporal? But is this not to deny the values of earth? If the supernatural is our only end, why were we not placed in an extratemporal order to begin with? Is there not something wrong with the present order of things in which the majority of Christians spend most of their time in the temporal order when logically they should be spending it all on the things that matter—the supernatural? And why is it that only a minority of mankind—the religious—are able, as a matter of fact, to devote themselves completely to man's end? As long as the temporal order is made to seem a sort of prison, the consequence of original sin, the layman cannot help but feel that he is a second-class Christian, condemned to spend his life in the secular world while his vocation is to the extratemporal.

The traditional formulation of two orders—the supernatural and the natural—results in tension not only on the level of understanding but also on the level of activity. For how can the layman devote his time wholeheartedly to the temporal when he does not find his salvation there? Natural work, he is told, has no power to redeem him; of itself it is non-salvific. Religious leaders accuse the laity of being second-class intellectuals. How can they be first-class intellectuals if they do not see a justification for devoting themselves wholeheartedly to the things of earth? How can they devote themselves to science when true perfection is to be found in the sacred disciplines, the sacred liturgy; when to be perfect is to be superterrestrial rather than terrestrial? On the one hand they are told that the present life is just a time of waiting, and on the other, that they must involve themselves in the affairs of the world. The result for the modern Christian is a schizoid type of spirituality. Let us hear Teilhard de Chardin's diagnosis of this modern state:

> I do not think I am exaggerating when I say that nine out of ten practicing Christians feel that man's work is always at the level of a "spiritual encumbrance." In spite of the prac-

tice of right intentions, and the day offered every morning to God, the general run of the faithful dimly feel that time spent at the office or the studio, in the fields or in the factory, is time diverted from prayer and adoration. It is impossible, too, to aim at the deep religious life reserved for those who have the leisure to pray or preach all day long. A few moments of the day can be salvaged for God, yes, but the best hours are absorbed, or at any rate cheapened, by material cares. Under the sway of this feeling, large numbers of Catholics lead a double or crippled life in practice: they have to step out of their human dress so as to have faith in themselves as Christians—and inferior Christians at that.[2]

Neither is the religious who is a scientist immune to this tension. In fact, it is in him that the tension becomes more acute, since by vocation he is consecrated to the service of the supernatural. He must give time to his religious duties and, at the same time, be outstanding in his field of specialization. This is not easy to realize. Teilhard felt the problem most acutely. His calling was to be a scientist, in the natural order, but at the same time he was by vocation a religious and a priest, in the supernatural order. There was a schism in his soul between the most legitimate demands of the world and of his Christian faith which required that he forsake the world. In Father Teilhard's first writings we find a passionate expression of this decisive experience of being torn apart:

For after all must one renounce being human in the broad and deep sense of the word, bitterly and passionately human, in order to be a Christian? Must we, in order to follow Jesus and to participate in His celestial body, renounce the hope that we are getting the feel of and preparing a little bit of the Absolute each time when, under the blows of our labor, a little more of determinism is mastered, a little more truth is achieved, a little more progress realized? Must one,

2. *The Divine Milieu* (Harper & Row, 1960), p. 34.

in order to be united with Christ, keep himself disinterested concerning the progress peculiar to this cosmos?

At once so intoxicating and cruel, this progress carries us along with it and comes to light in the consciousness of each one of us. Does not such a process risk making mutilated, tepid, and weak personalities of those who apply it on themselves? This is the existential problem in the heart of a Christian where the divine faith which supports all human effort, and the terrestrial passion, which is its sap, inevitably collide.[3]

In his spiritual autobiography, Teilhard again dramatizes the conflict he himself experienced between the best of his human aspirations and a certain spirituality of flight and escape:

I find the first traces of this opposition during my years at secondary school in my pathetic effort to reconcile my interest in nature with the evangelism (certainly too narrow) of *limitation* whose texts nourished my morning prayers. Later as a scholastic at Jersey, I seriously considered a total renunciation of mineralogy, about which I was then very enthusiastic, in order to consecrate myself to the activities called "supernatural."[4]

Teilhard's experience exemplifies the tension in the layman of today, and we mean "layman" in the sense given to the term by Yves Congar who has said that the true layman is one for whom the things of this world are really interesting in themselves, for whom their truth is not as it were swallowed up and destroyed by a higher reference.[5]

Those who believe in the truth of Christianity know that this conflict could not be essential to it; that true Christianity could not be in conflict with the values of earth. But

3. Cf. "La vie cosmique," 1916. I quote this from Claude Tresmontant's *Pierre Teilhard de Chardin* (Helicon, 1959), p. 79.

4. "La coeur de la matière," 1950. Cf. Tresmontant, *op. cit.*, p. 79.

5. Cf. his book, *Lay People in the Church,* trans. Donald Attwater (Westminster, Md.: Newman Press, 1957), pp. 17-21.

the Christianity that is practiced today produces this conflict, it would seem, and the tragic thing about it is that non-Christians judge us by what we believe Christianity to be. Teilhard describes the objection brought against Christianity:

> The great objection brought against Christianity in our time, and the real source of the distrust which insulates entire blocks of humanity from the influence of the Church, has nothing to do with historical or theological difficulties. It is the suspicion that our religion makes its adherents *inhuman*.
>
> "Christianity," so some of the best of the Gentiles are inclined to think, is bad or inferior because it does not lead its followers beyond humanity, but away from it or to one side of it. It isolates them instead of merging them with the mass. Instead of harnessing them to the common task, it causes them to lose interest in it. Hence far from exalting them, it diminishes and distorts them. Moreover, don't they admit as much themselves? And if one of their religious, or one of their priests, should happen to devote his life to what is called profane research, he is very careful, as a rule, to recall that he only lends himself to these secondary pursuits for the sake of conforming to a fashion or an illusion, to prove that Christians are not the most stupid of men. When a Catholic works with us, we invariably get the impression that he is doing so in an insincere way, condescendingly. He appears to be interested, but in fact, because of his religion, he does not believe in the human effort. His heart is not really with us. Christianity creates deserters and false friends: that is what we cannot forgive.[6]

The only way to cope with modern naturalism and secularism is, therefore, to situate the supernatural at the very heart and center of nature. In this way it canot be ignored; it ceases to be an option and becomes a necessity if man is to be fully man and thus perfect himself. In order to cope with communism, it is necessary to show that the end of

6. *The Divine Milieu*, p. 38.

matter is a spiritual reality. And to justify the involvement of Christians in time and thus counteract the spirituality of withdrawal and escape, we must place Christ at the very center of reality. Our spirituality must be temporal rather than extra-temporal. In other words, as long as a dualism between nature and supernature is maintained, the result seems to be that naturalism, secularism and communism are kept alive by this very dualism, and Christians live a schizoid existence. In the context of our modern world, the whole brunt of Christian renewal must be directed toward showing that man (and not only man but the whole material universe) is naturally Christian, as Tertullian, with great insight, observed long ago. Christ must be seen as already present in the beginning and not just at a particular moment in history.

In the opinion of many Christians today, the world-view of Teilhard de Chardin, especially as presented in his last book, *The Phenomenon of Man,* seems to be the answer to Christian renewal. From their point of view, the worth of Teilhard's synthesis is not so much its scientific value (which is a point of dispute) as its offer of a probable working hypothesis, a modern formulation of the scriptural view that Christ is head of the whole universe—a formulation which enables the Christian to articulate his faith in the context of the modern evolutionary world.

Teilhard's world-view is summarized in *The Phenomenon of Man.*[7] He first presents his discovery, the law of complexity-consciousness.[8] This law implies that reality evolves towards complexity and then converges towards consciousness. In other words, the direction of evolution is towards consciousness. With this new law, he introduces a revolution

7. Translated by Bernard Wall (New York: Harper, 1959). Note: from here on, the work shall be referred to as *PH,* an abbreviation of the original title, *Le Phénomène Humain.*
8. *Ibid.,* p. 48ff.

in thought by giving centrality to consciousness, which in past traditional scientific thought was considered purely as an epiphenomenon, an accidental, isolated occurrence of little weight in the intellectual reconstruction and formulation of reality.[9] With the new law, Teilhard is able to organize phenomenal data which before were held as merely disparate.

The law of complexity-consciousness is ontologically founded on the *without* and the *within* of things. The *without* is the material aspect and the *within,* the spiritual aspect of a thing. The dynamism of the material aspect Teilhard calls tangential energy, which brings the thing into solidarity with all elements of the same order; the dynamism of the spiritual aspect he calls radial energy, which draws the thing in the direction of convergence in the future. The material aspect or the *without,* then, is the basis for complexification; the spiritual aspect or the *within,* the basis for convergence.

If the law of complexity-consciousness is applied to the phenomenal data gathered by all the disciplines—science, philosophy and theology—we find that there is one single process of evolution. Within the single process there are critical thresholds, or points which are the result of previous complexification and centration. These thresholds produce a qualitative change or rebirth to a new dimension of being in process. It is necessary to adopt a space-time continuum of millions of years for the law of complexity-consciousness to be observable and applicable.[10]

First, then, there was pre-life[11] which complexified till it reached a critical threshold, at which point life emerged.[12] The evolution of pre-life is properly called cosmogenesis-

9. *Ibid.,* p. 56.
10. *Ibid.,* pp. 215ff.
11. *Ibid.,* pp. 67ff.
12. *Ibid.,* pp. 77ff.

geogenesis.[13] This in turn gives way to biogenesis,[14] or the complexification of life. At this point, the law of complexity-consciousness takes on a specific form. It becomes the law of cephalization. We are thus able to see the direction of life in terms of the development of the cephalic region of the living body.[15] Biogenesis reveals itself as a psychogenesis— the emergence and development of mind.[16] Psychogenesis in its turn leads to man.[17] Man is distinguished from other animals by the emergence of self-consciousness or reflection. This means that man not only knows like other animals, but that he also knows that he knows. With man, evolution becomes a self-directing process.

Evolution does not end with man. To the biologist this would seem so, for he sees only man's body, consciousness being an epiphenomenon. But the law of complexity-consciousness shows that evolution now takes place at the level of self-consciousness. Mind is the next layer; it is the noösphere.[18] But instead of cells as units, which we find in the biosphere, we now have personal centers of consciousness which tend, not to a biological, but to a spiritual synthesis. This process of complexification is called noögenesis.[19] The terminus of the process is a humanity consciously centered on the Omega point which is the level of super-personality, super-humanity, super-consciousness, the supernatural.[20] Teilhard identifies this Omega with Christ, finding confirmation for this view in the Scriptures, especially in St. Paul and in St. John.[21] The whole process of evolution from pre-life

13. *Ibid.,* pp. 46ff.
14. *Ibid.,* pp. 139-40.
15. *Ibid.,* p. 146.
16. *Ibid.,* p. 181.
17. *Loc. cit.*
18. *Ibid.,* p. 182.
19. *Ibid.,* p. 181.
20. *Ibid.,* pp. 257-63.
21. *Ibid.,* p. 291ff.

(cosmogenesis) to life (biogenesis) to conscious life (psychogenesis) to super-consciousness (noögenesis-Christogenesis) is really the story of man—hence the apt title of Teilhard's great work—*The Phenomenon of Man*.[22]

Even in this very cursory sketch of Teilhard's world-view, we can see the foundations for a formulation of Christian truth quite unlike the medieval formulation, which was based on the hypothesis of two worlds. That hypothesis is not only unscientific (because nonevolutionary), but unscriptural, for it implies that Christ is head only of the supernatural order. In Teilhard's view, the whole evolutionary process tends towards Christ-Omega. Thus Christ is not confined to the supernatural order; rather, there is only one cosmic process of which Christ is the heart and center, the force and the finality. In Teilhard's formulation, the dualism between nature and supernature is dissolved. There is only one process which is neither natural nor supernatural (in the traditional sense of these terms). Consequently, there being no purely natural order, there is also no area for a wholly profane science. As Teilhard notes, science leads to adoration.[23] Science, philosophy, theology, mysticism—all are situated in one and the same Christogenesis, although at different levels.

Christ is essential for the total intelligibility of reality, because he is the culmination of the whole process. Scientists and naturalists cannot claim that they are able to arrive at the truth of reality apart from Christ. They can make this claim only under the traditional view, for according to that view nature is autonomous, possessed of its own natural end, and therefore intelligible apart from Christ.

In Teilhard's view, involvement in time is justified because Christ is found in time. Furthermore, to him the world is not

22. *Ibid.,* p. 34.
23. *Ibid.,* p. 284, also pp. 278, 283.

merely a place for waiting but rather for the building of the kingdom, since the cosmic process is not yet finished. And because man in this view is not so much the end of the process as its spear-head, he has a principal role to play in guiding the whole process towards its Omega. We are advancing, not towards a communist utopia on earth, but towards the new earth in Christ. It is through the Church, the mystical body, that the world is led towards the *pleroma Christi*—and on this basis is founded the role of the Church in the modern world.

The modern Christian finds Teilhard's world-view appealing. It is also meaningful because he is able to integrate the truths of his faith within it; through it, he is able to see his role; there is a significance to human activity because the split between natural and supernatural activities is healed. He finds dependence upon Christ increased, because in this light he can see clearly that apart from Christ he has no essential intelligibility or existence.

However, before the heart can peacefully and confidently embrace Teilhard's world-view, the intellect must first be satisfied. It is here, however, that objections arise. We are interested in only one of these, but this one is, in the opinion of many, one of the central obstacles to the final acceptance of Teilhard's synthesis. It is this: If evolution is a natural process which tends towards Christ, then it would seem that this natural process is able to attain Christ-Omega as supernatural by its own natural powers. But this view seems to contradict the irrevocable and express teaching of the Church that the supernatural is gratuitous, hence unattainable by the natural powers of man or by the evolutionary process. Christ cannot be the fruit of the evolutionary process.

The traditional view postulates a hypothetical natural end

for the cosmos, to which a supernatural end is gratuitously superadded. Granted, this formulation does safeguard the gratuity of the supernatural. But the position of Teilhard is that there is in the universe only one center,[24] one end of a single process,[25] that "the world can no more have two summits than a circumference have two centers,"[26] that the universe cannot be "bicephalous,"[27] that the Omega is both immanent and transcendent.[28]

Teilhard, according to C. Mooney, shows that the immanence of Christ-Omega to the universe is that of a "physical" center. By "physical" Teilhard means that Christ forms a union with the universe that is opposed to all that is juridical, abstract, or extrinsic to reality.[29] But the term "physical," or "ontological," does not solve the problem of the intrinsic relation of Christ to reality. We can still ask: how immanent?, or how ontological? Is he so intrinsic as to be essential to and constitutive of the intelligibility and existence of the natural process of evolution? If so, then Christ ceases to be gratuitous; he becomes attainable by the natural powers of the process; God becomes obligated to give Christ as the goal of the process, for God cannot create a nature in vain. He must give it all that is essentially needed for its perfection.

On the other hand, if Christ as physical center is not essential to the intelligibility of the process, then he is not really intrinsic and immanent to the evolutionary process, in spite of the obvious connotation of the term "physical." In the end, to avoid calling the natural process unintelligible (which we would have to do if it had no natural end), we must

24. *Forma Christi* (1918), p. 5.
25. *Christologie et évolution* (1933), p. 10.
26. *The Divine Milieu*, p. 151.
27. *Super-humanité, super-Christ, super-charité* (1943), p. 9.
28. *PH*, p. 270.
29. Mooney, *op. cit.*, p. 592.

postulate a hypothetical natural end. We can go on asserting that in actuality Christ is the only end of the evolutionary
process, but we cannot at the same time say that he is the
essential intelligibility of the process, a conclusion which it
was the very purpose of Teilhard to reach and which seems
to be the view of St. Paul. Even with this evolutionary view,
Christ still remains, as in the old formulation, an accidental,
superadded plenitude of the evolutionary process.[30]

Other opinions on the relation of the supernatural to the
evolutionary process are faced with the same dilemma that
we noted above. Thus, for example, if the supernatural is
the second phase of one evolutionary process of which the
natural order is the first phase,[31] we still have to ask: Is this
second phase essential to the completion and intelligibility
of the first? If so, then the supernatural ceases to be gratui-

---

30. C. Mooney's book, *Teilhard de Chardin and the Mystery of Christ*
(New York: Harper, 1966), came into my hands too late to make use
of it in the body of the text. Mooney's study strengthened my opinion
that Teilhard has not really shown how the gratuity of the supernatural
is safeguarded in his evolutionary view, despite the fact that he has in
many places affirmed that it is. It is one thing to affirm the gratuity of
the supernatural; it is another to show its philosophical and theological
possibility. But this problem cannot be ignored if Teilhard's view is to
be considered theologically orthodox.

Mooney comments that in Teilhard's view "Christ makes evolution
possible by giving meaning to the world" and that "the world in evolution thus cannot be explained except by Christ" (p. 177), that the natural process of evolution "is not autonomous but has Christ also as its
Centre and *raison d'être*" (p. 212). Now, if Christ as supernatural end
is essential to and constitutive of the intelligibility of the natural process
of evolution, then it would seem that God *must* give this supernatural
end to nature, for God cannot create a nature in vain. What is constitutive of the essence is exacted by that nature; it has an exigency for it.
But if God must give it, then the supernatural is not really given gratuitously, despite affirmations to the contrary.

Anyone who considers Teilhard's world-view orthodox and valid cannot ignore two questions: Is the movement of evolution toward Christ
as supernatural end an intrinsic ordination or not? Is the gratuity of grace
minimized if Christ is essential to the intelligibility of evolution? Mooney
has not addressed himself to these central questions.

31. Cf. Hulsbosch, *op. cit.*, p. 28.

tous; on the other hand, if we say it is gratuitous, then it is not essential to the very meaning of the process of evolution.

Another opinion states that the supernatural is "not just a superadded glorification of nature but a new degree of that creative Presence which gives nature its being, the principle of which is the love of God freely given."[32] But this statement, which apparently reconciles the gratuity and immanence of the supernatural, really hides an inner contradiction. For if the supernatural is not superadded, then it is essential to and constitutive of the fulfillment and intelligibility of nature. But this is also to imply that the supernatural is not freely given. Tresmontant asserts that Teilhard does not confuse the order of nature and the order of supernature, but rather expressly reserves a place for the free gift of God by attempting to describe the preparations with respect to this supernatural end on the part of the world.[33] But Tresmontant leaves the crucial problem unsolved: If the supernatural is a free gift, then how is it truly immanent to the evolutionary process?

De Lubac also takes pains to show that Teilhard is careful to avoid confusing the two orders of nature and supernature. Teilhard, notes de Lubac, knew very well that the universe is capable only of receiving Christ and that one cannot look for the love and kingdom of God on the same level as human affections and progress, that the human sense of convergence is not sufficient to engender the center necessary for religion.[34] These rejoinders of de Lubac do indeed save the gratuity of the supernatural for Teilhard, but at the expense, it seems to me, of the teilhardian insight that Christ is intrinsic and essential to the meaning of the evolutionary process.

The difficulty concerning the problem of the supernatural

32. Cf. Chauchard, *op. cit.,* p. 147.
33. *Op. cit.,* p. 70.
34. *Op. cit.,* pp. 127-28.

connected with the teilhardian world-view is well expressed by the following passage:

> ... we are here in the almost polemic heat of controversy centering on the work of Teilhard de Chardin—if the history of man has an intimate connection with the history of the universe, even the physical universe, what will be the point of union of the two domains? And how will the fashioning of the world—a world in evolution, a world being constructed by man—enter into the supernatural economy of salvation? The reactions we have seen so far to Teilhard's great work show that there is not yet any general agreement on this interpretation of the science of the universe and that different "spiritualities" are the point of departure for the positions taken.[35]

There is only one way in which evolution can tend towards Christ according to Karl Rahner. Rahner has observed that "it would not be extravagant, as long as it was done with prudence, to conceive the evolution of the world as an orientation *toward Christ,* and to represent the various stages of this ascending movement as culminating in him as their apex. The only danger to be avoided is the suggestion that such evolution is an ascent which the world accomplishes by forces which are wholly its own."[36] But Rahner does not elaborate on this assertion.

The main question remains unsolved. How can a natural process attain to Christ as its apex? Can we say that nature is intrinsically ordained to the supernatural or is it in the nature of things that Christ and the supernatural are not essentially necessary to the existence and intelligibility of the natural order? Is Teilhard's world-view an impossible hypothesis because it is theologically and philosophically unsound? To answer these related questions we need to know

35. Marie-Dominique Chenu, O.P., "Time in Theology," *Theology Digest,* 10 (Autumn, 1962), p. 205.
36. Quoted from C. Mooney's article, *op. cit.,* p. 610.

the history of the problem of the supernatural; to study the premises, both theological and philosophic, that influenced the traditional assertion; to discover what is of faith and what is purely philosophical. We cannot arrive at true answers if our reflection is not well guided by tradition and history. Hence, our next step is to review the history of the problem of the supernatural.

CHAPTER II

The History of the Problem of the Supernatural

An enormous volume of literature has been written on the theological problem of the supernatural, both on its historical[1] and doctrinal[2] aspects. But the philosophic presuppositions of the problem have received little attention. The traditional approaches to the problem of the supernatural have been theological because the subject of the supernatural has been considered outside the province of the philosopher. Thus, historical surveys of this question have consisted of a recording, analysis and commentary on the theological controversies and problems concerning the supernatural and the various emphases made at certain periods. But to understand the evolution of the theological formulation of the

1. On the history of the theology of grace for the past twenty-five years, we refer the reader to the list made by Karl Rahner in his book, *Nature and Grace* (New York: Sheed and Ward, 1964), footnote 5, pp. 144-146. N.B.: The section "Nature and Grace" of Rahner's book mentioned above is also found in another translation in *Theology Today* I, ed. Johannes Feiner et al (Milwaukee: The Bruce Publishing Co., 1965), pp. 1-26. The bibliographical list is on pp. 6-8.

2. On the controversy which centers mainly on the historical and theological works of H. de Lubac, again we refer the reader to Rahner's listing in *Nature and Grace,* footnote 13, pp. 147-149; or in *Theology Today* I, p. 20.

There is also a very useful select bibliography on nature and grace in *Theology Today* I, pp. 245-48, prepared by William J. Weiler, S.J.

Additional articles are noted by Karl Rahner in his *Theological Investigations* I, trans. Cornelius Ernst (Baltimore: Helicon Press, 1961), pp. 297-317.

concept of the supernatural, a philosophic approach is indispensable, because any view of the supernatural is dependent on philosophical concepts of nature and the world. While most theologians are aware of this fact, they have not, as a rule, taken it into account in practice. It is this neglect that has frustrated the efforts of modern theologians to deal successfully with the problem of the relation between nature and supernature. It is my firm belief that the key to the final resolution of the problem is ultimately a renewal in philosophy.

Our philosophic-historical study of the supernatural may begin with a consideration of the origin of the word itself. Abbé de Broglie has pointed out that the word *supernatural* does not belong to the language of the gospels but is a theological term of later origin:

> The word *supernaturalis* appears for the first time in the Latin translations of Pseudo-Dionysius made by Hilduin, and by Scotus Erigena [d. 875?]. For a long time after, theologians did not know the word. Peter the Lombard [c. 1100-1160] does not use it. Only with St. Thomas does its usage become general. And, as is usual, only later still does the word find its way into ecclesiastical texts; we meet it for the first time in the decrees of the Council of Trent and in the twenty-first and twenty-third propositions of the Bull of Pius V condemning Baius [1513-1588].[3]

But although the term itself is of rather recent origin, the meaning conveyed by the concept (allowing for the evolution of the term) was present in the Old and New Testaments and in the early Church. In terms of meaning, the supernatural is God's redemptive call to the creature to share in the divine life. More specifically, in the Old Testament, it is the call of Yahweh to Israel (representing humanity) and

3. Quoted from Edward Brueggeman, S.J., "A Modern School of Thought on the Supernatural," *Theological Studies,* 6 (1945), p. 6.

in the New Testament, it is the call of the incarnate God to share in his life—hence the Christian life. In a transferred sense, the supernatural is often applied to the one who calls, so that Yahweh or Christ as God is spoken of as the supernatural. But in the strict sense, this is an improper way of talking. The supernatural is the sharing in the divine life, or Christian life. God, or Christ, does not share in the divine life; he is the divine life. However, from the point of view of man's tending towards God or Christ as his goal, there is a certain justification for speaking of God or Christ as the supernatural. We can also speak in a transferred sense of the recorded call or message of God's continuing offer to man, and the organized structure that dispenses this offer, as supernatural. Hence we speak of revelation and the Church as supernatural.

Let us take the meaning of the word supernatural in the strict sense as God's divine call,[4] and trace its history. It is often forgotten by those possessed of an ahistorical outlook that the divine call was a historical event. The supernatural —as the divine call to man to share the divine life—took place in time; it was given to a particular people, at a particular time and place. Hence one cannot study the supernatural apart from the people who receive the call. If the culture and language of the given people are quite primitive, then the message cannot achieve its fullest meaning. The message becomes clearer only as the people themselves are purified, their culture grows, and their language becomes more precise. There are many factors that effect growth in a people, among which is the divine message itself purifying the people to whom it is given; in fact, it is one of the main influences in the people's growth. But, at the same time, the unchanging spirit or ethos of a people could hamper their

4. As Rahner notes, the essence of the supernatural is God's self-communication in love. See *Theological Investigations* I, p. 307.

deeper understanding of the divine call. The only method then by which human understanding of the call could develop is by its transmission through another people possessed of a higher civilization and culture and of a less restricted world-view.

In order to gauge and evaluate properly the contribution and also the shortcomings of a given people in their reception and formulation of the divine message, we will take a concept of the supernatural which we will presuppose is the most evolved form to date. Thus, through the discovery of evolution, we are able to understand today that men participate not only in their own redemption (as we have always believed) but also in the redemption of the whole cosmos. We could not understand our part in the building of the new earth—and consequently God's plan of redemption could not be fully realized—if we did not understand through the discovery of evolution that the infra-human is really, and not merely metaphorically, groaning until now to be redeemed.

Using this approach, we can now trace the evolution of the concept of the supernatural. The divine call was first given to all men through the gratuitous act of creation. But as St. Paul says, although it was possible to come to know God through creation and thus adore him, yet clouded by passions and misled by false gods, the polytheistic worshippers could not know the true God, Yahweh. From the amorphous mass of peoples, a given people was chosen. The Hebrews heeded the divine call and through them, the true God became known.

Why the Hebrews were chosen is basically a mystery. But the fact is that the divine call was planted as a seed in the culture of this people. It germinated and grew. In the course of the history of this people, from the nomadic Abraham to the leader Moses to the kingly David on to the prophets, the people's understanding of the precise nature of the divine call as the union between God and man gradually evolved. At first they thought of Yahweh as their tribal God who ruled them justly, but over the course of centuries they came to know him as the gracious spouse of Israel, ever-faithful to his union with his people. This union was known as the old covenant; its laws were given on Mount Sinai. Through the purification and growth of Israel and the saving acts of Yahweh, Israel gave birth to Jesus. Thus in the New Testament, the divine call to union reached a new level—the old covenant gave way to the new in Christ. However, there came a time when this divine call could not grow any longer within the Hebrew cultural soil. For one thing, redemption was too strongly conceived in a purely political context, in which the Messiah was interpreted as coming to conquer all nations, making Israel the lord of them all.

In Christ the divine call was clearly addressed to all men. Under the inspiration of the Holy Spirit, Paul speaks also of material creation groaning until now to be delivered; it too is going to be redeemed. But Paul did not see how this was to be accomplished. He did not see the meaning of his statement in the context of evolution. Paul's interest in the world of nature was only in so far as it had religious meaning; he had no desire to elaborate a cosmology as such, hence no intention whatsoever of explaining how Christ is Lord of the Cosmos.[5] Paul's situation is much the same as the prophets of the Old Testament who knew the literal meaning of the statements they made but, not having the more

5. Mooney, *op. cit.*, p. 606. Care must be taken that we do not read into Paul (or other past thinkers, for that matter), modern ideas and new awareness.

The term "cosmology" in this chapter means simply a scientific view, without necessarily implying the scholastic distinction between a natural and a supernatural order.

adequate perspective of the New Testament, did not realize their fuller meaning as prefiguring Christ. Thus Paul, without the concept of evolution, could not realize that the redemption of material creation was going to be accomplished only by men participating in the affairs of this world, busying themselves in the pursuit of scientific knowledge and the practical use of it, promoting culture and unity, in short, by the whole of mankind seriously and passionately undertaking to build a new earth.

A full realization of the extent of redemption was hindered not only by a primitive cosmology but also by the current view that the second coming of Christ was imminent, hence that there was no need to involve oneself in the affairs of this world. Accordingly, in practice at least, the divine call was still narrowly interpreted to mean the redemption of mankind only.

But if in the divine plan of redemption man must participate in redeeming himself, and if man forms one evolutionary unity with the material universe, then in order to fulfill God's plan, we must recognize this unity, this oneness with the whole universe. Historically, it was through the discovery of evolution that God made known to man the fuller extent of the divine call. But a condition to the discovery of evolution was the development of science, and this the Hebrews did not have. It took about two millenia for science to develop to such a degree that man's awareness of evolution could become a possibility. But the first step in this direction was the planting of Christian faith in Greek cultural soil, which had the most developed cosmology at the time. It was from Greek classic science that Western science was later to grow. But it was the philosophy of the Greeks rather than their science that immediately influenced the evolution of the concept of the supernatural. As far back as the intertestamental period, Greek philosophic thought had been influencing Hebrew thought. Later, when the apostles preached the gospel to the Greek world, the apostles had to formulate their faith in Greek categories.

In the early Church, the reigning philosophy was platonic. Thus the Christian faith was platonized, and with it, the notion of the supernatural. The basic characteristics of platonic philosophy deeply influenced theological formulation and Christian understanding. In platonic philosophy, time was understood as a moving imitation of eternity[6] and thus was thought to be negative and noncreative. Such a view made of this world a region of contingency and change, possessed of no real ontological value. Whatever value it had was in its being a copy of another world—the world populated by pure forms or ideas, a world unchanging and eternal, and the basis for true knowledge. Hence to attain true value and meaning, one had to depart from this world, this "cave," through contemplation. Now this ontological and epistemological outlook was congenial to the eschatological temper of the early Fathers who, still hoping that the second coming of Christ was imminent, considered involvement in the world unnecessary.

The Greek platonic framework was generally adopted both in theory and in practice. In theory, the Christian God was equated with the platonic good, the plotinian nous, the sun; creation was, as it were, rays from this sun. Knowledge came through divine illumination from this sun and not through the senses, for the world was dark and shadowy. In practice, since value was in the other world of pure forms (for the Christians, heaven) this present world was shunned; people withdrew into deserts and became anchorites and hermits. Christians were advised to forego public duties, the true life being a life of contemplation. Since for Platonism the supreme value was in the other world, the Christians

6. *Timaeus,* 37d.

quite logically located their own supreme value—the supernatural—beyond this world.

The advantage of the platonic framework was that it
raised people's minds to spiritual values, preventing them
from being too materialistic. The framework was valid to a
certain extent in that it portrayed strongly the transcendence
of the supernatural. Its inadequacy, however, lies in its
inability to convey the immanence of the supernatural and
the character of the world as good and worth redeeming.
It also produced a view of Christian spirituality as being one
of escape from this world. A rational explanation for involvement could not be given.

Before we can come to the more mature view that scientific
knowledge of the world is redemptive and not just profane,
we must first arrive at the conviction that we can attain to
"profane" knowledge of it. More specifically, before we can
come to the view that man is man-and-his-world, it is necessary to reach the lower level, namely, that man is his human
nature, substantial rather than merely mythical—a copy and
a shadow of the ideal man. But this knowledge presupposes
the admission that this world can be known in and for itself
and not merely as a copy of the world of pure forms. The
only way value could be given to this world was for man to
evolve to a higher stage of philosophy.

The movement from Platonism to Aristotelianism was a
gradual process produced by the tension resulting from the
platonic dualism of two worlds. Men held on to the common
sense view that the world is after all real and that the world
of pure forms is purely mythical—a creation of the human
mind. Furthermore, increasing knowledge about the world
proved the platonic framework philosophically inadequate.
There was just too much data that could not be explained
within this framework. Hence men began to look for resolu-

tion elsewhere. It is to Aristotle's great credit that he effected this resolution. Besides being a philosopher, Aristotle was a scientist in the classic sense of the term. Thus he was able to synthesize the emerging view of his times with the traditional view of Plato. His philosophy was not so much a throwing out of Platonism and the fashioning of a new system—a false view of the relation between Platonism and Aristotelianism—as the presentation of platonic philosophy in a new light. By incarnating the pure forms as the essence of things, he relocated the platonic world. These essences became the aristotelian universals. In this way, he removed the basic objection to platonic philosophy—its opposition to this world—while at the same time preserving the best in Platonism, the ideas or pure forms.

By this stroke of genius, Aristotle was able to give some value to this world. Since the pure forms of Plato were now seen as the universals in things, the world ceased to be shadowy. It was now understood as existing in its own right; there was now reason to know it and build a science about it. Knowledge was now understood to be not by reminiscence, but by conception, which reaches to the essence behind phenomena. The prime category of the real was essence, the unreal was the phenomenal, the accidental. Essence was called substance in so far as it was a substratum for accidents; nature in so far as it was a principle of operation; and in itself it was that which makes a thing what it is, hence a principle of intelligibility.

Christian theology and spirituality followed the evolution in Greek philosophy. From augustinian-platonic theology and spirituality the middle ages tended more towards the scholastic-aristotelian type, which in its highest expression may be characterized as the aristotelian-thomistic. The genius of St. Thomas was to take over aristotelian philosophy, which had already integrated the mathematical and physical sciences, and to add theology in order to obtain a coherent and closely-knit view of the universe.[7] Diagrammatically, the medieval world-view was a series of concentric circles or spheres, the center of which represented the region of highest reality or importance. We may justly characterize the medieval world-view as ptolemaic. Thus on the physical level the earth was at the center and the planets at the periphery—the sun, moon and stars revolving around the all-important and stationary earth. At a higher level— the biological—species were considered as universals, eternal and unchanging, and placed at the center to conform to the position of the earth, while around the stationary species were the contingent particulars or individuals.

Aristotelian philosophy both conformed to and explained this pattern by furnishing the category of substance and accident. Substance (nature or essence) was situated at the center as permanent and stationary while at the periphery were the nine accidents that inhere in and revolve around substance. The center, then, was also substantial or essential, the periphery was accidental or nonessential, contingent, temporal, phenomenal. Theology in its turn placed theological or revealed truths at the center and called them the *substantia fidei* (the substance of the faith) to show their central, eternal and unchanging character. At the periphery were the empirical and contingent truths of science. From this framework, incidentally, we can see why the medieval theologians thought that they had the right to pronounce judgment on scientific matters, for in their view they possessed the center on which peripheral truths depend.

Within the context of this world-view and from its philosophic categories, the notion of the supernatural was understood and formulated. Thus the super-cosmos *(huper-*

7. F. Crowe, S.J., "On the Method of Theology," *Theological Studies,* 23 (1962), 638.

kosmos) of the early Christians became the super-natural *(supernaturalis)* of the scholastic Christian. It was not so much outside this world (as were the platonic forms) as in this world, like the aristotelian essences; however (unlike the aristotelian essences), it was not constitutive of nature but over and above it. Another way of speaking of the supernatural was to call it metaphysical, transphenomenal, extratemporal. It was within this philosophic framework that the word supernatural itself was derived. This framework was also the foundation for the dualism of two orders: the natural and the supernatural. Within the supernatural order were supernatural realities such as revelation, grace, the Church, and God as savior.

The various uses of the word supernatural within the scholastic framework are observable in St. Thomas' use of the term as summarized by Brueggeman:

> For St. Thomas, God is the supernatural Truth: "contemplatio patriae, qua supernaturalis veritas videtur," He is supernatural cause, i.e., "rebus naturalis causa essendi," He is the supernatural principle, "the agens supernaturale"; and He is such by essence, and not only when He produces certain kinds of effects which today we call supernatural. St. Thomas speaks also of "substantiae supernaturales" and of "substantiae supermundanae" in the same sense as of pure spirits and "formae separatae." Metaphysics, he says, which is only another name, corresponding to another aspect of *theologia* or *scientia divina,* is distinguished from *scientia naturalis,* because the objects of the former study are "res transphysicas et divinas."[8]

In the scholastic context the divine call to union becomes an entitative perfection of human nature. The gratuity of this entity is safeguarded by saying that it is above nature and beyond the powers of nature to attain. To capacitate nature for this perfection the creature is endowed with an

8. Brueggeman, *op. cit.,* pp. 6-7.

obediential potency which can be actuated by God alone. The common problem within the scholastic tradition now becomes the understanding and definition of the nature of the relation between nature and supernature.

In very broad outline we may say that this scholastic problem had two stages: first, the classic one in which the problem of relating nature and supernature was formulated in terms of the nature of the natural appetite (desire) for the beatific vision, and second, the more modern one of the natural exigency of nature for the supernatural. In both cases the question boils down to the problem of whether the supernatural is intrinsic or extrinsic to nature. Thus in the classic dispute the question was whether or not the natural desire for the beatific vision is innate. For the most part, discussion of this question has been centered on an exegesis of a few famous texts of St. Thomas where he speaks of man's natural desire to see God. It seems that in certain texts, St. Thomas founded the possibility of the beatific vision on a natural desire for it; while in other groups of texts he seems to base man's meriting of the beatific vision on the fact that he had no natural desire for it.[9]

The classic dispute came to a head in the baian controversy. Baius refused to admit any elevation or divinization of nature by grace.[10] St. Pius V, in condemning Baius' errors, gave the first declarations of the Church on the supernaturalness of grace; that is, on the fact that grace is not due to the exigencies of created nature.[11] Supporting Baius was Jansen who thought that the beatific vision was the only end possible for an intellectual creature.[12] Because Baius

9. Patric Bastable, *Natural Desire for God*, (London: Burns Oates, 1947), p. 31. For a more lengthy study covering the period 1274-1534, cf. Juan Alfaro, S.J., *Lo Natural y Lo Sobrenatural* (Matriti: 1952).

10. See *The Church Teaches* (Herder: 1955), pp. 246-249.

11. *Ibid.*, p. 247.

12. *Ibid.*, pp. 249-50.

considered grace to be natural, Catholic theologians were at pains to show it as supernatural and transcendent. The Catholic camp itself was divided among the innatists (including the scotists, Soto, Toletus, and the augustinians) and the noninnatists (including the thomists, Durandus, Cajetan, Medina, Bañez, Francis Sylvester of Ferrara, and Vasquez).[13] Because of the polemic against Baius, the latter group prevailed.

Since the time of Cajetan, the thomistic doctrine on this question has been fairly well established. Briefly it is this: Man's natural desire to see God is not innate. It is divinely elicited, conditional and, of itself, inefficacious. Formally, it is a desire to see God as author of nature. But there is no faculty in man which tends to the beatific vision as to its fixed terminus; man has only an obediential capacity for this vision.[14] The possibility of a state of pure nature having as its end an abstract knowledge of God was an idea first introduced by Cajetan. It became incorporated into the tradition of western theology through its use as a polemic against Baius and Jansen.[15]

But the thomistic view did not have peaceful possession for long. After the polemic against Baius died down and theologians could approach the problem more calmly, they realized that their necessary emphasis on the transcendence of grace left in relative obscurity the other aspect of the total doctrine of the supernatural—the fact that grace, remaining an utterly gratuitous gift, does actually perfect nature. Similarly, emphasis on the fact that nature has no slightest claim to this gratuitous perfection obscured the complementary fact that nature is somehow open to receive

13. Bastable, *op. cit.,* p. 83.
14. *Ibid.,* p. 82.
15. Richard Bruch, "The Problem of the Supernatural," *Theology Digest,* 8 (winter, 1960), p. 26.

it.[16] Thus the "new system" had unfortunate consequences. As Bruch notes, the supernatural began to appear more as something accidental and extrinsic to nature, an accretion to the natural order. Christianity became something of an ornament of nature.[17] As for Christian spirituality, the practicing Christian was left with the idea that elevation to the supernatural was, as it were, a divine afterthought.

This relatively extrinsic notion of grace which has found its way into modern theology[18] did not do much to stem the growing belief in the omnipotence of science. In fact it helped the cause of scientism and naturalistic humanism. It seemed to justify the autonomy and self-sufficiency of nature by stating that there are two orders extrinsic to one another, and that the natural order is the radical order; it is primary and fundamental—the pattern, so to speak, of the supernatural order.[19] It was this extrinsic notion of the supernatural which made Christ appear as an "accident of history" that stimulated Blondel to write a whole philosophical treatise on Christ as the substantial "bond" linking together the whole universe and giving life to all creation.[20]

It was not any theological or philosophical argument, however, that turned men's minds again to the need of making the supernatural central to nature. Rather, it was the experience of World War I which engendered a certain distrust in the ability of the forces of nature to bring about by themselves any progress in culture and civilization.[21] As a result, emphasis was increasingly placed on the notion represented by Scheeben: "Nature was created by God only that it

16. Brueggeman, *op. cit.,* p. 9.
17. Bruch, *op. cit.,* p. 26.
18. *Ibid.,* p. 27.
19. *Ibid.,* p. 25.
20. See Mooney, *op. cit.,* p. 609.
21. Bruch, *op. cit.,* p. 25.

might serve as a substratum and organ of the supernatural life." God created nature only to have a place where he might share his own inner life with others.[22] Thus philosophically and theologically, the classic controversy was resuscitated, but the emphasis now was not so much on the nature of the natural appetite to see God as whether nature has any claim or exigency to the beatific vision. The modern problem becomes: Even before a man receives his first salutary grace, is he internally affected by the supernatural?[23] Over this issue, theologians are divided into two groups:

> We may call the first group "extrinsicalists." They may be said to represent the theory of the supernatural that has been dominant and largely unchallenged in the schools up till recent years. These theologians would deny that the supernatural has any internal influence on man before the reception of the first internal grace. The second camp gathers in the many modern theologians whom we may call "intrinsicalists." These theologians represent a more recent movement in theology. They challenge the conception of the extrinsicalists on the ground that it makes human nature a self-enclosed system to which the supernatural can be added only as a sort of gilding or veneer. They urge that, if God has summoned men to the beatific vision and established it as man's exclusive end, that divine call must find some response in man, even before he receives his first salutary grace. They affirm that it is the end that commands everything; that, if God assigns a final destiny, that destiny simply must find some ontological counterpart in man. God's almighty call to man cannot leave man indifferent. He may in the end freely reject it; but his being must echo that call. In some sense the call to vision must be inscribed in man's structure.[24]

The intrinsicalist view was decisively influenced by Pierre

22. *Loc. cit.*
23. J. P. Kenny, S.J., "Reflections on Human Nature and the Supernatural," *Theological Studies,* 13 (1953), p. 280.
24. *Ibid.,* pp. 280-81.

Rousselot who in turn was influenced greatly by Blondel's philosophy and by Christian immanentism.[25] In his doctoral dissertation, *The Intellectualism of St. Thomas,* Rousselot tried to show that to be intellectual is to be capable, in some way, of the vision of God; for from his analysis of the activity of the intellect he concluded that the intellect-as-such is, by definition, "the faculty of the divine."[26] Then in 1924, Guy de Broglie added impetus to the intrinsicalist movement by holding the thesis of Rousselot on the nature of the intellect and its tendency to the vision of God, but argued that there is no right to that vision, nor exigency for it, in the order of existence.[27] He held that the tendency to the vision of God is a velleity that is implicit and necessary, and that this implicit desire in the whole conscious life of man must have some metaphysical implications.[28] This view of de Broglie safeguards the absolute gratuity of the supernatural vision of God. The same position, with only the slightest variations, was taken about the same time by Marechal, in the now famous Volume Five of his great work, *Le point de départ de la métaphysique.* He affirms that there is a metaphysical tendency to the beatific vision.[29]

The next significant step in the development of intrinsicalism was the publication in 1946 of *Surnaturel* by Henri de Lubac, and the consequent issuance in 1950 of the encyclical *Humani generis.* Father de Lubac tried to show that our natural desire for God guarantees with certainty that we are actually elevated to the supernatural order and are destined to the beatific vision, that human destiny to the beatific vision is necessarily connected with the existence of a spiritual creature, that God could not in accordance with

25. Brueggeman, *op. cit.*, p. 20.
26. Bastable, *op. cit.*, pp. 114-15.
27. Brueggeman, *op. cit.*, p. 19.
28. Bastable, *op. cit.*, p. 117.
29. *Ibid.*, p. 119.

his wisdom and goodness ordain man to any inferior good and that therefore modern theology should discard entirely the useless, unfortunate, and dangerous hypothesis of pure nature. The conclusion he came to is that human nature has an absolute exigency to the supernatural, yet this exigency is inefficacious.

The general critique of de Lubac's theory may be summed up thus: If God cannot refuse the supernatural to a spirit he has willed to create, then supernature seems due this spirit and is an object of an exigency, or a right inscribed in its very absolute desire. Furthermore, if the supernatural is an end without which a nature is inconceivable, then it cannot be an end that surpasses nature.[30] In this view one has not exalted the supernatural; one has abolished it. De Lubac's thesis would finally lead to the conclusion that the gratuity of the supernatural is reduced to the gratuity of creation in the case of finite spiritual beings. For if God cannot destine angels and men to any end other than the beatific vision, as de Lubac would seem to hold, this is tantamount to the restriction of God's liberty to the mere creation of finite spirits and the exclusion of choice as to their destiny. God has no liberty of choice, only of spontaneity. Concerning the stand of *Surnaturel, Humani generis* has issued a warning. It states that one's theory should not endanger the gratuity of the supernatural by asserting that God cannot create a rational nature without an exigency for the beatific vision. The encyclical, however, does not forbid speculation on the supernatural. Neither does it brush away the legitimate claims of intrinsicalism or settle the question between extrinsicalism and intrinsicalism.

No doubt, by safeguarding the gratuity of the super-

30. See for example Donnelly's critique (which makes much use of Boyer's excellent critique in *Gregorianum*) in *Theological Studies,* 9 (1948), 213-49; 554-560.

natural, extrinsicalism is in perfect harmony with *Humani generis*. But it labors under several quite significant disadvantages. It denies any intrinsic determination of man prior to grace. Yet there are three reasons that seem to suggest that even prior to grace the supernatural must affect man intrinsically.[31]

First, if God has summoned men to the beatific vision and established it as their exclusive end, that divine call must find some response in man even before he receives his first salutary grace. This view affirms that it is the end that commands everything; that if God assigns a final destiny, that destiny simply must find some ontological counterpart in man. God's almighty call cannot leave man indifferent.

Secondly, extrinsicalism does not square well with the traditional Catholic doctrine of original sin. The Council of Trent says that original sin is internal to man. Now original sin is the deprivation of the supernatural. How then can original sin be internal to every man—unbelievers included —if the supernatural was not somehow internal to all in the first place?

Thirdly, the Catholic Church's doctrine on hell—that the excruciating punishment which the damned suffer is an internal pain of loss and an internal fire that burns the very depths of the soul—is hardly explainable (and an occasion for unbelievers to accuse God of being unjust) if the punishment is meted out to human nature for failing to reach an end established by an absolutely external decree. Hell cannot be explained otherwise than by showing that the soul, by sheer stress and energy of its existing being, longs for the possession of God in the beatific vision.

These three arguments, taken together, give considerable support to intrinsicalism. Hence there have been many

31. The following three arguments are taken almost verbatim from J. P. Kenny, *op. cit.,* pp. 281ff.

recent attempts to show that nature is open to the supernatural, that the supernatural is somehow intrinsic to nature. Such theories have been proposed by Hans Urs von Balthasar, Malevez, Gutwenger, Alfaro, and Karl Rahner. Since all these theories take their point of departure from the same basic aristotelian-thomistic framework, a representative theory will suffice to illustrate their common philosophic premise of nature and supernature.

Let us consider the theory proposed by Karl Rahner. In his view, the supernatural is seen as existential. According to Rahner, God created man with a destiny to receive in himself the divine plenitude; this necessarily gives rise to an *affinity* in man to the end towards which he is destined. This affinity is the "central and abiding existential of man as he really is" (". . . *das zentrale und bleibende Existential des Menschen, wie er wirklich ist*").[32] This profound affinity does not detract from the gratuity of the supernatural since it is not constitutive of nature. Rahner's view is called by Kenny moderate intrinsicalism,[33] a theory midway between extrinsicalism—which would make the supernatural dependent purely on an external decree of God without any ontological counterpart in man—and radical intrinsicalism—which would make the supernatural constitutive of nature. While not constitutive of nature, the supernatural existential is nevertheless natural, but "natural" in the pre-scholastic sense of what was there in the very beginning as original equipment. This ontological entity was concreated with human nature.[34]

We conclude the scholastic phase of the problem of the supernatural by simply noting that all the theories, whether extrinsicalist or intrinsicalist, agree that nature cannot be

32. See his *Theological Investigations* I, p. 312.
33. Kenny, *op. cit.*, p. 281ff.
34. Bruch, *op. cit.*, pp. 27-28.

intrinsically, i.e., constitutively, ordained to the supernatural if they are to make any claim to orthodoxy and be
in harmony with *Humani generis*.

Let us look back now at the history we have sketched and
again ask the question we posed at the end of Chapter One:
why cannot evolution tend to Christ-Omega as supernatural? From a review of the history of the problem we see
that the scholastic objection is based on a philosophical
premise, not a theological one, that nature has an exigency
or claim for its end. That end towards which nature is intrinsically ordained is attained by its natural powers. Hence it
is a natural end and being so it ceases to be gratuitous. If
then we say that evolution tends to Christ as to its end—to
which it is intrinsically ordained, there being no other end
either actual or possible—it would mean that evolution
attains to Christ by its own natural powers; nature can claim
its end as its due so that Christ and the supernatural cease
to be gratuitous and transcendent.

Must we say then that Teilhard's view is heretical and
unsound? Yes, if we hold that the scholastic philosophical
framework is an absolute one giving us an essential philosophic formulation of reality as it necessarily is. To depart
from this philosophic framework would mean then the dis-
tortion of reality, and any conclusion derivable from another
framework would be false. In practice, scholastics have
identified their philosophy with the way reality necessarily
is, hence it has not occurred to them to question its philosophic premises. From our study of the scholastic formulations of the supernatural, we can see that even when scholastics questioned previous formulations, the questions were
framed within the scholastic framework; when new formulations were proposed, scholastic categories were still used.

But we have also seen that the question of the supernatural is wider than its scholastic formulation; its history broader than the scholastic history of it. We have seen, too, that a new formulation of the supernatural was incited by tensions felt by Christians between new world-views and old formulations that did not harmonize with the new views. We saw that theology followed on philosophy, that when a new world-view was adequately formulated philosophically there followed a theological rebirth, new theological systematizations and formulations. Given this wider vantage point, we can legitimately and meaningfully ask whether our world-view is so radically different from the medieval one as to require a new philosophical formulation, and, if so, whether the traditional formulation of the supernatural needs revision. We can further ask whether the tensions felt by the modern Christian and the uneasiness within Scholasticism itself over the traditional formulations are not indications that we have indeed a new world-view which traditional categories cannot adequately express.

But it may well be advised that the search for a new formulation should be undertaken only when the traditional formulation has been proven inadequate and unable to assimilate new data. This advice is good, hence our next step is to examine the adequacy of the traditional scholastic formulation as an answer to the requirements of the modern world and that of the Christian faith itself concerning the supernatural.

CHAPTER III

A Critique of the Scholastic Formulation

Our new awareness of the full extent of the supernatural call to redemption enables us to see that it includes all material creation. The discovery of evolution has opened our eyes to the deeper meaning of Paul's words that even material creation is groaning until now to be redeemed and that Christ is head not only of men but of the whole universe. With this new awareness we find upon a cursory examination that the present scholastic formulation is too narrow since according to it the supernatural call is given only to man; in other words, man alone is destined for redemption. Thus in scholastic treatises on the supernatural, the problem is treated exclusively as the problem of the relation of the supernatural to human nature, never to inanimate nature. Furthermore, the emphasis is on the salvation and redemption of souls with little attention given to the resurrection of the body, which, after all, is the belief we confess in the Creed. The redemption of material creation and the building of the new earth are not mentioned at all in these treatises.

Thus from our vantage point today, the scholastic formulation is inadequate. However, this inadequacy need not be a reason for abandoning the formulation as long as the scholastic philosophical framework has the capacity to accommodate our new awareness by giving a rational explanation for the redemption of material creation.

But it would seem that within the scholastic framework, such an attempt would be impossible. Theologians may be able to give convincing and rational explanations for the redemption of material creation, but their explanations then cease to be scholastic. One has to abandon the scholastic categories to make the attempt. Fundamental to the scholastic framework is the notion of matter as the opposite of spirit. Thus for matter to attain the supernatural, which is spiritual, it has to be restructured into non-matter. But such a restructuring is its very destruction. Instead of being perfected it is destroyed. Or the opposite result could happen, namely, that the supernatural received in matter becomes materialized, so that instead of elevating matter, the supernatural is degraded, according to the dictum, *quidquid recipitur secundum modum recipientis recipitur* (whatever is received is received according to the mode of the receiver). This consideration explains the traditional tendency to refer to man's salvation as the salvation of his soul rather than as the resurrection of the body.

The only way matter could be spiritualized and redeemed, it would seem, is for it to have a dynamism towards spirit. Teilhard explains this by saying that matter evolved towards consciousness in man and that matter in the beginning was already pre-conscious. But this view of matter is no longer scholastic. Besides, in the nonevolutionary view of Scholasticism such a position cannot be maintained without destroying the dualism between matter and spirit so basic to its framework.

This notion of matter is the basic obstacle, but not the only one, to the assimilation by Scholasticism of our new awareness of the nature of the universe and of redemption. For example, the dualistic view of the natural and the supernatural order assigns creation to the natural order, not the order of grace. Hence, it has its own natural end. Natural activities are not redemptive. Man alone by an obediential potency is elevated to the supernatural. Coupled with this dualistic view is the narrow equation of the supernatural and the redemptive process with the reception of grace and the final gift of the beatific vision. In this narrow concept, the building of the new earth, the billions of years of evolution and the thousands of years of human culture are considered irrelevant.

We conclude that if we are to stay within the scholastic framework, we must perforce explain Paul's statement that creation is groaning until now to be delivered as purely metaphorical.

Let us next examine the scholastic formulation of the relation between man and grace. We shall take the theory of moderate intrinsicalism as a representative example. But first, let us establish the requirements which any adequate formulation must fulfill:

1) It must safeguard and explain two basic truths concerning the supernatural itself, namely, a) that it is gratuitous, and b) that it is the highest perfection for man.

2) It must conform to, rather than contradict, other Christian truths such as that of original sin, the punishment of hell, etc.

3) It must be significant and meaningful for modern man.

We can summarize these three points by stating that the supernatural must be shown to be both immanent and transcendent with respect to man. The baian controversy has led theologians to stress the transcendence of the supernatural, ignoring its immanence. Today, however, forced and pressured by the needs of the present situation in which Christianity is losing its relevance to the modern world, theologians are beginning to stress the immanence of the supernatural, thus justly stressing its other aspect, namely, that it is the highest perfection of nature. Let us evaluate the formulation of moderate intrinsicalism according to the three points above.

First of all the term "moderate" seems to recommend itself while the term "radical" (implying an extreme position) at once disqualifies itself, for truth must comprehend the whole. But such terms as extrinsic or intrinsic are relative terms. What is intrinsic to one thing may be extrinsic to another. Thus in an order in which C is innermost, B in the middle, and A outermost, then B is intrinsic to A, but extrinsic to C. Of course, the presupposition of moderate intrinsicalism is that B, which represents its position, is the true norm, the true level of intrinsicalism. Hence, relative to it, A is extrinsic while C is radically intrinsic. The problem then becomes that of determining whether moderate intrinsicalism is really true intrinsicalism.

Since the terminology of moderate intrinsicalism is meaningful only within the scholastic framework, it will have to be scholastic philosophy that will determine whether it is true intrinsicalism. Now in scholastic terminology the constitutive parts of essence, namely, matter and form, are properly designated as intrinsic to being because, first, they are the intrinsic principles (formal and material cause) of being, and secondly, they belong to the category of substance. Again in scholastic terminology, it is substance that is designated as properly intrinsic to being, while the accidents are designated as extrinsic. No doubt, both substance (matter and form) and accident belong to a given concrete existent substance and for this reason they are both intrinsic to this concrete existent substance, but this is an imprecise use of the term "intrinsic." Also in a loose sense, we can speak of some accidents called properties (i.e., a predicable as opposed to a predicamental) which are more intrinsic or necessary than others because where there is an essence these accidents are found also. But in the strict sense it is matter and form alone which are intrinsic to or constitutive of nature.

Using again our A, B, C designation to analyze the levels of a given being, essence would be at the deepest level (C), property is just above it (B), and above property are the other accidents (A). But Scholasticism does not view property (B) as the normative intrinsic and essence (C), in relation to it, as radically intrinsic. Nor are the other accidents (A) viewed by Scholasticism as extrinsic to property. Rather, it is essence which is viewed as the norm and is properly designated as intrinsic to the being, while the accidents, whatever degree of association they have with the essence, are all designated as extrinsic. They have to be parts of the essence to be really intrinsic and constitutive of it. But an accident cannot be constitutive of the essence, hence it is improper to designate an accident as intrinsic to the being.

If we work within the scholastic framework, we cannot abandon its terminology to suit our own purpose. Thus, using the term "moderate intrinsicalism" to describe a view which founds the supernatural on an existential which belongs to the category of accident is really a misnomer and quite misleading. To be perfectly honest about it, this view should be properly designated as a more intrinsic form of extrinsicalism. For as long as the supernatural is founded on an accident—if we adhere strictly to scholastic terminology —the supernatural is extrinsic and this view of the supernatural is some form of extrinsicalism. All the traditional and accepted scholastic theories on the supernatural are really only different forms of extrinsicalism. The only difference, perhaps, is that some are closer to being intrinsic than others.

Having cleared the semantic problem, let us proceed to

the problem which really counts: whether moderate intrinsicalism is able to explain the immanence of the supernatural. Judging from its assertions it would seem that it
does, for it claims that "man was created in order to share
in God's own trinitarian life. Hence he must have a real
potency for this supernatural gift. This potency is at the
very core of man, the central existential element of man as
he really is."[1] Thus the supernatural existential is supposedly
at the very core of man. If so, it cannot be an accident, for
an accident cannot be found at the core of being; rather,
the core is substantial matter and form. Some argue that the
core of being-in-the-concrete is the act of "to be" which is
in the substantial order and that the supernatural existential
is at the core of this act of "to be." This argument places the
supernatural existential in the substantial order, making it
constitutive of being.

But as Bruch notes, speaking of Rahner's view: "He insists
that grace is not at all a gift to which nature can be indifferent. But he does not agree that the orientation of man to
the vision of God is so basic to human nature that the latter
cannot be conceived apart from it."[2] Now the last sentence
is quite revealing. It really contradicts the first statement.
For if this potency is not so basic that human nature cannot
be conceived apart from it, then it cannot be at the core of
man's being. I agree, therefore, with Bruch when he says
that to him it seems that Rahner postulates this supernatural
existential principle in man without a sufficient foundation.[3]
"It is not clear," Bruch adds, "that the call itself of man to
the beatific vision must effect some real modification in
human nature."[4]

1. Bruch, *op. cit.,* p. 27. See Rahner, *op. cit.,* p. 311: "To this extent
this 'potency' is what is inmost and most authentic in him, the centre and
root of what he is absolutely."
2. *Loc. cit.*
3. *Ibid.,* p. 28.
4. *Loc. cit.*

Moderate intrinsicalism would like to locate the supernatural at the very core of man's being, and rightly so if the aspect of the supernatural as the highest perfection of man is to be properly explained. For by all the rules of logic and common sense that which is highest must also be deepest in man. But what justification can moderate intrinsicalism offer to back up its assertion that the supernatural existential is at the core of man's being if it still belongs to the category of accident? Words do not change facts. One can call an accident central and intrinsic, but it is still an accident and as long as we locate the foundation of the supernatural in the category of accident, then for that very reason the supernatural is an accident of the being in question. To make the supernatural truly central to reality, it must be taken out of the category of accident. If we insist on situating the supernatural in the category of accident, then we must desist calling it central and claiming that it is at the core of man's being. We cannot have our cake and eat it too.

Within the scholastic framework, to take the supernatural from the category of accident is to put it into the category of the substantial, thus making it constitutive of nature. In so doing, we achieve immanence and as a consequence are able to explain and justify the other aspect of the supernatural as the highest perfection of man and as central to reality. But the experiment, though satisfactory in itself, is performed at the cost of sacrificing a dogma—the gratuity and transcendence of the supernatural. What then? The only other alternative, it would seem, is to take the supernatural out of both the categories of the natural order —substance and accident—but in so doing we proclaim the utter discontinuity and incompatibility of the natural and the supernatural and thereby deny the divine call to the supernatural. We thus end up in an insoluble dilemma. And this is not the only one.

A premise that has exercised a tremendous influence on the theologian's thinking concerning the supernatural is the dictum: God does not create a nature in vain *(Deus non creavit frustra; natura non potest esse inane)*. We do not question the dictum itself which is perfectly valid, for it would be against the wisdom and goodness of God to do otherwise. What we do question is its application within the scholastic context.

What follows from this premise, according to Scholasticism, is that those things necessary for the perfection of the creature are due the creature; nature has an exigency and claim for them. It follows too that the creature cannot be conceived apart from them. Now the supernatural, given this line of reasoning, cannot be necessary if it is to preserve its gratuity. But on the other hand, how could the supernatural be the highest perfection of man and yet not be necessary? Reason itself compels us to assert that it is the most necessary thing for the rational creature. If it is not necessary, then it cannot be the highest perfection.

From another point of view, if indeed the supernatural is the highest perfection, then why is it merely accidental, not essential? For is not the essential a higher perfection in the creature than the accidental? Is this not to create a nature in vain when it is commanded by a divine decree to tend to an accidental perfection when the dynamism of its being as put there by God is to tend to its essential perfection? Is this not to accuse God of contradiction? Unless we are going to surrender our reason, we have to hold that if the supernatural is the highest perfection then it is also the most necessary, and if the most necessary, also essential, not accidental. But, we are reminded, we have to protect the gratuity of the supernatural. Indeed, we must, but let us admit that we can do so only at the expense of the other aspect of the supernatural which must also be safeguarded.

What to do? Before we invoke the easy way out and call the whole situation a mystery, there is need to re-examine scholastic premises. If the supernatural is gratuitous and also the highest perfection then these aspects must be compatible. If they are not seen as compatible, then the most likely area to question is not the truths of faith but our philosophic framework.

Let us examine another contradictory aspect of the scholastic formulation. Among the many factors that could alienate one from the scholastic formulation is its conclusion that man can exist and be understood apart from Christ and the supernatural. Thus, for example, Alfaro holds that we must say that man could exist and thrive as a creature even though he were not destined to see God. In drawing this conclusion, he says, we are stepping out of the realm of formal revelation into that of theological reasoning.[5] And Rahner says that there is in man a reality "which must have a meaning and a capability of existing, even when the supernatural existential element is not there."[6] Rahner gives the reason: "otherwise, this existential element would necessarily be demanded by nature itself."[7] Thus, there is always the philosophic premise: if a thing is necessary, it is demanded; then the theological reasoning: the supernatural cannot be demanded, therefore, it is not necessary. And since God cannot create a nature in vain, the creature must be able to exist and have intelligibility apart from the supernatural.

What is passed over and ignored by the above reasoning is the abundance of assertions in Scripture that the creature

5. Alfaro, Juan, "The supernatural: immanent and transcendent," *Theology Digest,* 8 (winter, 1960), p. 31.

6. Bruch, *op. cit.,* p. 27.

7. *Loc. cit.*

is nothing without God, that without Christ we are nothing. Thus Joseph Huby describes the all-inclusiveness of Christ's lordship in his commentary on Colossians:

> In Him all has been created as in a supreme Center of unity, harmony, and cohesion, which gives to the world its sense, its value, and therefore its reality. Or, to use another metaphor, He is the focus, the "meeting point" as Lightfoot put it, where all the fibres and generative energies of the universe are organized and gathered together. Were someone to see the whole of the universe, past, present, and future, in a single instantaneous glimpse, he would see all beings ontologically suspended from Christ and completely unintelligible apart from Him.[8]

Now how can we reconcile this statement with the previous statements we quoted, that "man could exist and thrive as a creature even though he were not destined to see God" or that man has a "meaning and a capability of existing, even when the supernatural existential is not there"? How are we to reconcile the opposed views? Shall we say that Paul's assertions are metaphorical? Then how is the Christian going to convince himself that Christ is the most necessary reality in his life? Is it heretical to say and believe that a man cannot exist and have meaning apart from grace and Christ? Fortunately the great number of Christians are not fully aware of this part of the scholastic formulation. Most Christians see no contradiction in holding on the one hand that grace and the incarnation are gratuitous events, and on the other that Christ is the life of the soul, the vine without which the branches will die.

Thus the view that man has intelligibility apart from grace and Christ does not square well with Scripture and the constant belief of Christians. Another consideration that will show the falsity of the view that man is intelligible apart

8. Quoted in Mooney, *op. cit.,* pp. 604-605.

from Christ and the supernatural is a reflection on the meaning of redemption itself. Now, redemption is at bottom self-knowledge, original sin being the loss of one's image and evil being the lack of knowledge of oneself. If then man is able to attain to a knowledge of himself apart from the supernatural, and this knowledge is essential knowledge (the matter and form of human nature being *animal rationale*), then man is not only able to redeem himself but indeed is already redeemed. But the whole purpose of Christ's coming is to restore the image we lost. In Christ lies our meaning. Redemption is the giving of a name—Christ "knows" us (in the Hebrew sense of "to know") and in knowing us we are redeemed. To those who are unredeemed Christ says: Depart from me you cursed into everlasting fire; and the reason Christ gives: because I know you not.

If redemption consists in essential self-knowledge and man possesses an essential definition of himself, as scholasticism claims, then what need have we of the supernatural? Thus the assertion designed to save the supernatural ends up denying the necessity of the very thing it is trying to justify. Implicit in the effort of the secular humanists and naturalists to attain to self-knowledge apart from the supernatural is the premise that once self-knowledge is attained, then peace and salvation ensue. Man is redeemed. Are we not siding with them and defeating our own cause, betraying it, when we claim that man has intelligibility apart from the supernatural? In fact are we not the more rabid naturalists, for we claim that we already possess an essential meaning of man while they hold that they still have to search for it?

It is not only the aspect of immanence of the supernatural that is endangered by the scholastic formulation but also the aspect of gratuity. This point can be shown by an analysis of the notion of a gratuitous gift. For a gift to be gratuitous two conditions must be fulfilled. First, the giver must be free to give the gift; it is not something owed; there are no obligations on the part of the giver. In other words he does not have to render the gift; there is no necessity on his part. On the part of the receiver there must be a lack of exigency, claim or title for the object received; the object is not only undeserved but beyond the ability or means of the receiver to obtain. The second condition for gratuity is that the gift be valuable or significant to the receiver so that, in receiving it, he will have something to be thankful for. For the quality of gratuity in the gift lies precisely in its ability to cause gratitude in the receiver. But how can the receiver be grateful if the gift is valueless for him? Common sense is sufficient to show that when we select a gift for a loved one we want it to be something he desires.

It is to be noted further that the capacity of the gift to cause gratitude is in proportion to the desire of the receiver. Hence it is not sufficient that the giver give freely for the gift to be gratuitous. For example, a rich man may freely throw pearls before swine but we would hardly call the act and the object given gratuitous. The swine has to want the object, or to put it more philosophically, it must be structured for the object. A gift may be of great value in itself but if there is no desire for it on the part of the receiver, the object cannot really be gratuitous no matter how willingly and freely the giver may part with it. Thus it is not only the degree of freedom with which the gift is given that measures gratuity. An essential requirement of gratuity is also the condition that the receiver desires the gift. On the part of the receiver we can also conclude that the greater the desire the greater the gratuity. It follows too that the greater the gratuity of the object, then the greater the ordination in the receiver for the object. Ordination towards the gift is a necessary condition of gratuity.

Having made the above observations on the necessary conditions for gratuity, let us now apply them to the scholastic formulation on the gratuity of the supernatural. Does the scholastic formulation really explain the gratuity of the supernatural? Let us start with the first condition. How freely is the supernatural given? On this point we need not delay for it is precisely this condition that the scholastic formulation has been designed to safeguard. Thus God is totally free to give the gift or to refuse it. Let us rather go to the second condition. How greatly is the supernatural desired or needed by human nature?

As Christians we believe that the supernatural is of absolute necessity for man; without it he goes to hell and suffers excruciating pains at the very core of his being for this great and irreparable loss. The Scriptures also tell us that man is unintelligible apart from Christ who is the central supernatural gift of God to man. The Scriptures again tell us that it is because of love for his son that God created the world and man; that if God loves his creation it is because he loves it through, with and in Christ. We are also told that nobody goes to God except through, with, and in Christ. Thus if Christ is all-important for me (I owe my existence, my meaning, my very destiny to him), then I can see that indeed the supernatural gift of Christ to mankind and all of creation is totally and infinitely gratuitous, at least insofar as gratuity is measured in terms of the significance of the gift for the receiver. I have everything to be thankful for; my gratitude is complete and total. In return I could not but offer the whole of my self—my whole mind, heart, and soul to God.

But if we move now from the level of lived truths to that of abstract formulations, the scholastic formulation seems unable to show the significance of the gift of the supernatural. No doubt the scholastics agree that the supernatural is the highest perfection of man. If so then it must also be man's deepest need and desire towards which he is intrinsically structured in the very depths of his being. I do not see how else the gift could be significant for me. I do not see how the gift could really be totally and absolutely gratuitous from my point of view if it is not an essential need of mine. The gift may be of absolute value in itself but if I have no essential need for it how can I be truly thankful for it? If that gift is God's offer of love, how can it arouse in me a similar gift of love such that I give my all to God unless I owe everything to that gift? If the gift is purely accidental to me since it answers only an accidental need in me, God is demanding more than he gives if he asks my whole being in return. But this is contrary to the nature of God who always gives more than he asks.

The scholastic formulation, in spite of all the difficulties mentioned above, insists nevertheless that the supernatural is not essential to my perfection, for it is not part of my essence, it is not constitutive of my nature, I am not intrinsically ordained to it. The supernatural is an accidental perfection of human nature. But does this not lessen the gratuity of grace? In order to increase the freedom of the giver to the infinite degree, the scholastic formulation depreciates the value and significance of the gift for the receiver by making the gift detachable from my essential intelligibility and existence. But in so doing how can Scholasticism also maintain that grace is the most gratuitous gift in the sense of the gift I am most thankful for? If it is merely an accidental perfection, I do not see much to be thankful for. How gratuitous is the gift really? If the gift is absolutely and infinitely gratuitous then it must be something I am totally and wholly thankful for, but to be grateful to this degree also implies that the gift answers my most important need, that it fulfills my very depths. And this means that the gift cannot be detachable from my essential intelligibility and from my very existence. If the gift is detachable from my existence and intelligibility, which are the deepest realities in me, then it cannot be fully gratuitous.

Thus we see that any given thing is really gratuitous only if it is immanent to the receiver; thus the greater the gratuity the greater the immanence. If grace is absolute in gratuity then it must be absolutely immanent. If this is not so, then the gratuity of grace and the incarnation are really insignificant. Men will be unable to realize that what they are and what they have are all due to Christ and to grace. This is precisely the situation we are in today.

We are aware, of course, that in the scholastic framework to view grace as an essential need of human nature is to view it as nongratuitous on the part of God. God, then, must give grace, for the creature cannot be frustrated. But this is to destroy the gratuity of the supernatural on the part of the giver. Thus in the scholastic framework the two aforementioned conditions of gratuity are incompatible. But it is nevertheless true that any adequate formulation of gratuity must reconcile the two. In Scholasticism we reach an impasse.

Let us pass on to the third point of our evaluation. Is the scholastic formulation significant for modern man? The scholastic solution may have been meaningful for men of the middle ages. According to the aristotelian framework, value is in the extra-temporal and Christian spirituality is a matter of going beyond the temporal to the extra-temporal where the supernatural is situated. But today we have come to realize the value of the temporal because our knowledge of evolution has shown time to be positive and creative. Time does not so much destroy as build. As Robert Johann notes, we can no longer deny the new awareness of contemporary man:

Time and the world are no longer preliminaries to the main event; they help to constitute it. Time is not simply duration, the continuance of what already exists, a span given man to prove himself worthy of heaven. Time is the creative process itself, in which the real is coming to birth. And the world is no mere stopover on the way to somewhere else. It is the very stuff of man's life, asking to be shaped by him and shaping him in its turn.[9]

Unless the supernatural is truly intrinsic and immanent, it can be of little significance to the values of earth, to human activity. The traditional formulation and our new awareness of the value of temporality have caused a tension in modern man. As Father Johann describes it:

This awakening of man to the creative possibilities of this life and to his here-and-now responsibility for achieving an ever more human world has occasioned a new wave of religious skepticism. For there is the widespread feeling that traditional religions, with their emphasis on extratemporal salvation and the rules for reaching it, have served to distract the mass of men from wholehearted commitment to enhancing the present scene and really meeting its needs.[10]

A similar view has been expressed by Walter Ong:

We are living in an age in which man is identifying himself more and more with the material universe by pinpointing the network of connections between himself and the rest of God's material creation. Darwin's discoveries mark a stage in this movement whereby man finds himself more and more truly by finding the cosmos in which he lives. This movement is the contrary of that of Platonism and other ancient philosophies which drift away from a consideration of this world to a world of separated and supposedly "pure" ideas.[11]

9. Cf. his column, "Philosopher's Notebook," in *America,* (Feb. 27, 1965), p. 287.
10. *Loc. cit.*
11. Cf. *Darwin's Vision and Christian Perspectives,* ed. W. Ong, (New York: Macmillan, 1960), p. 145.

It is highly probable that the tension felt by the modern Christian is the contradiction between his scholastically formulated concept of the supernatural (valid and significant for a medieval world) and his actually experienced world, which is not medieval and for which scholastic formulations have become insignificant. The source of most of our tensions in theology and the spiritual life is, then, the attempt to think in the context of the medieval world while actually living in this world. We try to withdraw from the real world to overcome the conflict, but in so doing we become unrealistic; hence we are driven back to the real world which, because we lack the proper intellectual categories to grasp it, becomes unintelligible for us. We are unable to integrate the truths of our faith with reality so that they become insignificant for us unless we again withdraw into the medieval world, but once again we find ourselves in unreality; hence the acute tension resulting from this vicious circle.

From the point of view of the needs of non-Christians, the formulation of moderate intrinsicalism is no recommendation for Christianity to them. For atheistic communists and naturalistic humanists, the world is all important; they do not believe in a supernatural beyond. They can heed the supernatural only if it is shown to be constitutive of nature, situated at the very core of it, and its highest perfection, without which it is unintelligible. But as long as the supernatural is left in the category of accident, then what is emphasized by this formulation is the transcendence of the supernatural, whether or not that is our purpose. What needs to be emphasized, however, is the immanence of the supernatural, but the best of scholastic formulations is unable to do this.

Because the supernatural is put by the scholastics in the category of accident, the logical and inescapable conclusion is that it is not essential to or constitutive of nature; nature can be conceived apart from it and is basically self-sufficient and autonomous; in other words, we can take it or leave it. The atheistic communists and naturalists, of course, choose to leave it, and they are quite within their rights; their position is logical and justifiable. And if the supernatural is not really necessary to nature, then we have a hard time explaining to them why the Christian God would place in hell anyone bereft of the supernatural by his own free choice. The doctrine on hell makes sense only when the supernatural is shown to be constitutive of nature; then we can say that nature is intrinsically ordained to the supernatural so that man has a natural duty to tend towards it. The free choice of denying what is of nature, indeed the very core and perfection of nature, would proportionately merit the highest type of punishment or sanction. The scholastic formulation is unable to make the doctrine on hell reasonable.

Thus evaluating the position of Scholasticism and of moderate intrinsicalism in particular according to the three points outlined previously, we find that both are inadequate. The scholastic formulation is unable to explain how the supernatural is the highest perfection of man, for it cannot show that it is at the very core and center of his being, constitutive of his nature, and the goal towards which his nature is intrinsically ordained. It is unable to resolve the tension in the modern Christian whose new awareness is that time is redemptive, creative, positive, for this formulation tells him that value is in the extra-temporal, transphenomenal, metaphysical, metempirical. And finally, it is unable to meet the needs of naturalism and secularism, because it is unable to present the truths about the supernatural in a meaningful and significant way, or in a way that is harmonious with the other truths of Christian faith. All that the scholastic formulation is able to explain is the transcendence of the supernatural. True, the supernatural is transcendent; this is not to be denied. But why go on emphasizing it when the need today is to emphasize its immanence? We do not deny that in scholastic thought the immanence of God and of the supernatural is affirmed. We can find abundant testimony to this in all scholastic writings. This has always been the view of Christianity. But again, as we noted in the beginning, it is not the belief of Christians we are questioning; rather, it is the formulation of that belief. It is one thing to affirm the immanence of the supernatural; it is another to show its philosophical possibility. But, to date, attempts to show this possibility have failed; if we question the scholastic formulation, it is because it does not conform to the universal and continuous belief of Christians.

Resolution of the dilemmas consequent upon the scholastic formulation, it would seem, requires much more than a reshuffling of scholastic categories, all the while using the same basic philosophic framework. We have been at this problem for well over seven centuries but the closest we have come to showing that the supernatural is immanent is to assign it to the category of accident. Perhaps modern scholastics would consider the categorizing of the supernatural as an accident a caricature of their position—a view one would not find even on the textbook level. Be that as it may, it is nevertheless true that the older scholastics considered the supernatural (grace) an accident:

> Theologians, for a variety of reasons, including the need to do battle with Luther and Calvin, concentrated so much attention on the transformation of the soul through grace (they called it, God forgive them, "a supernatural accident") that they hardly noticed that the transformation is effected by the indwelling Spirit, who is present because the person concerned has become one with Christ.[12]

12. Most Rev. Denis E. Hurley, D.D., "Love, Law and Creation," *Pax Romana Journal,* 1965, No. 4. See also University of Dayton *Catholic Action Studies,* Oct. 1965, Study No. 216, pp. 1-2.

Having been rightly accused of extrinsicalism and being quite sensitive about it, modern scholastics now shy away from calling the supernatural an accident. But the older scholastics might well ask how the supernatural should then be categorized. They would remind the younger ones that between substance and accident *non datur tertium*. Consequently, if the supernatural is not an accident, then it can only be substantial to man. But if this is so, then it is part of man's essence. This conclusion, however, would destroy the gratuity and transcendence of the supernatural. Thus the older scholastics, in calling the supernatural an accident, were at least more logical than the younger ones. The "new breed" of scholastics have yet to give us a more satisfactory formulation.

As we close our sketchy critique, we are aware that there will be scholastics who will say we misrepresent the scholastic formulation and that our critique of it is unfair. But we are sure they will agree that Scholasticism has not yet achieved a satisfactory formulation of the relation between nature and supernature. As the theologian Bruch notes, "In conclusion we admit that the problem of the relation between the natural and the supernatural in man remains a problem and demands continued theological research."[13] For my part, I believe that we have exhausted the possibilities of the scholastic framework. And the reason for the failure of a great theologian like de Lubac to show the immanence of the supernatural is that he was cramped and imprisoned by the philosophic categories he took for his point of departure. An attempt made within a new framework may resolve the dilemmas and prove the feasibility of Teilhard's synthesis.

13. *Op. cit.,* p. 29.

PART TWO

The Philosophy of Process

CHAPTER IV

Philosophy and Christian Renewal

This second part of the study requires a few words of introduction. The aim of the second part is to effect a not too rough transition from scholastic philosophy to a philosophy of process. For we believe that a philosophy of process is a more adequate philosophical framework for the formulation of a modern conception of the supernatural, which is implied in Teilhard's world-view.

There is, understandably enough, great resistance on the part of scholastically trained Christians to change from one philosophic framework to another. People usually love what is familiar and distrust the new. But there is also much risk involved in espousing the new, for it requires great intellectual, emotional and psychological effort to effect a change from one mode of thought to another, and in the end that effort may be unsuccessful and result only in confusion. But risk is the necessary condition for growing up. And the greater the end sought (such as the growth of the mystical body towards the *pleroma Christi*), the greater the risk.

It is not only for the sake of the modern world that we must search for a new philosophical framework, but for the sake of truth itself. We saw this in our review of the history of the concept of the supernatural. The growth of truth among men requires new formulations. Past formulations are but the starting point for more adequate ones. What should be put away from the mind is the false idea that change is always dangerous and that truth lies in the unchanging. The more objective and realistic position is that within an evolving universe change is the necessary condition for growth. Not to change is to die. Of course for one who persists in living in the framework of the middle ages truth is in the atemporal and eternal; he may achieve peace of mind but it is a false peace, for every man's vocation is to serve the world in which he lives. To withdraw into the world of the middle ages is to be unrealistic, and therefore, unChristian. Karl Rahner speaks of the artificial existence of those who still escape into the imagined world of yesterday, into the dead corner of history—the middle ages—instead of living in this concrete world (which is the only real world we have).[1]

If we are to live in the modern world, then we must be prepared to look at all things historically and evolutionarily. Even realities which we have traditionally considered supratemporal and metempirical evolve—dogma evolves, the Church evolves, philosophical frameworks evolve, theological formulations evolve. And the formulation of the supernatural has evolved. Historically, there was an evolution of philosophic framework from Platonism to Aristotelianism with a corresponding change in the formulation of the supernatural. These changes were pressured by the tensions in men seeking to grasp their world intellectually. New discoveries and advances in culture change the world radically for a man. That change creates a tension in him, compelling him to harmonize his intellectual framework with the world as he knows it. Thus new philosophic frameworks develop. But a new philosophic framework in its turn forces a man to harmonize all levels of his knowledge, including his religious or theological constructions.

1. Cf. *Theological Investigations,* V (Baltimore: Helicon, 1966), p. 149ff.

The medievals followed precisely this procedure. The ancient world-view had proven itself inadequate; the world had evolved to such an extent that new philosophic categories were required if men were to comprehend and synthesize it. Hence they took the aristotelian philosophic framework and used its categories for the formulation of truths. St. Thomas was great precisely because he was in touch with his times. If he had been an ultra-conservative he could not have produced the precedent-setting *Summa*. He expressed the truths of Christian faith in categories which for that age were modern, achieving a synthesis that harmonized very well with the physical and mathematical world-view of the time. Because of his modernity, St. Thomas met opposition from his ultra-conservative contemporaries, especially among those in positions of authority and even among members of his own order. There was resistance to Aristotle and the effort of Thomas to "aristotelianize" theology. History, however, has vindicated Thomas. He was able to resolve the moral and theological crisis of his time, effecting a transition from platonic-augustinian to scholastic-aristotelian theology.

Today we are in a similar state of crisis which demands a similar renewal in philosophy and theology. The tension felt by the modern Christian, the rise of communism, naturalism, and secularism are tell-tale signs of the emergence of a new world-view that is forcing the Church to adapt to the modern world or else lose all influence. As Cardinal Döpfner warned at the Munich Congress, masses of the faithful have been lost because the Catholic Church has appeared to them as "an institution that enslaved freedom" and as "a superannuated souvenir from a past age."[2] It has spoken to men in an ancient tongue, in incomprehensible rituals, and in

2. Cf. *Time,* February 7, 1964, p. 66.

concepts that have no relation to current life. Instead of
penetrating the world, the Church has seemed to sit "in a
self-imposed ghetto, trying to build its own small world
adjoining the big world." Tied to "antiquated forms,"
Catholicism has often given the appearance of resenting the
inescapable presence of ideological pluralism, political
democracy and modern technology. The Church which the
Cardinal described is the medieval Church, valid for that
age but no longer for ours.

Our world has changed radically, as radically as in the
time of Plato and Aristotle, if not more so. Thus there has
been a shift from the ptolemaic to the einsteinian at the
physical level, from the static universal species of Aristotle
to the evolving species of Darwin at the biological level,
and, at the cultural level, from the ahistorical outlook of
the medievals to the modern historical outlook. The new
dimension in our world today is that of evolution. In all our
constructions what differentiates us from the medieval man
is our historical and evolutionary approach. Thus we have
begun to look on revelation as a history of salvation rather
than as an unchanging body of propositions enshrined for-
ever in scholastic summas; the Church is now seen as an
evolving reality rather than a purely static juridical structure; man is considered in his historicity and temporality
rather than in his unchanging essence.

The change in world-outlook cannot but affect a change
in theology calling for theological reformulation and integration. The connection between the change in world-view
and in theology is highlighted by Charles Henkey:

> Change in theology has followed on the change that human
> existence has undergone generally. From a static universe,
> closed in by time and space and ruled over in stoic majesty
> by a remote spiritual power, a universe comprehensible by
> the Aristotelian categories, we have come into a new,

entirely dynamic universe, indefinitely open to space and time. The human spirit no longer conceives its perfection in a Platonic aloofness and withdrawal from the turmoil of material existence. This existence is now conceived as a function of the spirit, and thus gives our personal existence and our theology a cosmic broadness.

This great change in attitude obviously did not come about just within the last decade, nor were such revolutionary books written during this period as to constitute the beginning of a new age. Still we can say that it was during these past ten years that the faith of the Church became explicitly aware of the fact that our existence had passed over the threshold of a new age. Pope John did not act merely on the basis of private, personal insight in calling Vatican Council II; he expressed what the Church felt, a feeling which came to something like a boiling point in his reign.

These changing dimensions in human existence call for theological integration. We live in a new age, whatever we call it: the space age; the age of internationalism, in which the barriers hitherto separating nations and races and creeds are slowly disappearing; the age of personalism, and consequently of pluralism, in which the person is emerging from the closed social formations which formerly harbored him.[3]

In spite of the obvious connection between a new worldview and the need for philosophical and theological adaptation to this new world-view, there is great reluctance on the part of many to transcend Thomism. One of the reasons for this reluctance is the belief that Thomism is perennial and able to assimilate everything within it. It might be well to re-examine the foundations of this belief. For in the context of an evolving universe, it would seem that there is no such thing as a perennial philosophy except perhaps the collective thought of mankind.

Philosophy, in our view, is evolutionary. Our premise is

3. Cf. his article, "Roundup—the Church," *Perspectives,* 9 (Nov.-Dec., 1964), p. 180.

that creation is going on even now, that species evolve, that reality is in process, hence unfinished, and that the fullness and essential meaning of reality will be revealed only at the end of the process. Philosophically this means that the intellect cannot arrive at the essential meaning of reality for the present. It would be a falsification of reality to present it as finished when it is still evolving (unless, perhaps, the intellect had prophetic powers that could transport it to the end of the process so that it could see the fruit of the process). If truth is conformity to reality, then conformity to present reality has to present it as evolving. All our philosophical formulations must necessarily be evolutionary if they are to conform to evolving reality. Does this mean that there is no absolute truth? By no means. The absolute truth of reality is synonymous with evolved truth, which, however, is found at the end of the process. But more on this when we come to treat of the philosophy of process directly and in detail.

If our premise is true—that creation is going on even now and that the essential meaning of reality cannot be found till the end of the process—then no philosophy can claim to know the essence of reality now. Consequently, no philosophy can claim to be finished and to have said the last word. We do not yet have an absolute formulation of reality. Philosophical systems are but partial formulations of reality, valid for a certain age of collective human consciousness which is itself in process of evolving towards maturity.

We are in effect submitting a view on the nature of philosophy which contradicts the hellenic individualistic view. According to this individualistic view, each philosophical system is independent and autonomous of every other system. In our view (which I believe to be more traditional) we introduce the notion of corporate personality or collective human consciousness. The evolution of this consciousness, or noögenesis, to use Teilhard's phrase, is philosophy. Thus the various philosophic systems are not independent of one another but are related as stages of one philosophic consciousness.

The failure to look at philosophical systems this way is one of the main reasons for a stubborn adherence to one system and the reluctance to embrace another. In the individualistic view of philosophy, the transition from one philosophy to another is like the abandoning of one religion for another. This outlook breeds deep-seated allegiance. And since philosophy is the search for truth, the choice of one philosophy over another is an implicit declaration of the falsity of the other. In the evolutionary view, however, the transition is the transition from one stage to another. Hence, the transition from one stage to the higher is not an indication that the earlier stage is wrong; it is not an abandonment of the earlier stage; nor is it being unfaithful to the former stage. In fact, to be faithful to the former one has to transcend it; one has to transcend it in order to preserve it. Growth is the law of philosophy as it is of being.

From the foregoing considerations we can see that the transition from hellenic thought to a more evolved perspective does not prove Hellenism wrong. Its best insights are taken over into the new view; however, to take them over means to evolve them into a new framework. Just as adolescence is no longer childhood, although childhood somehow exists in it, so Hellenism in the context of a more adequate philosophy is no longer recognizable as Hellenism. If adolescence can no longer be called childhood, and if the seedling no longer called a seed, neither can a more evolved philosophy be called hellenic or thomistic. Or to use a theological analogy, to accept the new law or new covenant is not to deny the old law or covenant, but to accept it in a deeper and more intimate way. However, it is important to note that the earlier stage does not continue to exist in a formal way; the old law has been transcended; it can no longer be taken as it is. Or, the adolescent can no longer use the framework of childhood. The error, it seems, in judging philosophical systems is in taking one as absolute instead of as a stage. While it is valid to say that Thomism lives on in a more evolved philosophy, just as the old law lives on in the new, this does not mean that we go on thinking in hellenic categories, any more than Christians go on simply following the old law or the adolescent goes on thinking and acting like a child.

Given this evolutionary view of philosophical systems, there is no need to fear that moving into a more adequate philosophy will prove that the Church was wrong about Thomism. To express this fear is to manifest that one is still very much ruled and influenced by an individualistic view of philosophy. Rather, what the transition signifies, if and when it happens, is that the Church is growing up. After all, the Church has gone over from Platonism to Aristotelianism in the past. There is no reason why Catholic Christians cannot change from Thomism to another philosophy if we judge that the move is for our best interest.

The mistaken belief that the magisterium cannot change its philosophy has arisen from a misinterpretation of the position of the Church with regard to Thomism. The true attitude of the Church is explained by an eminent theologian when he says that "the Church's preference for the work of Aquinas is primarily intended to provide, at a time of spiritual dissolution, a sound philosophy by which the abiding, naturally known antecedents of the faith are eminently validated; it is not aimed at forcing theology into a determined form. The Church did not mean at all to put an impassable obstacle in the way of reshaping theology by the search of new philosophies."[4] And one of the foremost European

4. Joseph Ratzinger, "Theologia Perennis?", *Wort und Wahrheit,* 15 (1960), 179-188. For a digest see *Theology Digest,* 10 (1962), 71-76. The quote is from the digest.

theologians says that "Thomism does not exhaust the liberty of Christian thought."[5]

Again, Daniélou remarks that "when Karl Rahner, S.J., suggests that existential philosophy helps us to understand the hypostatic union, when André Fessard, S.J., shows us that dialectic is a valuable instrument for understanding history and free choices, when Father George Morel founds an anthropology that articulates the facts underlying the experience of John of the Cross—they accomplish excellent theology and are eminently traditional."[6]

Our mistake has been to absolutize Thomism and the middle ages. This absolutizing of the middle ages, according to Leslie Dewart, originates from a hellenic complex which, Dewart explains, Christianity acquired by adopting Greek and Roman cultural forms. But now, he continues, it has wrung those forms dry. They have become inadequate for the continued life and development of the Christian faith. He concludes that the Christian crisis of this age is definable in terms of the inadequacies of the hellenic complex.[7]

Dewart is not alone in pointing out the need to transcend hellenic categories for "the continued life and development of the Christian faith." Francis X. Murphy, a *peritus* of the Second Vatican Council, notes that what is needed today is a new metaphysics, a substructure for a new approach to theology. He observes:

> What seems obvious from the strictures of a large number of bishops is that much of the scholastic methodology has proven inadequate to the requirements of our age. This is apparently what Pope John meant: the need to expound and study Revelation and doctrine through the methods of

5. Jean Daniélou, "Unité et pluralité de la pensée chrétienne," *Etudes,* 312 (1962), 3-16. I quote from *Theology Digest,* 10 (1962), 69.

6. Cf. *Time,* Dec. 14, 1962, p. 60.

7. *Christianity and Revolution* (New York: Herder, 1963), p. 286.

research, and through the literary forms of modern thought. . . . What seems to have taken place at the last session of Vatican Council II was the death agony of a type of theologizing that simply refused to let go of the old, safe-and-sound structure that came down from the Middle Ages and is now decrepit.

The great lack thus far stems from the failure of theologians generally to provide what can only be called a meta-theology as a basis or foundation for the transition from the scholastic method of dealing with theological concepts. The scholastic method was the logical development of conceptual propositions culled from the SS and Tradition, or postulated on an Aristotelian observation of natural phenomena and erected into "natural laws."

Now there must be a transition to the type of theology that the force of events is forming among the forward-looking bishops; a theology that starts with the principles of revealed truth but applies them with great respect for the facts of life instead of trying to force the facts of life to fit what are logical conclusions, legitimately deducible from revealed data, but useless or even harmful to the Church at this time since they have no true relation to modern life.[8]

The whole point of Murphy's argument is that "what is needed right now, as the conciliar discussion amply indicated, is a courageous assertion of the fact that this older type of theologizing is finished."[9]

Similar sentiments to those expressed by Murphy have been voiced by John L. McKenzie. Speaking of writers on seminary training he says:

What these writers and observers are implying is that the scholastic dialectical system of dogmatic theology be displaced from the central position it has held for so long. Sooner or later someone is going to say this explicitly and probably the suggestion, once made, will receive more support than might be imagined. The opinion (or conviction; or mere feeling) that dialectical theology is less relevant to

8. See his article, "Vatican II Needs a New Approach," *Catholic Mind,* 52 (April, 1964), pp. 25-26, 30.
9. *Ibid.,* p. 29.

the modern priestly ministry is very common, even if it is largely inarticulate. Quite possibly it remains inarticulate because it is like attacking motherhood, and also because one feels that one should not wreck such a venerable structure without offering something to replace it. But revolutions occur in the intellectual world as well as in the political world. The advance of learning sometimes throws a whole body of erudition into the scrap heap, and a period of unsteady growth follows. In the natural sciences materials become antiquated before they can be synthesized in textbooks. A parallel in theology is the one revolution it has experienced, the scholastic revolution of the thirteenth century. There the genius of St. Thomas met the need with a synthesis; but it took some time for the synthesis to win general acceptance. It should be recalled that the writings of St. Thomas were condemned by the hierarchy in the very city where they were written. What will happen to the present generation, and has begun to happen already, is that scholastic theology will be more and more neglected until it finally perishes by erosion. It simply does not win interest.[10]

The conviction that the medieval synthesis is no longer significant for men today is shared by modern Protestants. Thus Walter M. Horton notes that "the medieval synthesis has been disrupted, both as a unity of mind and as a unity of society."[11] For Theodore M. Greene the modern question is: "How can we, with complete integrity, reinterpret religion and, through such reinterpretation, recapture the spiritual and cultural vitality which modern secularism has so largely lost?"[12] He continues: "Can we reinterpret God and religious belief, man and human reason, reality, finite and ultimate, in such a way as to make the concept of a

10. Cf. his article, "Theology in the Seminary," *Perspectives,* (Nov.-Dec., 1964), p. 174.

11. Walter M. Horton, "Tillich's Role in Contemporary Theology," *The Theology of Paul Tillich,* ed. Charles W. Kegley and Robert Bretall (New York: Macmillan, 1959), p. 44.

12. Cf. his essay, "Paul Tillich and our Secular Culture," in *The Theology of Paul Tillich,* pp. 50 and 57.

new theonomy meaningful and plausible? Can faith and reason be so reinterpreted as to make honest and informed religious dedication possible? Can a belief in God as the Source and Ground of all our being be reconciled with a belief in human freedom, initiative and responsibility? Can the central claims of Christianity be made credible in the light of modern science and modern philosophical reflection? Can the Church be revitalized and thus enabled to revitalize our culture?"

Thus among Catholics and Protestants alike there is the belief that the medieval synthesis is no longer adequate for today because our world has changed and requires its own categories. The Protestants have gone ahead to map out the contour of this new world of ours. With regard to the special problem on the supernatural, the Protestants, unencumbered by fidelity to any given philosophic framework, have been more successful than Catholics in the search for new categories with which to reformulate the truths of Christian faith. For example, Paul Tillich, whom Gustave Weigel called the outstanding Protestant of our time,[13] made it his life work to show the immanence of the truths of Christianity in nature. Tillich himself said, "I have fought supranaturalism from my early writings on, not in order to support naturalism but because I tried to overcome the alternative between naturalism and supranaturalism. I still hold emphatically to this position which could be called self-transcending or ecstatic naturalism."[14]

The opinion that Christians today need a new philosophy as an alternative to Thomism has been strengthened by Vatican Council II. In reviewing the work of the Council,

13. Cf. his article, "Protestantism and Paul Tillich," *Theological Studies,* 11 (1950), p. 185.
14. Paul Tillich, "Reply to Interpretation and Criticism," *The Theology of Paul Tillich,* p. 341.

Hans Küng indicated that the major trends of thought exhibited there may be of greater significance in the next few decades than the actual decrees.[15] Among these are 1) the theology of the neo-scholastic schools showed itself incapable of dealing with new problems, and 2) the Church has given up characteristically medieval positions in regard to civil society, the state, political life and Scholasticism.

There is no finished and worked out philosophical framework that theologians can use today in the way St. Thomas was able to use aristotelian philosophy. We have Teilhard's world-view which integrates the supernatural into the modern world. But what is required is to systematize the philosophy of an evolving universe. This Teilhard did not expressly do, though such a philosophy is implicit in his system. The work of explicitation we will attempt to do in the next chapter.

It may be objected at this point that the philosophy of process we are going to propose is not teilhardian; furthermore, that in using this philosophy, we are going outside the teilhardian vision to solve the problem of the supernatural. I believe that the philosophy implicit in Teilhard's synthesis is one of process.[16] Whether Teilhard would accept the philosophy of process as we present it here is another question. But that he would approve such an attempt as in conformity with his basic vision is quite clear from one of his letters:

> You are, quite rightly, concerned with the question of "essences." But you must realize that since we have now to advance from a "metaphysic of the cosmos" to a "metaphysic of cosmogenesis," the question is not exactly how to

15. Hans Küng, "What Has the Council Done?", *Commonweal* (January 21, 1966), pp. 461-68.

16. I tried to demonstrate this in my doctoral dissertation. Cf. *infra*, Chapter IX, p. 267, n. 2.

preserve but how to transpose (into an additional dimension) the notion of the *fixity* of essences.

In cosmogenesis, essence becomes genesis: so that what is fixed is direction—this constant direction being accompanied by an accentuation of certain characteristics—and operating through certain steps or thresholds (separating domains that are essentially different: for example, the preliving and the living, the simply living and the reflectively living—physics is full of such "steps"). (18 May 1954).[17]

Of particular importance in this letter is Teilhard's observation that we have now to advance from a metaphysic of the cosmos to a metaphysics of cosmogenesis; that the question is not so much how to preserve the notion of the fixity of essence as how to transpose it into an additional dimension. This is exactly the task I have set myself to in the succeeding chapters—a transposition of the category of substance or essence to that of process which is a new ontological dimension, and the analysis of this process into what Teilhard would call thresholds or domains. That a philosophy of process is the authentic view of Teilhard is noted by Claude Cuénot when he says that Teilhard urges us to abandon traditional ontology—the metaphysics that deals with essences. The result of this transposition to a process philosophy is a revolution in philosophy, observes Cuénot, as far-reaching as the existentialist emphasis on existence at the expense of essence.[18]

17. I quote from the masterful work of Claude Cuénot, *Teilhard de Chardin* (Baltimore: Helicon, 1965), p. 369.
18. *Loc. cit.*

CHAPTER V

The Basic Category of Process Established

The prolegomenon to a philosophy, far from being incidental, may indeed be the most important part. For the philosophy that follows is merely a development of the conditions and assumptions laid down at the beginning. Thus I shall begin with a discussion of my approach to philosophy and the problem of its methodology.

Because of the inadequacy and perhaps impossibility of any rationalistic system to comprehend the depth, complexity and mystery of the universe, many philosophers today shy away from system-building. They content themselves with the examination of a small portion of reality, for example, an analysis of language or of human temporality. While this new trend toward piece-meal philosophy is justifiable, it can also be overdone. The urge to synthesize into some sort of order the chaotic multiplicity of facts and phenomena is a demand not only of knowledge, but much more so of life itself, which requires a continuous adjustment at all levels of one's relation to the world.

Philosophy in this deeper sense of the term is the formulation of a workable world-view for the guidance and direction of human existence. Hence, philosophy is not so much for contemplation as for life. Such a philosophy is valid as long as one does not consider the synthesis closed, and as long as one accepts the possibility of many systems each expressing in its own way a view of the world but none completely exhausting the meaning of reality.

From two methodological approaches to present reality are derived two general philosophic views, one a philosophy of being, the other a philosophy of becoming. While the former does not deny becoming, it nevertheless considers becoming relative to being and, as a consequence, it assimilates movement and time within what it considers to be the more basic category, that of permanence and atemporality. Conversely, while accepting the fact of permanence in experience, the latter nevertheless emphasizes becoming as more basic, thus assimilating permanence and atemporality within temporality and history. Since the philosophy of process presented here approaches reality as process, it may be classified methodologically in the latter tradition; however, in terms of the result, since for this philosophy becoming terminates in being, it may also be called a philosophy of being. Thus, the philosophy of process may be viewed as a synthesis of the traditional philosophies of being and becoming.

There is a strong impression current among traditionalists that philosophies of being are to be preferred over philosophies of becoming since the former are based on self-evident principles, for example, the intuition of being, while the latter has no basis since it views reality as flux. The former, therefore, yields absolute and certain truths, while the latter yields only relative truths, if any. The answer to the question ultimately comes down to the nature of the starting point of philosophy. Is philosophy postulational, or is it based on self-evident ontological principles?

If we decide the matter purely historically, it would seem that philosophy is postulational. In the past, several philosophical systems claimed the self-evidence of their respective ontological starting points. But given one and the same reality, how can there be so many self-evident starting points which are often contradictory to one another? How determine the true one when what is self-evident to one philosophy is not to another? Today, philosophers tend more to the view that there is a plurality of systems, each founded on a basic assumption or postulate. This is not to subscribe to the view that reality is pluralistic, that it is nothing else but what we make of it.

I believe that reality is one; however, at the present, since reality is still evolving, no one can arrive at a final formulation of what reality is. The most we can do is to postulate its probable outcome and then organize facts and direct our actions accordingly. Communists, for example, postulate a communistic materialistic utopia as the end of the process; Teilhard, Christ as Omega. Even the thomistic starting point, the intuition of being, is based on a postulate or assumption that reality is finished; hence one can intuit being. But if reality is indeed evolving, then the intuition of being is not self-evident; we do not have a self-evident starting point.

To judge a philosophy that openly asserts that it is based on a postulate as less adequate than one that claims it is based on self-evident principles is to judge falsely, since the view that one can have self-evident starting points is itself not self-evident. But should not the more sensible stand be to withhold judgment until all the facts are in? It would be if we were doing science purely, for we cannot give as scientific fact what is unsupported by empirical evidence. But it is unfair to demand this of philosophy if we understand philosophy as we have described it here. In the task of directing one's life, or relating oneself to the world, we do not have absolute certainty; we have only a working hypothesis. The whole man does not live by science alone; we cannot reduce the whole man to the scientific man, although this seems to be the trend today.

At the deeper level, human life is based largely on

assumptions: as to our origin, our nature, our destiny. Atheism is based on the assumption that there is no God, theism, that there is; naturalism is based on the assumption that there is no after-life, supernaturalism, that there is, and so on. We have to make a commitment; we cannot just stand still and do nothing. We are caught in the forward march of life and we have to act. But the foundations of our actions are questions which science cannot answer; only the naïve and positivists would object that such assumptions and the philosophies derived from them are of no value because they are not based on scientific facts.

In line with the foregoing considerations, let us consider a specific objection to Teilhard's synthesis. It is contended "that Teilhardian views are mostly assumptions, are entirely unproved, and not worthy of acceptance as a serious philosophy."[1] The objection is elaborated:

> Teilhard's structure is like a beautiful or intriguing painting or a landscape. It is fine to look upon—and even enjoy. But let us suppose an engineer sought to build a road through that landscape. He would not be able to base his plans on that landscape. He would have to make a minute scientific study of the reality of the country he must cross. There is no evidence Teilhard's view is more than a landscape. The scientific study is lacking.

The objection contains the speaker's requirements for a valid philosophic synthesis, namely, that it must have a self-evident starting point and be supported by scientific evidence. According to these requirements Teilhard's synthesis fails, hence it is not a serious philosophy. The objector has the secure feeling that Thomism, on the other hand, is based

1. This is the view of Father Michael Stock, O.P., as reported by the *Catholic Telegraph* in an interview with one of its reporters. See the May 14, 1965 issue, p. A 12.

on self-evident principles and conforms to scientific study.

If we judge the thomistic synthesis by the requirements of the objector, we find that it, in fact, is deficient. For the claim to the possession of a self-evident starting point is itself an assumption. Furthermore, Thomism is based on a fundamental assumption that reality is substantially finished, an assumption which is of lesser probability than the assumption that it is unfinished. And if we compare Teilhard's synthesis to Thomas's on the point of fidelity to modern science, doubtless it is Thomism that is lacking in scientific foundation since this philosophy was made to harmonize with a ptolemaic universe. On the other hand, not only was Teilhard a scientist of the first rank, but his synthesis, which takes account of evolution, is by that fact "scientific," while philosophies that lack an evolutionary viewpoint lack scientific support.

But the objector reveals an even deeper misunderstanding of the nature of synthesis. It is necessary to distinguish between what we might call micro-synthesis and macro-synthesis. The former joins together in an intelligent way elements derived from analysis. The formulation derived cannot go beyond the elements of the synthesis; the synthesis must be grounded on the result of the analysis. This type of analytic-synthetic method is employed in all disciplines—science, philosophy and theology.

There is another kind of synthesis, employed at the macro- or large-scale level, which aims to achieve a harmonious and integrated view of a whole discipline or even of all the disciplines. No doubt such a synthesis must also be grounded on facts derived from a previous analysis. But it is much more than the result and explanation of the previous analysis since it provides the starting point for a new level of analysis by suggesting new approaches or methods of research for the discovery of new data. At the level of science, Einstein's synthesis is an excellent example. Now who will complain that it contained unproved assumptions, that it went beyond presently known facts? It is of the very nature of this type of synthesis that it goes beyond present facts, that it contain assumptions. In Einstein's synthesis, creative imagination and insight played a vital part in the formulation. In fact, the basis not only for great scientific discoveries but also for great philosophic and theological syntheses is precisely the creative imagination or prophetic spirit. The positivist is never a great discoverer or synthe- sizer because he never goes beyond present facts.

Teilhard's synthesis is not a micro- but a macro-synthesis. Furthermore, it is not a scientific synthesis on the macro- level, but a *Weltanschauung,* that is, a world-view. Hence, scientists who evaluate Teilhard's view usually make two kinds of mistake: they equate it either with micro-synthesis or with macro-synthesis at the scientific level. In the first case, they complain that it goes beyond presently known scientific data and therefore lacks scientific study; in the second, that it goes beyond scientific methodology by includ- ing Christ-Omega in it.

Coming, then, to the synthesis which is a *Weltanschauung,* there are two kinds depending on the basic methodological approach to reality. There is a static approach (which we believe is the approach of Father Stock) in which every- thing is finished, the universe is substantially complete, essences are given. The function of a philosophic synthesis in this case is to give us a completely mapped out picture of reality, so to speak, for the purpose of contemplation. But in an unfinished universe, the purpose of a synthesis is to forecast the direction reality is tending; hence it is a work- ing plan that guides and directs the collective human effort in the building of the new earth. And because it is a plan, it is of its very nature based on assumptions. In a finished universe, however, there is no reason to assume anything; in fact, it would be wrong to do so since everything is given.

Now, Father Stock assumes that there is only one approach to reality—his approach—and then judges all philosophic syntheses by the requirements of his approach. But the question is: which approach is more in accord with reality? If reality is unfinished, then all syntheses—scientific, philosophic or theological—are unfinished and necessarily based on assumptions. Today we consider synthesis not as a finished picture but as a working plan. Even in theology, we are beginning to look upon theological formulations as but the starting points for further clarification and reflection. What makes Teilhard's a great synthesis is not only the unification of previously known data on all levels of our systematizations, but its creative and prophetic insight in pointing out to men the direction human endeavor should follow in the context of an evolving universe.

We are going to derive the philosophy of process from the evolving universe which is at once teilhardian, copernican, einsteinian, darwinian and spiritually oriented. Needless to say, Teilhard's synthesis is just a probable one, hence all we are claiming for our philosophy is that it is probable.

An objection to a philosophy of process that might be made at this point is that it is an extrapolation from biological evolution and that therefore it has only metaphorical value. Besides, the objection might continue, such a philosophy is not able to stand alone because it depends for its certainty on whether evolution is a theory or a fact. To answer this objection, it is necessary to discuss the nature of extrapolation.

Extrapolation is a valid means of arriving at truth, especially in science. It suggests new methods, new approaches that often give surprising results. But then the philosopher comes along and speaks of truths arrived at by extrapolation as purely metaphorical. But hardly would cosmogonists and cultural evolutionists consider their respective sciences metaphorical. An important distinction has to be made, namely, between the method and the result. Just because the method is extrapolation, that does not mean the result is extrapolated, hence metaphorical or figurative.

To show this let us use a philosophic example. When a child begins to know, the first level of knowledge is sense knowledge; only later does he progress to intellectual knowledge. (Sense knowledge reveals intellectual knowledge, because intellectual knowledge, being more immanent, is not as apparent as sense knowledge.) Now intellectual knowledge is an extension of sense knowledge at the historical or methodological level, but not at the ontological level. In other words, intellectual knowledge is not secondary. Hence, intellectual knowledge, though secondary in point of discovery, is first in point of ontological value. What comes later from the point of view of discovery or emergence is not necessarily the least, otherwise we would have to reduce man to matter. Again, to use another example, the seed is first historically, hence at this level the fruit is reduced to the seed; but at the ontological level, the seed is reduced to the fruit. Extrapolation is not a deduction in which the conclusion cannot be greater than the premise. The process of discovery often starts with what is superficial and proceeds to the more profound: from sense to intellect; from seed to fruit; from child to adult.

Biological evolution is but the most apparent instance of process; it is the one closest to us. As a point of departure, a principle of discovery, it is first. We do extrapolate, in the sense that we extend the notion to other levels. But the result is not metaphorical, secondary, and valuable only analogically, biological evolution being the prime analogate or norm. As well might we argue that sense knowledge, being the first in order of discovery, is the prime analogate of knowledge, intellectual knowledge being analogical and reducible to it. To speak of the result of extrapolation as metaphorical is really another form of reductionism by which, for example, life is reduced to mechanism; consciousness to vitalism, etc.

No doubt, then, it was biological evolution that historically gave impetus to the search for large-scale processes at other levels of reality. In the process of discovering these other levels, the very notion of evolution itself was deepened, in much the same way that sense knowledge is deepened into intellectual knowledge so that the former is reduced to the latter as its prime analogate. It is from this deeper and wider notion of evolution that we look at biological evolution as simply an instance of evolution. Historically, the notion of evolution was founded on the discovery of biological evolution, but ontologically, it is founded on higher and more immanent instances of evolution. It is false, we believe, to freeze the concept of evolution, applying it univocally only to biological evolution and calling all other uses of it figurative. In the context of process and discovery, the concept itself grows. Its full meaning outgrows its first instance.

When we use the term evolution in our study, we are using it in the full sense of the term and not as an extrapolated concept from biological evolution. Evolution in this full sense is synonymous with process. Process is founded not on biological evolution alone but on other instances of process as well. Biological evolution is but one among many instances; in fact, its data are secondary to the data supplied by higher levels of reality. For example, theology reveals the fact that revelation is a history of salvation, that is, a process that is creative, and not just a mere succession of time; there is also the evolution of dogma; and the Church is understood as a mystical body that evolves towards the *pleroma Christi*—which is not metaphorical language at all. On the level of rationality, there is the fact of cultural evolution, the evolution of ideas and world-views. Thus the testimony of science to evolution at the lower levels, though important in itself, is for our construction a purely secondary source of data. Therefore, we do not have the false problem of building a philosophy of process on a biological notion or the consequent problem of accomplishing a transition from a scientific notion, which is empirical, to a philosophic one, which is supposedly metempirical.

If we base our philosophy of process on theological data such as Christ-Omega and revelation as a history of salvation, is this not being unphilosophical? The objection imposes a purely conventional notion of what it is to philosophize, a notion which defines the area of philosophy by cutting it off from the scientific, poetic and religious aspects of reality. We depart from this hellenic view which considers these aspects of reality as of no philosophic value, as well as that mentality which considers science as the ideal which philosophy must imitate in its results and methods. For us, extramental reality is naturally poetic and religious. Our data will be whatever truth is found, without discrimination as to the source. As Bertrand Russell well notes, "a philosophy which is to have any value should be built upon a wise and firm foundation of knowledge that is not specifically philosophical. Such knowledge is the soil from which the tree of philosophy derives its vigor. Philosophy which does not draw nourishment from this soil will soon wither and cease to grow."[2]

Thus, to arrive at a synthetic view of reality, openness to

2. Borrowed from T. A. Goudge, *The Ascent of Life* (Toronto: The University of Toronto Press, 1961), p. 11.

all truth is the necessary condition. Suppose reality as a process really does terminate in Christ as its Omega, then how can we understand that process without knowing its end? How shall we know what an unknown seed is unless we know what its fruit will be? But by the hellenically influenced definition of philosophy and its goals, we have cut ourselves off at the very start from the source of truth. But we are mixing methods, it may be objected. Let us consider, however, whether reality itself should not dictate the proper method to arrive at an integral synthesis.

It may be further countered that nature is autonomous, intelligible apart from the theological or supernatural. But where, may we ask, is the foundation for such an assertion? It is not revelation; it is not even science. It is just a probable assumption deriving from hellenic philosophy and scholastic theology which create a dualism between nature and supernature. We will not deny its possibility, but neither should the possibility of the opposite be denied. Again, it may be objected that such an approach confuses disciplines. I think, however, that we should be more concerned with arriving at the truth than with preserving our neat distinctions and our professions. Hence, I do not hesitate to use theological data, as long as they are part of history, part of this world. And the incarnation of Christ, as Teilhard notes, is a fact which stands before us; it has its place among the other realities of the world.[3]

The same objection proferred above is often made from another angle, namely, that reason attains only the natural; hence to use theological data is to go beyond the realm and capacity of reason. But this view of reason is again purely conventional and as valid as the distinction between a natural order and a supernatural order. For us reason is ordered not to the natural, but to the world. And if the world tends

3. *PH*, p. 292.

to the supernatural as to its Omega, then reason is ordered to that, too. This is not to say that reason attains to the supernatural of its own power. This is what we would seem to be saying if our statement is judged according to the hellenic view that nature necessarily attains its proper end by its own power alone. But we will show—and this is the central philosophic point we are going to make—that the hellenic concept of nature is a false one.

Reason for us is not only scientific or natural, but poetic, religious, imaginative. In fact, as we noted earlier, it is often the imaginative reason that gives insight into reality, as confirmed by the great discoveries of science. Hence it is this synthetic reason that we will use in our approach to reality, which is the same as saying that it is the whole man that must philosophize, not the compartmentalized specialist. The scientific approach and the traditional philosophic approach give only the impersonal and objective aspects of reality, and not its intimate and incommunicable depths. The reasonable (because truly human) approach to reality is attained only by the existential, living individual who does not deny his emotions, beliefs, and aspirations both poetic and religious; the man who is at peace with the world and himself. It is this approach that is best able to probe the depth, richness, beauty and truth of reality. On the other hand, the so-called reasonable and objective approach that employs only a part of man—the cold light of natural reason alone—is really unreasonable and at most a myth.

Comparing the philosophy of process with other dynamic philosophies, we might note that it is not heraclitean or bergsonian because time for us is not an interminable flux or flow without direction and purpose. Nor is it a philosophy of evolution if by this is meant a philosophy based purely on scientific ideas (or facts) such as biological evolution, relativity physics and quantum mechanics. Hence it is unlike the philosophies of Whitehead, William James, John Dewey or Samuel Alexander, although it is not to be denied that there are many points of similarity between it and them. It is similar to the philosophy of Hegel in that it terminates in spirit, but it differs from his in the location of this spirit. Thus Hegel's spirit starts outside time as an idea and also ends outside time as absolute spirit, while Teilhard's Omega is in time and remains in it as its fullness. The philosophy of process is also similar to that of communism in that the goal in both is in time and remains in time, but they are dissimilar in the nature of the goal proposed. In communism, the goal is a materialistic utopia; in the philosophy of process it is a spiritual redemption of the earth.

With regard to the presentation to be made, it may be useful to point out that since our age has just emerged into a new world, an analysis of its philosophic structure such as will be attempted here is obviously exploratory. We could not, nor do we aim to present a perfect alternative to Thomism. Thomas was in a much better position in relation to his world than Teilhard was in relation to his. For Thomas had a ready-made philosophy, that of Aristotle, which had already mapped out for him the philosophical structure of a static universe. But Teilhard was his own Aristotle. In this task he was a pioneer. What remains for us to do is to make explicit the philosophy implicit in his world-view.

It should be noted besides that since we are not presenting a philosophy of process in itself but only in relation to the problem of the supernatural, our treatment of the philosophic categories of an evolving universe is going to be selective; we will discuss only those categories which are pertinent and useful for the elucidation and solution of our problem. A fuller treatment of a philosophy of process will have to be made at another time and place. In spite of this selective approach, however, an attempt is also made to show the synthetic unity of the philosophy, since one of our aims in this presentation is to recommend this philosophy to others, especially to theologians. With them in mind, an attempt is made to indicate possible applications of the categories of process to other areas of theology besides the one at hand, in order to show the feasibility of the philosophy for theological reformulation and Christian renewal.

ONTOLOGICAL BASIS OF THE CATEGORY OF PROCESS

The main characteristic of modern thought is its historical rather than timeless view of reality. This historical view is applicable on all levels and is being achieved progressively. The conversion on the scientific level has already been made—a shift from egocentrism to a centering in the opposite: from the earth to the sun, from the past to the future, from matter to energy—which shift effects also a change from the static to the dynamic. On the philosophic level no comparable transition has yet been made. Before theology can attempt a conversion from the timeless to the historical, philosophy has to furnish that framework. Hence, our purpose is to effect a conversion from aristotelian categories to those of process.

1. *Operational definition of process.* Process is motion and it is change, but not all motions and changes are processes. Negatively, we eliminate from the notion of process transitory motions such as the flight of an arrow to its target, the rolling of a ball, changes in temperature, putting on and off of clothes, etc. By process we mean growth from within, hence immanent motion. To avoid confusion with scientific terminology, we observe that the term "process" has for us a wider connotation than the scientific term "evolution" since it includes what science would refer to as development. In science, the term "development" is reserved for individual

growth, as for example the germination of a seed, the development of an embryo, etc., while the term "evolution" pertains to the macrocosmic level. Philosophically, this distinction is immaterial. For us, both are processes and can be similarly analyzed philosophically. When we use the term "evolution," it is used in its wider sense as including what science would call development.

This operational definition of process is enough, we believe, to situate us in the proper semantic context. We shall develop the notion of process as we go along.

2. *Conversion of the notion of substance into the notion of process*. This conversion[4] is not going to be easy due to the conditioning of centuries. Besides, aristotelian philosophy is a philosophy based on common sense observation just as the ptolemaic and euclidean views of physical reality are based on common sense, which explains their persistence and appeal. But we can learn from the sciences, for if science had stuck stubbornly to the evidence of common sense it would still be in a backward state today. Progress in science was phenomenal once the evidence of the external senses, so naïvely thought in the past to be the final arbiter of what is right and wrong in the external world, had given way to intellectual evidence. The copernican view of the earth as revolving around the sun is an example of the triumph of scientific thought over the naïve evidence of the external senses.

But it was a hard-won battle; it took a long, long time before the aristotelian-influenced clergy gave up absolutizing the framework of common sense and using it as the ultimate norm for what is right or wrong both in science and in philosophy. In the framework of common sense, Galileo

4. The choice of the word is of no great importance. One could very well substitute for it such synonyms as change, evolution, transition, etc.

was clearly wrong, but the point of Galileo was precisely that his statements could not be properly judged within the common sense frame of reference. Again, on the level of the infinitesimally small, progress in the knowledge of matter and the consequent harnessing of the atom proceeded only when physicists went beyond ordinary sense observation and expressed in mathematical formulae data that transcended sense-perceptible phenomena.

What all these examples illustrate is that reality is not always what the senses reveal, that the profounder depths of reality are in the infinitesimally small and the infinitely large which are beyond the grasp of the external senses. It is characteristic of modern scientific syntheses that they are based on data that are not directly observable by the senses. Modern atomic theory, for example, is based on concepts of data that are not directly observable. While the sciences have gone beyond naïve sense observation, traditional philosophy still sticks to the "ptolemaic" or common sense view of reality. The philosophy we are going to propose, however, goes beyond the directly observable and in this respect is more in line with modern science.

To help the reader in understanding this philosophy, it might be helpful to remind him that Teilhard's synthesis and the obstacles to its acceptance are an exact parallel of the Galileo case. Hence, to understand Teilhard and the philosophy derivable from his synthesis, a necessary condition is the giving up, at least for the duration of the study, of the aristotelian-thomistic framework as absolute and as the ultimate norm of philosophical acceptability. If this philosophy is deeply ingrained and has become second nature in one's thinking process, there is all the more need for great intellectual and conscious effort in checking its influence, for inevitably it will creep into our philosophic thinking and evaluation. The philosophy we are going to propose should be judged by its own categories and within its own framework.

To make the transition from the category of substance to that of process, let us start by considering the evidence for the former. Thus from common sense observation, mountains and valleys are models of changelessness. The species of plants and animals seem eternal and unchanging. The reason for this is that the time scale of our frame of reference is so small that within that scale we can perceive no changes in these things. Within this static context (static relative to evolution) we see objects, not processes. The result is a world of objects. Walter Ong notes this common sense approach taken by platonic and aristotelian thought and contrasts it with the modern view influenced by Darwin:

> This reliance on vision yields a world of "objects" which are "clear and distinct," and quite directly produces the old Platonic and Aristotelian notion of "species," each cut off from one another, or, to use the more standard word signifying the same things, "define" one against the other. Darwin's discoveries represent a direct assault on this visualism, for in his account of the origin of species the old distinctness is lost in a blur of variants, potentially infinite in quantity and always at least incipient in the mere differentiation of individual from individual, although how far incipient depends somewhat on how far macro-evolution dominates micro-evolution (if the two are effectively distinct at all).[5]

The category of substance was devised to explain the central experience of permanence of common sense observation. To explain the experience of activity proceeding from the subject, happening to the subject and perfecting the subject, the category of act and potency was devised.

5. Cf. *Darwin's Vision and Christian Perspectives,* ed. W. Ong, S.J., (New York: Macmillan, 1960), p. 145.

Thus we have a philosophy whose basic category is substance and whose dynamism is act and potency. Substance is the ultimate substratum which is not predicated of anything else[6]; it exists of itself and not in another and is the substratum of accidents.[7] It is a dynamic principle of identity, activity and organization[8]; as a principle of activity and organization, it is called nature and as a principle of identity it is called essence.

This analysis of reality is valid for everyday common sense experience of the world, and as long as we stay within its time-frame reference our statements are true relative to it. In practice, however, this common sense experience of permanence has been extrapolated, the conclusion being that, irrespective of time scales, reality conforms to our common sense experience of it. Hence aristotelian-thomistic philosophy, which is the philosophic expression of this common sense experience, is taken to be absolute and perennial.

There is a simple way of testing whether our extrapolation is valid. Let us take a time scale of, say, a billion years and then determine whether the experience of permanence in the small time scale is still valid in the large one. If it is still valid, then the philosophical analysis in the small time scale is indeed absolute and the systematized philosophy of this framework is likewise absolute. What modern man has discovered, however, is the evidence for macrocosmic process. But this evidence is not based on the senses; we do not observe this process actually taking place, not because process has stopped but because these evolutionary changes are so slow that, within the time scale of the senses, they are imperceptible. It is not necessary to go into the technical aspects of the problem any more than it is necessary to

6. *Metaphysics*, V, 8.
7. I *Sent*. d.xxiii, q. Ia; II *Sent*. d. xxxv, q. 2, a.1 ad 1.
8. *Sum. Theol*., Ia, Q. 4, art. 2 & 3; Ia, Q. 2, art. 3.

understand the complex mathematical calculations of Einstein for us to believe the convertibility of matter and energy.

The impact of the new awareness is that what we called permanent in what may be called the two-dimensional context (2-D) of common sense observation, is really process in a three-dimensional (3-D) or evolutionary frame of reference.[9] This is indeed a revolution in human thought similar to the revolution caused by the discovery that the earth revolves around the sun, rather than the sun around the earth. In both these intellectual revolutions, the theologians and philosophers were jolted the hardest and were the slowest to capitulate. Old and comfortable ways of thought gave way slowly.

Philosophically, the new awareness of process proves that the two-dimensional experience of permanence is not absolute, and that therefore the 2-D category of substance which denotes permanence is likewise not absolute. Discovery of the third dimension reveals that everything is in process or, better still, all things are processes, not substances. To help us in this shift of outlook, we may consider the statement of physicists that matter is really energy. This statement contradicts the testimony of the senses. Energy, to common sense, is dynamic; movement is discernible. Hence we do not say that the chair before me is energy. Rather, we speak of the chair as being a material substance, while the rocking of the chair would be classed as energy. We say the chair is distinct from its motion because they belong to different categories, one to the category of substance; the other to

9. The choice of the term 2-D and 3-D was purposeful. But it should not be confused with the mathematical notions in which 2-D is a surface, 3-D a cube and 4-D the dimension of time. The dimensions we are speaking of are those of process. Thus in the context of process there are four kinds of time: 1-D which is mythical time or false eternity where, e.g., dwell the platonic forms, the mythical events of SS., etc.; 2-D is the time of common sense and of activities perceived by the senses; 3-D is evolutionary time, and 4-D is the fullness of time or true eternity.

that of accident, and that neither of these two categories is convertible. But at a higher level of investigation we find that the chair is really a field of energy composed of whirling sub-atomic particles. In much the same way, at a higher level of investigation what is seen as substance in a two-dimensional context is really process in a three-dimensional frame of reference. We might say that just as matter is coagulated energy, so substance is coagulated process.

Our conclusion, then, is that substance is process. There is no contradiction here unless one takes the statement out of the 3-D context. But even with this distinction, the statement may not be correctly understood. That in fact evolution or process is falsely classified and hence falsely understood can be shown from the views of modern thomists who believe that it can be assimilated into the thomistic context by equating it with the accidental category of motion. Thus for example:

> I do not question that St. Thomas made no systematic use of the idea of development or evolution in the modern sense of these words. But for one thing, that idea itself is neither enlightening nor fertile except in the context of an ontological analysis of reality. . . . To enclose a metaphysic in a compartment of history is not a way to give evidence of a sense of history; and it is no proof of philosophic sense to think that there is nothing more in a metaphysic than the scientific imagery which, in a given era, permitted it to exemplify itself in the plane of phenomena, which plane never confined it.[10]

In the above passage evolution or process is relegated to the category of the accidental or historical as opposed to the metaphysical or ontological. This seemingly valid and logical identification is offered to support the adequacy of the

10. Jacques Maritain, *Existence and the Existent,* trans. by Galantière and Phelan (New York: Pantheon, 1948), pp. 45-46.

thomistic framework by proving the existence of substance, there being no motion without a principle of motion, which principle is nature or substance. Consequently, Maritain feels that evolution has not destroyed the thomistic philosophic structure but rather proves its perenniality in being able to assimilate new data. This leads him to say with confidence that even if St. Thomas did not make use of the category of development it is of no great consequence. Furthermore, having identified evolution with the phenomenal, he then logically concludes that what applies to phenomena applies to evolution, namely, that it cannot confine a metaphysic, while a metaphysic is able to assimilate evolution.

Again we find the identification of evolution with activity at the 2-D level in the following passage:

> The subject is the reality which is principal ... the power of operation is a complementary reality, secondary, subordinated, the principle of evolution of the individual, the principle of the "accidental" order, or the order of "secondary" perfection. It exists by the subject, in the subject and for the subject.[11]

In the passage just quoted, evolution is seen as a power of operation and as such is viewed as secondary and subordinated to the substantial subject which is principal; it exists by, in and for the subject, hence it is a principle of the accidental order. Louis de Raeymaeker similarly situates evolution in the accidental order when he says that it is an activity of the universe.[12]

From the views just cited, it is contended that evolution as a power of operation or as an activity cannot be the basic category of reality for it cannot replace the category of the

11. Fernand Van Steenberghen, *Ontology,* trans. Martin Flynn, (New York: J. Wagner, Inc., 1952), p. 127.
12. Cf. his *Introduction to Philosophy*, trans. Harry McNeill (New York: J. Wagner, Inc., 1948), p. 49.

substantial or metaphysical. On the contrary, it is a second-ary category which has meaning only in the context of an ontological analysis of reality. From the aristotelian-tho-mistic viewpoint, philosophy is of the metaphysical or onto-logical, hence to claim process as the principal category is to claim that the phenomenal can replace the metaphysical, the accidental the substantial, and that a metaphysic can be enclosed in a compartment of history—all of which claims are absurd. Besides, it will be argued against us that although we have shown that in immense time scales evolution is manifest, it is not clear how it can produce a revolution in human thought since all it shows is that we have discovered a new power of operation, a new activity of the universe. The "substance-accident" or "nature-operation" categories still stand and are perfectly adequate for the understanding of evolution. It is argued further that no thomist claims that substance is totally static. Evolution does not destroy the concept of substance; in fact it proves what thomists have claimed all along, that substance undergoes accidental changes and that under the category of nature, it is a prin-ciple of operation. If these assertions be true, how then can we effect a conversion from the category of substance to that of process?

To present our case, we cannot emphasize often enough that one has to make a supreme intellectual effort to forego, temporarily at least, the aristotelian-thomistic context. For in the arguments made against us above, what was done was to hold on to the 2-D frame of reference and then try to assimilate process or evolution into it. Thus the statement that reality is evolving or that substance is process is made to mean that first we have substance or a subject from which proceeds evolution as an activity. This way of grasping the meaning of evolution is logical to an aristotelian-thomist, for substance and accident are comprehensive categories, that is, a given reality is either substantial or accidental.

Now evolution is movement, hence logically it is seen as an activity of substance, proceeding from substance. This conclusion seems well enough supported by observation. Thus, eating, talking, typing, and so forth, are actions proceeding from the subject or substance. Evolution, too, is an activity proceeding from the universe as subject.

But let us approach the phenomenon of process or evolution without any preconceived categories in an effort to grasp its true meaning. Let us take a concrete case of a being that manifests the phenomenon of process and study it, for example, a being that is born, grows and dies—for birth, growth and death are the alpha, beta and omega, so to speak, of process—the beginning, middle and end of it. Right away, the given compels us to adopt a temporal approach in order to comprehend process. But if we started with a preconceived approach like that of 2-D, which is atemporal, then for that very reason we fail to comprehend process.

From the point of view of 2-D, birth is the coming-to-be of being, death, the cessation of being; hence they are considered as the limits of being rather than as being in themselves. Being, from the 2-D point of view, is that which is between birth and death and is defined as that which *is*. Thus, since that which is becoming or being born is not yet being, and that which is dead is no longer being, birth and death are systematically excluded from the two-dimensional analysis of being. Since being, by definition, includes everything that is, a philosophy of being seems to be all comprehensive; anything worth saying is founded on being, hence the categories of a philosophy of being must be able to grasp everything worth saying. Evolution, therefore, should be, theoretically at least, comprehended by a philosophy of being. According to the aristotelian-thomistic explanation, evolution is an activity that proceeds from being.

But now let us ask a simple question. Is birth like any of

the activities such as talking, singing, and typing which proceed from substance (nature) as their principle of operation? Can we say, for example, that birth proceeds from substance the way talking does? If so, then the level of phenomenal activities in 2-D can indeed assimilate process or evolution; then, too, substance would contain process the way it contains its activities. True, birth can be assimilated to the being which gives birth to another as its activity, but that same event pertains more basically to the being that is born as *its* birth. The question is, with respect to this being that is born, how is its birth related to it? Can we say that birth proceeds from this being the way activities proceed from it? Clearly, to say so would be a contradiction, much like saying that the chicken laid an egg from which it will develop. The birth of the given substance is not an accident that inheres in or proceeds from the substance that is born, because the substance in question does not yet exist, for birth implies the non-existence of that which is born. Substance, then, proceeds from birth and is contained, so to speak, in the process of birth. Furthermore, birth is not just a first event in the existence of the substance; rather, substance is continually born to the next moment, hence substance is always in the context of process.

It may be argued in defense of the thomistic philosophy of being that the event of "birth" is adequately explained by relating it to the being which gives birth as its activity, hence that evolution is an activity of substance or nature, and hence too that evolution is an activity of the universe. But let us look closely at the statement, "the universe evolves," and compare it with this other, "a being gives birth." In the first, the meaning is that the universe undergoes evolution— it is born, it grows; it is the subject undergoing process. But in the other statement, it is not the being-that-gives-birth which is being born and will grow, hence which is in process. Therefore we do not explain evolution by saying that first we have a being from which proceeds evolution as an activity. Macrocosmic evolution is not an activity proceeding from the universe, for if it did then the universe would not actually evolve but would be the source of evolution the way a being-that-gives-birth is the source of birth. But just as the being-that-gives-birth is not the one born, so if we assimilate the statement "the universe evolves" to "a substance acts" we are unable to express what is supposed to be expressed, namely, that it is the universe that is born and grows.

If then we must relate evolution to the being undergoing it in order to explain it, we find that the 2-D framework is unable to assimilate it to the substance-accident category. For as we have shown in our analysis of birth, evolution as a process of birth is not an activity that proceeds from or inheres in the substance undergoing the process. Thus from the analysis of birth alone, we see that evolution or process transcends the 2-D framework.

But let us continue our analysis and look now at the other end of process, namely, death. We can say simply that since life tends towards death, living is really a process of dying. Now dying can be either a complete cessation or a rebirth as, for example, in the germination of a seed. If death is a cessation, then since substance tends towards it, death contains substance, not the other way around. If it is a rebirth, then substance is contained in birth as our preceding analysis showed. Substance does not contain death as an accident because substance does not perdure—death presupposing the non-existence of that which dies. It is death that contains substance as the subject contains the predicate.

How then are things approached from the point of view of 3-D? Does it mean that the tree out there is no longer substance but process? But process is a flow, it might be objected, while a tree is not like a river that flows; it is standing solid and permanent. We do not deny the testimony of the senses that the tree out there is solid and permanent but we must hasten to add that the terms "solidity" and "permanence" have meaning and significance only when the time-frame reference is given. In the context of process, terms have no meaning and significance out of the time-frame reference. What is meant, then, when it is asserted that the tree out there is standing solid and permanent is that within a time scale which excludes birth and death, the tree *is* a tree. And if I take the same time scale I would also see the tree as a tree.

The point that we wish to make, however, is that the time scale proposed is not absolute, that if we want to look at the tree in its totality we have to adopt a wider time scale in which we will see that the tree was not always a tree, that at one time it was a seed, at another, a sapling, and so forth. In this wider context, the tree that we are now looking at, standing solid and permanent, is but a stage, a part of a process or, diagrammatically, of a line that has an alpha and omega. And we can take a still wider context in which to situate the tree. We can situate it in the context of the evolution of its species from which it takes its birth and consequently its meaning; the species in its turn can be situated in a still wider process—the evolution of plant life; and plant life can be situated in the widest possible time context—the evolution of the whole universe. Thus, processes are within processes of larger time scales, and all processes are contained within the single process of the evolution of the universe whose ultimate meaning is its Omega. But in all these processes, there is one methodological approach—all things are seen linearly, so to speak, having alphas and omegas, and not statically, like points.

In using imagery, however, we must be careful not to fall into the fallacy of imagining process as a given point that moves from *a* to *b*, or as a billiard ball, let us say, which rolls from a given place on the table to a pocket. Such examples are not processes. They are in fact examples of 2-D analysis. For the billiard ball remains itself in its transition, hence aptly conforming to the category of substance, while its motion conforms to the category of accident which is attributed to the ball as substantial subject. Even in cases of growth (say, that of a tree), as long as the tree remains quantitatively the same, it cannot be considered a process.

Perhaps a good example to illustrate the difference between motion as understood in 2-D and process in 3-D is to relate two-dimensional motion and three-dimensional process to a seed. Let us first take the statement, "the seed rolls off the table onto the floor." In this example the seed remains a seed, before, during and after the motion. Such a situation is aptly analyzed in terms of the substance-accident category of 2-D, for here the seed is a subject to which the motion can be predicated. But let us now take the case of a seed that is planted and goes through the process of germination. The result of the process of germination is the cessation of the seed as a subject of attribution. Hence we cannot relate the process of germination to the seed as subject the way we can relate the rolling off the table to it. The seed that rolls off the table is not in process even if it is in motion because the seed in this case remains a seed. Motion here is an accidental motion of the seed and is properly related to the seed as subject.

Given this case, Maritain can rightly say that the phenomenal analysis of motion cannot take over as supreme method because the metaphysical (substantial) subject is never confined in the plane of phenomena, and Steenberghen can truly say that the subject (seed) is the principal reality while the principle of motion is purely secondary and that, lastly, the motion exists by, in and for the subject. But it is false to generalize and say that evolution or process is an instance of 2-D motion. Process or evolution is not like the seed rolling off the table, but like the germination of a seed. We cannot apply the substance-accident category in the latter case because there is no permanent subject of attribution. As long as the seed remains the same it is the principal reality, and its motion is purely secondary. But we cannot say this in the case of the germination of the seed for, as we said above, germination cannot be related to the seed (once the process is accomplished) the way the rolling off of the seed can be related to it. In the case of germination, germination-towards-the-seedling is the principal reality and the seed exists by, in and for it.

Thus, contrary to the 2-D situation in which the metaphysical (substantial subject) is not confined in the phenomenal (its motion), in 3-D, the so-called metaphysical or substantial subject of 2-D (the seed) is confined in the phenomenal (the germination). 2-D analysis, both phenomenal and ontological, is valid only when the subject perdures; once it is the subject itself which evolves, we cannot grasp the phenomenon of evolution in this context whose basic presupposition is the perdurance of the subject.

Ordinary language supports the view that evolution is an activity that is related to a subject that perdures. Thus we speak of the seed becoming a seedling, growing into a tree and bearing fruit. In these instances, the seed is taken as the common subject of predication to which are related past, present and future events. But we cannot base philosophy on ordinary language. Linguistically, we can and do assume that the seed remains the same in the course of its evolution, but this mode of expression is as philosophical as the statement that the sun sets and rises is scientific. Ordinary language is ptolemaic in structure. The present is considered stationary and around it the past and the future are thought to revolve. This ordinary language finds philosophic expression in aristotelian metaphysics and logic. Thus the present is the place of the subject and of being or substance. Events, be they past or future, are related to the present. We speak of the future coming, instead of the present being in orbit and tending towards the future.

The ptolemaic structure of ordinary language and its philosophic expression are valid for a static universe or for very small time scales in which the subject is assured of perduring, hence for everyday life. But in the context of evolution, ordinary language becomes unphilosophical. For the fact is that the present is not the place of being and of the subject. The present is the region of becoming and of the predicate; the future, the place of being and of the subject. Coming back to the example of the seed, in the case of germination the seed tends towards the future; it is not a stationary and perduring center. Hence instead of relating germination to the seed as perduring subject, the seed is related as predicate to a future subject that will emerge and which, in relation to the seed, is its fullness of being. In this case the seed cannot be analyzed ontologically for it is not an enduring subject. Being a part of the evolution-towards-the-fruit, it is properly analyzed as process. If reality, then, is becoming, is unfinished, it is unphilosophical to analyze it ontologically because it is not yet being; it is not yet subject. It is properly analyzed as process.

Drawing together the results of our analyses, we find that process cannot be assimilated into the 2-D category of motion. The 2-D category of substance-accident is valid only as long as we abstract from birth and death. But when birth and death, which are the alpha and omega of process, are equated with activities like talking, typing and eating, we do so only at the cost of distorting the facts. Birth and death transcend both ontological and phenomenal 2-D analysis and, for this reason, show 2-D analysis to be inadequate and limited. Care must be exercised that we do not equate 3-D analysis, which is a temporal approach to reality, with the phenomenal analysis of 2-D as Maritain and others have done, for as we showed above, evolution or process cannot be reduced to the activity of substance in 2-D. In fact 3-D analysis is more deeply metaphysical than the ontological analysis of 2-D since process is the matrix of substance, so to speak, in that it gives origin, meaning and destiny to substance.

The fundamental difference, then, in the 2-D and 3-D explanations of evolution is that in the former, there is always something which is distinct from its process; in the latter that something is the process itself, or is part of the process. Again, in the former, to say that something evolves is to imagine a line from *a* to *b* and distinct from it, the thing which moves from *a* to *b*. In the latter, there is nothing other than the line. In 3-D, one looks at a tree and sees it as the mid-point of a line; it is one with its life. In 2-D, we take the tree here and now and attribute the past, present and future to it. In 3-D, this tree is but part of the life-span, hence the proper adequate subject of attribution is the process itself.

As long as Maritain and the other thomists quoted above are allowed to classify evolution as 2-D motion, they can go on claiming the existence of the category of substance and believing that the thomistic framework is secure and adequate to assimilate evolution. The challenge of evolution, however, is that it is not 2-D motion. It is motion, no doubt, but it is a deeper level of motion, one which, instead of proceeding from substance and being confined in it, underlies substance. We have tried here to establish this deeper ontological level from which the category of process is derived.[13]

Having established the ontological basis for the category of process, we may now turn to an analysis of the nature of existence. What is it to be in process? This analysis has very important implications for the solution of the problem of the supernatural, for it corrects the aristotelian individualistic view of nature—the main obstacle to the reconciliation of the gratuity of the supernatural and our intrinsic ordination to it.

3. *Transition from existence (act of "to be") as self-containedness to existence as union.* The second stage in the conversion of our outlook from 2-D to 3-D is to view existence as unitive. In 2-D, substance is considered as having its own act of "to be"; but at the deeper level of 3-D, to be in process is to be united. Existence is sharedness. Let us consider a few examples of processes to illustrate this point.

If we look at a plant and abstract from its rootedness in the ground, the plant seems to have its own act of "to be." But a little consideration is sufficient to show that it is the union of the plant with the ground which is the very existence of the plant. Uproot the plant and it is dead. Clearly there is no proper act of "to be" separate from the ground. All the objects that we see and categorize as substances, that

13. If after the above considerations the reader still thinks that the approach to reality in terms of process—birth, growth, death or rebirth—is unable to lay bare the depth of being and that 2-D ontological analysis is deeper, it might be helpful to consider that the Scriptures, which lay bare the deepest levels of reality, assert just the opposite, namely, that birth and death are the deepest categories, for on them are built the central mysteries of our faith: the incarnation (mystery of birth); grace (mystery of life and growth); passion, death and resurrection (mystery of death and rebirth). It is not through an ontological analysis of being but through the continued celebration of these mysteries—hence through a process of growth—that the Church attains the most intimate depth of being which, according to the Scriptures, is the trinitarian life of God.

is, as having autonomous existence, are really processes, enjoying their existence only as the result of union. Existence is not something bottled up within a being or substance. This is the impression we get in 2-D. We see a dog move around and we say it has its own act of "to be." But if we go beyond the unphilosophical view of the senses, we see that no concrete reality can be understood apart from the evolutionary unity of the universe in which it is situated and from which it takes its meaning and existence. Outside this context, it is not only meaningless but it is nonexistent.

God is not an aristotelian first cause that first thinks of essences—dog, cat, man—then creates each species and next puts them together to form a world. If this were the case, then the act of "to be" would indeed be self-contained. But it would follow, too, that these creatures do not really belong to one world; they are foreigners to it. Common speech and our common way of thinking help to perpetuate this abstractive and individualistic view of things. Thus in the statement, "The man is" or "The man exists," the act of "to be" can be considered in the 2-D context, in itself, that is, without implying any necessary relation to the world or to another man. The "to be" cuts off a being, thus giving it identity, intelligibility and definition. If man is related to the world and to other men at all, his relation is accidental. Not so in 3-D. Existence has evolutionary roots, hence it is the basis for one's belonging to the world. Thus in the 3-D context the statement, "Man exists," necessarily means that man is man-and-his-world-and-towards-others. The existence one has is not only an assurance of being one with the world, but also the foundation for one's identity, for it determines one's place in the evolutionary universe.

It is idealistic to think of a single object as having an existence apart from the world. In the only world we know, existence is sharedness. Things are not simply born; they are born into a world. Without a world there is no existence. The foetus is born into a womb which is its world, and its existence depends upon its continued union with it. When it is delivered, it is born into another world. Again, at a higher level of existence, that of human personality, existence is also relatedness—the union of the "I" with the "Thou." But more on this later when we come to treat of man and grace.

What is true of all individual beings is true as well of the universe as a single evolutionary unity. The universe is born and its continued existence is a process. But process is union or sharedness, hence the universe points to the need for an "other." Naturalistic evolutionists would disagree with this view. Unconscious of the hellenic pattern of their thoughts, they think that they are being scientific when they consider the universe as self-sufficient, able to evolve itself, hence without need of a Ground. But what basis is there in reality for this conclusion? Is there any process that is not sharedness, that does not need an "other"? Take again the example of the seed. Deprive it of its ground; leave it on the table and we can wait as long as we want but the seed will still be unable to evolve itself: to germinate, grow, flower and bear fruit—all by itself. It will not be in process. Process requires union. In the example, the seed needs the ground. The union of the seed and the ground is precisely the process. In the process, it is the ground that germinates the seed, makes it grow and mature, lets it flower and bear fruit.

Thus it is not only metaphorically but in a true sense that we call the earth "mother earth." In all cases of process there is always a union of that which is in process with its "ground," so to speak, or its "other"; furthermore, for there to be greater growth there has to be deeper and more intimate union. That the union between the seed and its ground cannot be bottled up is obvious. For union is the openness of the seed to its ground, this continued union being successively the seedling, the plant, the fruit. Thus, because the center of the seed is not itself, it is not self-sufficient. If, in fact, it stays alone, it dies—a profound truth which the Scriptures use as an example to show the need for openness and a rebirth in Christ into the new life of grace.

Just as the seed's being is literally rooted in the ground and ordered towards it, so the universe, if it is in process, must have its own "Ground"; otherwise we are saying in effect that it is its own ground, a case for which we can find no example. The seed is not its own ground, nor the foetus its own womb, nor the egg its own hen. And yet this inconsistency is preferred to admitting that the universe needs a "ground." If the universe does not need a ground then it is not in process; if it is in process it needs a ground, and we call this Ground of being, God. This Ground directs the evolution of the universe, not by wholly taking over, but through the conjunction of two freedoms: human freedom, which represents the apex of evolution, and divine freedom.

According to Nicolas Corte, it is Teilhard's view that "evolution demands the continuous action of creative Wisdom more imperiously than does Fixity (of species), for we are clearly concerned with an Evolution which has a purpose, a *directed* Evolution, an Evolution which itself suggests that once it has reached its summit, which is Man, it has nothing more to do but to stop and leave Man himself the task of following it through in the order of reflective consciousness."[14] And Teilhard himself said: "As early as in St. Paul and St. John we read that to create, to fulfil and to purify the world is, for God, to unify it by uniting it organically with himself. How does he unify it? By partially immersing himself in things, by becoming 'element,' and

14. *Pierre Teilhard de Chardin,* trans. Martin Jarett-Kerr (New York: Macmillan Co., 1960), p. 85.

then, from this point of vantage in the heart of matter, assuming the control and leadership of what we now call evolution."[15] Divine creativity, therefore, is not finished. Through man, the universe participates and cooperates in its own process of creation. In fact, God's omnipotence is grander if the creature can take part in his own creation than if, according to the traditional view, God creates once and for all. In what sense, after all, is man an image of God if he does not share in the creativity of God?

The result of our preceding analysis is a unitive view of reality. With existence converted from a self-contained act of "to be" (an individualistic view) to existence as process (a unitive view of being), we see that the notion of substance as self-enclosed and self-subsistent is an abstract construct. A life ruled by this construct can result only in inauthentic existence. But if "to be" is always to-be-with, then being is not an island but is always being-with-another. The shift in perspective may be illustrated by the example of the seed alone by itself and the seed in union with the soil. The existence of the seed alone by itself is inauthentic existence because it is a being-towards-death, while being-with-the-ground (or at a higher level, openness to the other) is authentic existence because it is being-towards-life. Because 2-D philosophy makes no distinction between authentic and inauthentic being, it builds its philosophy on a notion of being which is in fact inauthentic.

The objection could be raised by 2-D philosophy that if being is essentially being-towards-the-other, then individuality is lost. On the other hand, substance as a category preserves individuality. Again, the objection is valid only in the context of 2-D. Thus in a 2-D context to say that one being is essentially related to another is to say that they are

15. *PH*, pp. 293-94.

really one substance, in which case the identity of the other is lost. An example of this is the essential relatedness of the substantial principles, matter and form, whose union results in one substance. In 2-D, for beings to be distinct, there has to be substantial distinctness; relation in this case must be merely accidental.

Because in 2-D relation implies dependency, it is the category which a complete substance most abhors, for it is a threat to its substantiality and thinghood. Consequently, relation is the most ignored and least respected category. It is labelled as a *debellissimum ens,* that is, the weakest of beings, the borderline between being and non-being.[16] According to this view, essential dependence on another is loss of identity; individualization is freedom from essential dependency. In the 2-D context, then, to proclaim essential relatedness as the basis for true existence would be to proclaim a monistic view of reality. We would be denying the obvious differentiation and multiplicity of beings. Furthermore, to proclaim man's essential relatedness to God as Absolute Thou would be tantamount to pantheism.

In answer to these objections, we note again that the 2-D context is not an absolute framework. As a matter of fact the maligned category of relation is elevated in 3-D philosophy to first rank. To show that union does not result in a loss of identity but rather in the attainment of it, let us study several concrete examples. Thus, the more the foetus is united with the womb, the more it differentiates itself; the more the seed is united with the ground the more it unfolds itself, germinating into a seedling in which the roots, stem, branches are formed, until attaining to greater and greater

16. There seems to be an inherent contradiction in scholastic theology in accepting, on the one hand, that relation is the weakest of categories, as its philosophy points out, and, on the other, in using this category to portray the nature of the Trinity as subsistent relations.

growth, the seed arrives at its full identity in the fruit which reveals it for what it is.

If we go to a higher level of being, we observe that the more animals adapt themselves to their environment by the development of organs, the more they preserve and prolong their own existence and that of their species. In the case of man, the more he comes to know the universe, the more he comes to know himself. On the level of personality, the more the "I" is united with other persons the more personalized it becomes, while the more it withdraws from others, the less it becomes a person. In the relation of God and man, the more man relates himself to God the more man becomes truly man.[17]

The 3-D view that union differentiates is best summarized by Teilhard:

In any domain—whether it be the cells of a body, the members of a society or the elements of a spiritual synthesis— *union differentiates.* In every organized whole, the parts perfect themselves and fulfill themselves. Through neglect of this universal rule many a system of pantheism has led us astray to the cult of a great All in which individuals were supposed to be merged like a drop in the ocean or like a dissolving grain of salt. Applied to the case of the summation of consciousnesses, the law of union rids us of this perilous and recurrent illusion. No, following the confluent orbits of their centres, the grains of consciousness do not tend to lose their outlines and blend, but, on the contrary, to accentuate the depth and incommunicability of their *egos.* The more "other" they become in conjunction, the more they find themselves as "self."[18]

The biblical view supports this view that true being is relatedness or union. In the Bible, the covenant, which is the

17. The greatest union possible according to Catholic teaching is the eternal procession in the Godhead. So infinite is the union that it results in a differentiation of persons.

18. *PH*, p. 262.

most basic and central category, is a bond of union, and it is towards this union that all beings must tend if they are to exist and have meaning. Authentic being is covenanted being; both man and creation are covenanted. Outside the covenant there is only inauthentic being or death. Johannes Pedersen, one of the foremost authorities on Israelite culture, notes:

> For the Israelites, one is born of a covenant and into a covenant, and wherever one moves in life, one makes a covenant . . . if the covenant were dissolved existence would fall to pieces, because no soul can live an isolated life. It not only means that it cannot get along without the assistance of others; it is in direct conflict with its essence to be something apart. It can only exist as a link of a whole, and it cannot work and act without working in connection with other souls and through them.[19]

19. Cf. his *Israel and Its People,* I (Copenhagen, 1926), p. 308.

It might be said that Aristotle, too, had a view of man as a social animal since he held that the individual achieves independence and completeness of life only in the state. But Aristotle's assertions have to be understood in context. As John Dewey notes:

> Aristotle's assertions that the state exists by nature, and that in the state alone does the individual achieve independence and completeness of life, are indeed pregnant sayings. But as uttered by Aristotle they meant that, in an isolated state, the Greek city-state, set as a garlanded island in the waste sea of *barbaroi,* a community indifferent when not hostile to all other social groupings, individuals attain their full end. In a social unity which signified social contraction, contempt, and antagonism, in a social order which despised intercourse and glorified war, is realized the life of excellence!
>
> There is likewise a profound saying of Aristotle's that the individual who otherwise than by accident is not a member of a state is either a brute or a god. But it is generally forgotten that elsewhere Aristotle identified the highest excellence, the chief virtue, with pure thought, and identifying this with the divine, isolated it in lonely grandeur from the life of society. That man, so far as in him lay, should be godlike, meant that he should be nonsocial, because supra-civic. . . .

(Cf. John Dewey, in *The Influence of Darwin on Philosophy and Other Essays in Contemporary Thought* (Indiana University Press, 1965), pp. 48-49.)

The true philosophic view of existence, then, supported by the biblical view, is that existence is sharedness or union. In Teilhard's words (which we make our own) we must see reality such that "all around us, as far as the eye can see, the universe holds together, and only one way of considering it is really possible, that is, to take it as a whole, in one piece."[20] And again Teilhard observes that "the distribution, succession and solidarity of objects are born from their concrescence in a common genesis."[21]

Having analyzed the nature of existence as relatedness, the next logical step is to determine how this relatedness is attained, what powers being possesses to achieve union.

4. *Conversion of the dynamism of being from act and potency to the dynamism of love.* We have seen that consideration of existence as sharedness changes our view of being from self-contained and subsistent substance to being-towards-the-other. We would now like to show that the aristotelian category of nature as possessed of its own principle of operation is an inadequate explanation of the dynamism in being.

According to the aristotelian 2-D view of nature, there is a claim, exigency, or title in nature for its natural end. This claim is founded on the premise that this concept of nature attains its end alone. By the term "alone" we mean that nature treats the whole world (persons and things) as "its." The world is then related to nature itself as an autonomous center. Given the premise, it follows that nature must have the necessary means to attain its end; it follows too that God owes it to himself to supply the means by which nature attains its end; otherwise God would be creating a nature in vain, and that would be contrary to his wisdom and good-

20. *PH*, p. 44.
21. *PH*, p. 217.

ness. In line with this view, nature is fitted with operative potencies as immediate principles of operation (nature itself being the remote principle) by which nature is able to achieve its natural end. Thus the dynamism of nature is conceived in terms of the categories of act and potency, nature in this case being viewed as an objective potency *(potentia objectiva)* which perfects itself by receiving acts, or perfections, which actualize its potencies. Once the potencies are actualized, we have an autonomous, self-sufficient nature. The conclusions set forth are all valid within the 2-D context.

What we wish to question, however, is the basic premise that nature is able to attain its end alone. This premise is empirically based on ordinary habits of thought and common ways of speech. Thus we are so accustomed to thinking and speaking of a given object, say, a tree, and its activities —it grows, matures, flowers, bears fruit—as if the tree were the center to which everything is related; we forget that all these activities are really for the sake of the more basic dynamism of maintaining union with the ground—a dynamism of giving, not of receiving.

Again, on the human level we relate the whole world to the self as center. I see and judge everything as good or bad according as it is beneficial or harmful to my profession or station in life, forgetting that I am what I am basically because of the union I have with the world. Extrapolating these habits of thought, one comes up with the notion of the aristotelian first cause which, having made the world, left it to shift for itself, hence, autonomous. Scholasticism took over this view and "baptized" it by introducing the notions of creation and divine concursus, thus giving to the world a Christian God who is concerned about his creation. But the basic premise remains the same, namely, that creation is autonomous. This view is in line with the hellenic view that truth is in the extra-temporal and that therefore, to be properly infinite, God cannot act contingently or temporally. Creation, therefore, must be instantaneous, extratemporal. Hence species are eternal and self-sufficient to achieve their respective ends.

Of course the scholastic view does not claim that a being is already fully actualized as it leaves the hand of God. Rather, nature is said to achieve its fullness in time by the actualization of its potencies. Nevertheless, it is held that everything that will be actualized is already precontained in potency in the original equipment of nature. So strong is the view that there is really nothing new under the sun that even those who are sympathetic towards evolution are so influenced by this hellenic mentality that they explain evolution as the explicitation or unfolding of what was already there in the beginning. If this is so, then evolution is really comprehended by the aristotelian categories of act and potency, and can be expressed in terms of these categories. But the fallacy here is the extrapolation from the common sense view of things, which is monistic and individualistic, to the philosophic level, so that the universe is seen in its evolution as autonomous and self-sufficient. Compare the evolution of the universe to that of a seed. If the seed, left alone and apart from the soil and air, were still able to germinate, grow and bear fruit, then everything that unfolded would have to be precontained in the seed. There would be nothing else for anything to come from. But clearly, this never happens in reality.

On the contrary, we have shown that process, or the unfolding of being, always requires union or the "other." It is union which differentiates. Now the "other" is not precontained in that which evolves or develops; if it did, then the aristotelian category of substance would be adequate. But recall what we have already seen, that in all examples of development being is not its "other." Thus the seed is not its own soil, nor the foetus its own womb, nor the "I" its own "Thou." No doubt, the seed is ontologically structured for the soil and the "I" for the "Thou," but this is not to pre-contain the other, rather it is to facilitate union.

And even when being is united with its "other" or "ground," the whole resulting from that union does not come merely from one side, but from both. The union itself—which may be termed the "between" or the "we"—is not something precontained in either one taken singly. Furthermore, there are an "infinite" number of "betweens," corresponding to an "infinite" number of "others" to which one and the same being could be united, each relation producing a distinct differentiation in being. Even when the particular "other" has been determined, the type of differentiation which the "I" attains depends on how both are going to forge the union.

Take a concrete example. A particular seed does not have to be planted here or there. The facts that it was planted in this soil, by this particular farmer, at this particular time are chance events and are not precontained in the seed. But it is precisely these factors that determine how the seed is going to unfold. If the soil is barren or the farmer remiss, the seed may not germinate at all; or if it germinates, it may not reach full growth; or if it does, it may not bear fruit, or give only poor yield. Thus how this particular seed is going to develop does not depend on itself so much as on what we broadly call the "other."

What is true of the seed is also true, *mutatis mutandis,* of the human "I." In the first place, any "I" could be related to any particular "Thou." This relation is not something pre-determined. For example, that this man marry this particu-lar woman is not precontained in the man at birth, but depends on circumstances of time, place, temperament, and so forth. The way this man will develop in his personality is to a large extent conditioned not only by himself but by his partner, so that if she were B rather than A, this man would have developed differently. And in the second place, even after the union with this particular woman is achieved, it has to be properly nurtured, for the development of each personality is conditioned by each one's effort in enhancing the union. Being is not mechanistic or monistic.

Even on the level of natural species, the species that we know today, such as dogs, cats, horses, were not precontained in earlier species. It was the interaction of earlier species with their environment that determined in time what the species would be. And the same species surviving in the present are not static, merely unfolding what they precontain. They constantly react with the environment and thus continually develop and differentiate. The human species, for example, is not fixed, nor is everything that will come forth in time precontained in it. What the human species will turn out to be depends on the involvement and interaction of men with the world and above all with the Absolute Thou. Man is open; he is in a true sense still achieving his essence, and thus still making himself.

It might be objected at this point that actually nature in the aristotelian view does not achieve its end alone since it requires an extrinsic act to actualize its potencies. As a matter of fact, the objection continues, the very notion of potency implies or calls for an "other," since no potency can reduce itself to act. For if it could, then it would already be act, not potency, and if act, there would be no need to actualize it in the same order of perfection. It is a contradiction for a thing to be both in potency and act at the same time and in the same respect. Hence if a thing were in potency, it would require an act to actuate it. The objection is most logical.

In answer to the objection we note, first, that nature does

not treat the "other" as truly other, that is, as a *thou,* but as an *it.* Hence it alone is *self* in a world of *It;* it alone is subject in a world of objects. Everything is subordinated to nature as self and center. Even persons are treated as *its.* Secondly, nature does not really need the "other" in the sense that the "other" does not really contribute anything new. Everything that is educed comes wholly from nature. Thus in the hylomorphic view of nature, the perfective act educes the forms from nature taken as an objective potency or, on the macrocosmic level, forms are educed from prime matter. The defect in this view is that while it may explain the phenomenon of change, it is unable to explain real novelty, hence real progress. Let us listen to an excellent observation on the deficiency of the hylomorphic theory:

> Anyone who sees in hylomorphism the ultimate explanation of the material universe will inevitably find an evolutionary theory to be self-contradictory. For in the hylomorphic perspective, development must necessarily be conceived in terms of the transformation of an ultimately passive subject, prime matter. The transformation of such a subject, however, immediately entails an appeal to a cause already possessing, formally or eminently, the perfection which matter is to acquire in the process. Since matter is only the passive substrate of the change and therefore contributes nothing in the line of formal perfection to the process, the appearance of new perfection in matter must of necessity be attributed to the influence of a cause, which already has it itself and which is said to "educe" the same from the potency of matter. Such a theory, of course, makes an evolutionary conception of the world impossible.[22]

As Johann notes, that which is in potency is totally passive and therefore contributes nothing to the eduction of forms implicit in it; hence the actuation must come from the

---

22. Robert O. Johann, "The Logic of Evolution," *Thought,* 36 (1961), pp. 611-612.

influence of a cause possessing the form. But the perfective act does not give of its own form; it merely "educes" the same from the potency of matter. Thus there is no real novelty, for everything is precontained in the potency of matter. The "other" (perfective act) does not give of itself as in the relation of I-Thou which is animated by the dynamism of love. The eduction of forms is individualistic rather than communal. There is no true interaction. But it is through interaction, as Johann observes,[23] that evolution arises.

There is a third sense in which nature is said to attain its end alone, namely, that it is endowed with an exigency, title or claim, hence a moral power, so to speak, to attain its end. It does not have to go begging. Thus it does not wait on the "other" the way the "I" waits on the good graces and pleasure of the "Thou." That to which nature is intrinsically ordained, that it can demand. Consequently, nature has the wherewithal to attain its end independently.

The fourth sense in which nature attains its end alone is with respect to its final state. Thus, if it unites itself with a world of *It* (which in itself is not even a semblance of communion since there is no I-Thou relation) it does so only that it may attain definition and self-subsistence—which is a cutting off from dependency and essential relation. The end of nature is not communion but autonomy. Union is but the path to independence. On the other hand, union is the end point and resting place of beings whose basic dynamism is love.

From our preceding analysis, then, it would seem that in an evolutionary context, the hylomorphic view of nature with its dynamism of act and potency is inadequate. The view that the perfection of being is in the actualization of poten-

23. *Ibid.*, p. 608.

cies precontained in concrete nature or in prime matter is untenable and could lead to dangerous consequences.[24]

In contrast, we would like to submit the view that the basic dynamism of being is love. To show this, let us start by observing that since being tends to its "other" in order *to be* and be *true,* its dynamism is not a having (act and potency) but a giving (love). But care must be taken that we understand what we mean by love. Love in the popular sense is a sentiment and an emotion. However, it is in its natural dynamism and evolutionary significance that we deal with it here. Of love in this sense Teilhard says:

> Considered in its full biological reality, love—that is to say the affinity of being with being—is not peculiar to man. It is a general property of all life and as such it embraces, in its varieties and degrees, all the forms successively adopted by organized matter. In the mammals, so close to ourselves, it is easily recognized in its different modalities: sexual passion, parental instinct, social solidarity, etc. Farther off, that is to say lower down on the tree of life, analogies are more obscure until they become so faint as to be imperceptible. . . . If there were not internal propensity to unite, even at a prodigiously rudimentary level—indeed in the molecule itself—it would be physically impossible for love to appear higher up, with us, in "hominised" form. By rights, to be certain of its presence in ourselves, we should assume its presence, at least in an inchoate form, in everything that is.[25]

The dynamism of love does not destroy the dynamism of act and potency. What is objected to is the absolutization of the latter. The dynamism of act and potency is for the sake of the deeper dynamism of being which is the urge to union. No doubt the egocentric dynamism of act and potency is

24. For example, on the level of spirituality, we have the doctrine of predestination, according to which a man's total future is already precontained in his being at birth so that there is nothing he can do about it.

25. *PH,* p. 264.

necessary, but to posit this as the perfection of being is to tend towards extreme individualism in which the fullness of being is attained by the denial of all essential relatedness; this is isolationism. In 3-D, on the contrary, being is relatedness. Hence in its essence being is a gift, not a right.[26]

Existence is for the sake of giving. I do not exist in order that I may possess, rather I exist in order that I may give of myself, for it is in giving that I attain myself.[27] Being must first be a *we* before it can become an *I*. The seed must die to itself, give of itself to the ground in complete surrender of death, before there is a new and higher possession of itself. It cannot be emphasized enough that being needs its

26. Moral theology is predicated on the aristotelian concept of nature and its dynamism of act and potency. Just as the central categories for nature in relation to its end are exigency, claim, right, so moral theology is founded on the virtue of justice. In the context of justice, the virtue of charity is out of place. In traditional textbooks on moral theology, charity, the central teaching of Christianity and the foundation of the Christian life, is given a very minor place. Reformulation in moral theology, if it is not to be skin-deep, must be based on a sound philosophy of being whose dynamism is that of love.

Since scholastic theology is logically constructed, the same philosophy animating all its parts, the problem of extreme juridicism and casuistry that we meet in moral theology is basically the same problem we have in the treatment of the supernatural; there grace is related to a concept of nature based on exigency and justice. A reformulation here will necessarily affect the reformulation in moral theology.

27. The traditional doctrine on private property is based on the philosophical view that the ultimate dynamism of being is a receiving. The result is to make the mine-thine category the absolute and final structure of being, rather than the "we" category. In practice, this produces an inherent divisiveness in the capitalistic structure of the Western world. That perfection is in receiving is a very superficial view of things. True, from the 2-D point of view we see a snowball increase by adding to itself, a container becomes full by containing, a bank deposit grows by receiving, and so on. But at a deeper level of existence, that of personality, all property is ultimately for the sake of sacrifice. This is so because all property is for the sake of the self, but the self is for the sake of the Other. To attain the Other, the self gives of itself, offers itself in sacrifice to the Other. This is done by offering the "fruits" of our labor, hence our property (*proprium*), symbolized by the bread and wine, to the Divine Thou. Thus the dynamism of act and potency, which is a receiving, is for the sake of the dynamism of love, a giving.

"ground," for it is through union that selfhood is attained. The plant attains its end not by its own powers alone but more fundamentally through rootedness in its ground, so much so that the more it is rooted, the deeper it sinks its roots into the soil, the fuller and taller it grows. Again, to use other examples, the foetus attains its birth, hence a new being, through vital union with its womb; the feminine attains her fullness through union with the masculine; the "I" attains full personality through the powers of the "Thou" cooperating in the fruition. Being attains self-sufficiency only in union. Being is not proud; the basic attitude of being is gratitude. There is no being who can stand up and say: I did it alone.[28] Rather, the universe is in the framework of love.

The biblical view of the dynamism of being verifies our analysis. Thus the whole of reality from the lowest to the highest is covenanted, that is, united in a bond of love. The perfection of creation, which is seen as feminine, is within the covenant, conceived as a marriage bond between Yahweh and his creatures. Hence according to the Bible, too, the dynamism of being is that of love. The whole of Christian

28. Secularism and naturalism are based on the premise that the universe can do it alone, that is, save and redeem itself without supernatural help. Again, as we noted elsewhere, the aristotelian view of nature as being able to attain its end by its own powers alone, as having an exigency towards its end rather than a prayerful hope that the Thou will condescend to call, and whose dynamism is a receiving rather than a giving, supports the secularistic and naturalistic view. The posture of aristotelian nature towards the world is not prayerful but demanding and imperious. It is hard, to say the least, to build Christian morality, whose virtues are those of surrender and giving, on a nature whose dynamism is that of receiving. By the law of its very being, nature would repel these so-called virtues as threats; in fact they are vices to be shunned. The philosophy that has followed the implications of the hellenic view of nature to its ultimate conclusion is that of Nietzsche. It is a complete and absolute form of naturalism where the virtues inculcated to attain the superman are cruelty, cunning, pride, and ruthlessness—the complete opposite of the beatitudes.

spiritual teaching confirms the view that suffering, sacrifice, work, humility, hope, faith—all forms of giving and therefore acts of love—increase holiness when they are embraced gladly and willingly. Love as the dynamism of finite reality harmonizes the finite with the nature of God. Thus, if God is love as St. John says, love being an eternal procession in which one gives of himself totally to the other two, then we would expect creation in reflecting its maker to have this same dynamism.

CHAPTER VI

The Ontological and Epistemological Structure of Process

DEFINITION OF PROCESS

Negatively, it might be said that process is not a category of 2-D, hence not in the category of either substance or accident. It transcends these categories. Process is existence, but not in the aristotelian-thomistic sense. That existence is individualistic, that is, an act of "to be" in the substantial order, hence the primary act of being possessed by substance as its own. But existence as process is a being-with-another; it is sharedness, hence a "we."

Because process is a "we" it does not proceed from one source or principle. Process is not a mere succession of moments or a series of events, each autonomous and distinct from the rest; nor is it one single flux that is heraclitan or bergsonian. Process is cooperative, but it is not the cooperative activity of, say, two men putting up a structure or two horses pulling a carriage. In these cases, union is purely on the level of activity; the subjects remain the same and unevolved.

Process is a growth, hence it is oriented and structured. In its structure it has an alpha or beginning, a middle, and an omega or fullness. The process from alpha to omega is marked by qualitative changes or births to new levels of union and existence.[1] The increase is not mere accretion or addition from without like that of a rolling snowball. Nor is it a redistribution of purely external elements in the evolutionistic sense; nor is it the mere actualization of what was potentially contained in the beginning, for this would be a merely accidental and quantitative increase from within since the essence is already fixed. But the increase in process is at the level of existence itself; it is interior, creative, touching the very core of being. The whole purpose of process is the search of being for its essence and meaning, hence the essential unfolding of being.

CONVERSION IN THE PLACE OF BEING AND TRUTH FROM THE PRESENT TO THE FUTURE

We have noted that process has a beginning (alpha), middle, and end (omega). Now if a given process is still going on, then we approach it in the middle, so to speak. That which is to the left of the middle is its past, to the right of it, its future, and the middle itself is its present. Since the universe we are concerned with is still in process, our starting point is the present. From this methodological vantage point the universe has, besides its present, a past and a future. Let us clarify what we mean by past and future. When we speak of the past of a given process, we mean its alpha or beginning; when we speak of its future we mean its omega or end. Having outlined this basic structure of process, let us proceed now to show that the place of being is in the future, not the present.

Since present reality tends towards the future in order *to be,* its present is not the place of being; its future is the place of being, and hence of truth, too, since being and truth are convertible. The present is the region of becoming, and

1. *PH*, pp. 151, 168, etc.

becoming (it is obvious) is that which is not yet being. In other words, becoming terminates in being. What we say here may be totally confusing to one possessed of the 2-D framework. For such a person, anything that exists is being so that even that which is still becoming is considered as somehow being. There is logic in this semantics as long as we are aware of the 2-D frame of reference and the premise that motivates this outlook.

The 2-D mentality would imagine a vertical line which separates being from non-being. On the left of the line is the region of non-being, which in itself is a construct derived from the privation of being. On the right of the line is that which is possessed of existence. This is the region of the real. In the region of the real, the basic premise is that the world of things is substantially finished; each species is eternal; there is no evolution. Thus time is immaterial and inconsequential to what is already possessed of being. Whether being is in the past, present, or future, it is unaffected. In this static context, time has been emasculated of its power since it is not creative. There is no real becoming. The ancients and medievals had reason to divest time of any power since for them it was negative, that is, destructive of being and hence of truth.

On the other hand, in an unfinished universe, we cannot say that everything in it is being. We have to approach the universe as becoming. This must be our approach if we take evolution and process seriously, if we take our new awareness of time as creative and productive of novelty into consideration. If we were to use 2-D terminology in the context of an evolving universe, we would have to say that the seed, the seedling, the plant, and the fruit are all beings. But then it would be impossible to distinguish them as stages of one process, for in so far as they exist, they all *are*. One is not more than the other. Hence to take account of process one has to get outside the 2-D frame of reference.

In the 3-D context, *being* is applied only to that which is fully evolved, in this case the fruit. Conversely, that which is not yet fully evolved is non-being, but non-being does not mean non-existence. It means becoming or that which is not yet being, hence non-being. This terminology, I think, takes account of evolution. On the other hand, in the 2-D context, if one starts with being, then there would be no reason why this being should evolve; it is already being. If evolution is to be meaningful, so that it terminates in being, the starting point cannot also be being.

An objection that may be made against the identification of being with the future or omega is the obvious observation that the future is not yet; the present alone is being; hence the future is non-being, rather than being. This objection seems to be a formidable one, for obviously we cannot deny that the future is not yet. In reply, let us at least establish the fact that the future is not pure nothingness. For if the future were pure nothingness, then why would we fear it, make provisions for it, fear old age and death? Could we say more?

It seems that the future is not just midway between pure nothingness and the present which is supposedly being. It seems that the future is in a sense more real than the present. If we again take the concrete example of a seed, it is true that the seed here and now existing is more real than the fruit-to-be. Let us suppose, however, that we are assured of the succesful culmination of the process—that the seed will bear fruit—then would not the future be more real than the present, since the fruit is more real than the seed, as the adult is more real than the child? But the objection will immediately be forthcoming that we are never certain about the future outcome of things.

Let us make the objection more forceful and suppose that the end is not achieved at all. What then? Does it follow that the presently existing seed is more real than its future which will never come to pass? By no means, for to say that there is no future to the seed is to say that there is no life in it. A present without a future is tantamount to death or non-existence. It is only when a thing has a future that it exists, for it is the future that gives existence to the present. Take away the future and the present collapses like a pack of cards. Hence, the whole being of the present depends on there being a future.

Common sense observation leads us into the fallacy of imagining time as having independent reality. But time is the essential structure of the thing that is process. In this context, if the present stage is unable to reach the final stage, will the present have existence of itself? Common sense would say yes, because it not only atomizes time as a series of moments but sees the present as having an existence of its own apart from the future. The fact is that if the seed does not reach its final stage it does not have authentic existence, for it is a being-towards-death. The structure of the present is that of hope; the present hopes that there is a future, for without this hope the present is nothing. The reality of the present, then, is that of hope, but hope necessarily implies something unrealized. Hence, the present is not fully real. But if this is so it cannot be the region of being.

The Greeks were justified in situating being in the present because, to them, things were substantially finished. Hence, the future had value merely accidentally, not substantially. Such a view is re-enforced by ordinary speech. We say *"my* future," *"my* death," thus relating the future to the present. Again, ordinary speech speaks of the future as coming— the coming week, month, year. The metaphysical basis of ordinary speech is the view that the present is stationary, possessed of being, hence substantial and self-subsistent. It is the future that comes to the present. But this metaphysics is built on common sense observation which is ptolemaic in structure. In the context of an evolving universe, it is the future which is stationary; it waits for the present, which is tending towards itself.

Again, in the ptolemaic structure of Greek thought, the present is the region of presence, for beings, substantially finished, are manifest to themselves. But in 3-D, present reality is not present to itself. To be present to oneself is to be fully unfolded to oneself. But it is only in the future that full unfolding is attained. Hence, the future is the region of presence; the present, on the other hand, is, paradoxically enough, half-present, half-absent to itself. Appropriately the present order is the region of night and day, for this phenomenon is most symbolic of the ontological and epistemological structure of present reality as process. Things in the present partly reveal, partly hide themselves. This structure of the present is the basis for mystery.

Certain great thinkers have seen with great insight that present reality is not totally rational, that there is the irrational in it. But they lacked the proper categories to express this insight. Heidegger, however, emphasizes the concealedness of truth and holds that the task of reason is to uncover it. The revolt of the existentialists was precisely against the rationalism of past thought which had practically evacuated reality of its mystery. Nietzsche and Kierkegaard were the forerunners of this rebellion. But they went to the other extreme of emphasizing the irrational, the dionysian drunkenness of things and the leap of faith required to attain truth. The result was that they appeared anti-rational or anti-intellectual.

The problem of philosophy may be seen as the reconciliation of the rational and irrational aspects of reality. On the basis of emphasis philosophy may be divided into two major traditions. The first we may call the rationalists—those who emphasize the rationality of the universe; the second, the irrationalists—those who emphasize the irrational. The first choose rationalism perhaps because it would be intellectual suicide to found reason and truth on the irrational, or perhaps because such a view is more comfortable to reason. The second, on the other hand, choose irrationalism because the evidence for it cannot be denied and therefore truth is not necessarily more secure in rationalism or more congenial to it. Which side is right?

The difficulty, it seems to me, is not in reality but in the static hellenic framework which we have all inherited. We unconsciously imagine reality as finished, consequently we see the rational and the irrational as two finished orders or dimensions of reality, lying side by side. Hence the term "irrational" is made to point to a definite extramental object whose essence is precisely that it is irrational; the term "rational" likewise is made to point to what is rational. If this be the situation, then it is impossible to effect a reconciliation between the two. For if the irrational is essentially so, then it can never be integrated into a rational framework, and the claim that such a framework gives an essential explanation of reality is a dishonest one. Justly would the mind itself revolt against such a claim. On the other hand, what is essentially rational cannot be made irrational. Hence it would likewise be false to claim that reality is essentially irrational.

But perhaps it is possible to explain the irrationality of things in a 3-D context. Thus in 3-D, the so-called irrational element of reality does not co-exist with the present. It is the future aspect of things which reason, being situated in the vantage point of the present, cannot yet grasp. Hence, to reason-in-the-present the future dimension of reality is still a mystery or irrational, if we take this to mean that reason cannot make sense out of it. Let us emphasize that the object itself is not essentially irrational. Rather the irrationality we see in things is the projection by reason of its own irrationality.

In a static framework, to say reason is irrational would be the height of absurdity. It would be to accuse God of making reason defective. On the postulate that things come forth finished from the hands of God, nothing could be defective essentially. Hence reason cannot be irrational; irrationality could only be in the object. In an evolving framework, however, reason itself is evolving. While it is ordered to knowing reality, it does this progressively through the development of its capacity, which evolves from irrationality to full rationality. Reason did not come forth from the hands of God fully rational as tradition would have us believe; it did not come forth an adult; it evolved and is still evolving. We cannot emphasize enough that in an evolving universe, God does not have to create things in a finished state because he gives a future to them.

There is no such thing as an irrational element of reality, for in itself the future is not irrational. Considered in itself, the future is the region of being, hence the fullness of truth and rationality; considered in relation to us, however (that is, to reason-in-the-present), it is irrational. What is irrational to reason-in-the-present is not necessarily so to reason-in-the-future or to evolved reason, for once reason has reached the omega of a given process everything will be manifest with respect to that process; the "fruit" is revealed. With respect to the macrocosmic level, once reason reaches the Absolute Omega it will see all things clearly and not just "darkly" as in the present, to use a Pauline phrase.

What has to be taken into consideration, then, is not only the unfolding of the object of reason, but the unfolding of reason itself. We cannot exclude reason from evolution, as tradition has done and still does, for human consciousness is an evolutionary part of the universe, in fact, its *within*. The knower and the known are both processes, hence not only has the object of knowledge a future dimension and therefore is still a mystery, but reason itself as knower has a future dimension and hence is still a mystery unto itself. The true problem in epistemology is how to relate a knower and known which are both evolving, not the false one of relating them as static realities.

By way of summary of our preceding considerations, let us diagram the ontological and epistemological structure of any given process:

Alpha	Past	Present	Future	Omega
	non-existence	becoming	being	
	absence	half-present half-absent	presence	
	darkness *or* night	light and shadow *or* night and day	light *or* day	
	irrational	half-rational half-irrational	rational	

The structure diagrammed above is applicable, *mutatis mutandis,* not only to particular processes but to the macrocosmic one. In the diagram we observe that process has three levels: the past, the present and the future. The past has the character of non-existence, absence, darkness; the present is becoming, half-present, half-absent, the region of night and day, of rationality and irrationality, hence of mystery; and the future is being, presence, the region of day and rationality.

In contrast to the above structure, traditional ontologies and epistemologies consider the future as the region of non-being and locate the real, be it essence, being, noumenon (realists, Kant) or phenomenon (empiricists) in the present, or else in the absolute past (Plato, Plotinus). In a sense, 3-D philosophy is evolutionarily one with the past, except that now it relocates being or the real in the future. In 3-D, there is no essence or noumenon hiding behind the phenomenon in the present. Essence or noumenon is one with the future dimension or omega of a given reality.

The change from 2-D to 3-D is one of emphasis in which the future becomes a more basic category than the present. The future is not only included as an essential structure of reality but is considered as its deepest level. This future dimension—which appears as mystery from the vantage point of the present—is the region of the mystics, the prophets and the poets, of religion and revelation, of all synthesizers and theorizers whose task is predictive, whether in science or in philosophy. Since this dimension is unconceptualizable, those who deal with it use poetic, mythical, symbolic or allegorical language. It must be noted, however, that all those who deal with this dimension do not necessarily work on the same level, for the dimension of the future is itself tiered. There are different levels of omega, starting from the immediate future and ending with the absolute future where dwells the ineffable mystery of God. Hence different searchers have their own levels for which they use different methods: poetic, mystical, intuitive, and so forth.

For confirmation of this conversion, we note that for Teilhard the future is the region of fullest being, the region of Omega which is the future-universal and also hyperpersonal,[2] the irreversible culmination of the movement of synthesis,[3] the center of centers where the universe fulfills

2. *PH*, p. 260.
3. *PH*, p. 270.

itself.[4] We observe, too, the findings of depth psychology which show that at the deepest level of the psyche is the concern for future realities: death, completion or rebirth, love, eternity.

The Scriptures show that the weight of being is in the future. Thus the Bible represents the movement of creation (represented by man himself) as a journey towards the *land*. The word "land" has various levels of meaning: Yahweh, first of all, and, secondly, the dwelling place of Yahweh, hence Jerusalem, the holy temple, Christ, the Church, faith, heaven. But on all these levels there is a common symbolism, namely, that land is truth (the land of truth) and being (the land of salvation and redemption). To be possessed of no land is to be an outcast, to be of no substance. Man on earth does not yet fully possess the land. He is a "Hebrew" (which means wayfarer) and a tent-dweller. The same realities to which "land" is applied are also referred to as presence, light, life, truth, mystery. Thus Yahweh is called the presence, the supreme mystery who dwells in inaccessible light, and who manifests himself by his "glory." The Jews travelled to Jerusalem and the holy temple as the place of the presence, of mystery, truth, and light. In the new dispensation, Christ is the presence and, in union with Christ, so is the Church wherein Christ dwells. Christ is the light and the truth, this truth being the mystery of faith.

CONVERSION FROM TIMELESSNESS TO TIME

This conversion follows as a corollary of the preceding conversion. If time is the essential structure of reality, then there must be a conversion in our outlook from timelessness to time.

The hellenic obsession with the timeless is a result of the 2-D view of time; therefore a conversion from timelessness to time is the same as a conversion from 2-D to 3-D time.

4. *PH*, p. 294.

Let us consider first the 2-D view of time. Time for the Greeks was negative in the sense that it was not creative of new reality. For Plato, the world was shadowy because time was but a "moving imitation of eternity."[5] Nor was time creative for Plotinus since in his metaphysical system the genesis of the sensible is effected through a fall from the One[6]; time is but the measure of this degradation. Aristotle joined the chorus in lamenting the negativity of time. For him, time is the measure of change. According to Aristotle: "All change is by its nature an undoing. It is in time that all is engendered and destroyed. . . . One can see that time itself is the cause of destruction rather than generation. . . . For change itself is an undoing; it is only by accident a cause of generation and existence."[7] In another place Aristotle reiterates this view of time: "For we are wont to say that time wears, that all things age in time, all is erased by time, but never that we have learnt or that we have grown young and handsome; for time in itself is more truly a cause of destruction *(phthoras),* since time is the number of movement, and movement undoes that which is."[8] The implication in all this is that the world is substantially finished and therefore change can only undo "that which is."

To escape the destructiveness of time, the methodology for the attainment of truth and being was to go outside time. Hence, for example, the scholastics devised methods of metaphysical separation from temporality to attain being and the process of abstraction to arrive at the essence of things. This philosophical outlook affected spiritual methodology. As we noted in the chapter on the history of the supernatural, under the influence of Greek philosophy Christians withdrew from involvement in the temporal affairs of the world. They emphasized not action, which is tem-

5. *Timaeus,* 37d.
6. *Enneads,* 3:7,7; 3:7,11.
7. *Physics* IV, 222b.
8. *Ibid.,* 221a.

poral, but intellectual contemplation, which is immanent and supratemporal; the ideal man was for them, logically enough, the thinking and contemplative man; thought was placed before action. Philosophy became metaphysical and turned away from current and existential problems; theology became a "thinking" theology, instead of a history of salvation.[9]

By way of contrast, we find that in the 3-D view, time is a struggling, creative, irreversible process bringing forth ever novel forms of life.[10] Time has become positive. It does not undo; it makes and evolves. What follows from this is that in an evolving universe, to go outside time is to die. Permanence is falsehood; process is truth. The reason for this is that the region of being and truth is the future, and to attain the future there is need of process; to stay in the present claiming to be substantially finished is an illusion. To be outside time, then, is untruth; to be in time is truth. Instead of assimilating time into substance and destroying its reality, we bring substance into time, make it process and thus restore to time its reality. Here, then, is an ontological and epistemological basis for involvement in time.

Though the Hebrews were not aware of evolution, their notion of time corresponds to our modern view. Thus for them time has always been the region of truth. Timelessness is likened to a barren woman, and this state is untruth, death. To have time is to be true and is likened to a woman with child.[11] Time is salvific, hence positive, for it is in time that God works his saving acts. These saving acts have a term or fullness. Thus John L. MacKenzie observes:

9. Crowe, *op. cit.*, p. 637.

10. James Collins, "Darwin's Impact on Philosophy," *Darwin's Vision and Christian Perspectives*, ed. W. Ong (New York: Macmillan, 1960), p. 97.

11. Claude Tresmontant, *A Study of Hebrew Thought*, trans. M. Gibson (New York: Desclee Co., 1960), pp. 26-29.

In the Hebrew faith, events tended not to a circle, but to a term: a term which God wills and intends, and to which He directs everything. . . . All their traditions showed them that there had to be something more; and the belief in a future took form most distinctly in the very period when faith in the present was being shattered on the rocks of events. We shall have to see what hope the future held for the Hebrews, what form it took, by what process they believed that it would be realized; for this hope is the ultimate key to Hebrew belief and Hebrew history, which is unintelligible without it.[12]

This hope, this future of the Hebrews, is described by St. Paul as a "mystery" destined to remain hidden until the "fullness of time," that is, until the appearance of Christ— and Christ was in fact to be its essential content.[13]

An objection to our conversion of time from 2-D to 3-D is that if time is the place of being there is no basis for the notion of eternity. Is not eternity the place for true being, the habitation of the infinite? And do we not go outside time and temporality to attain our ultimate good? This 2-D objection forces us to define the meaning of eternity within the 3-D framework.

Earlier in this study we said that eternity was 4-D (fourth dimensional) time. 4-D time, however, has a wider meaning than the traditional notion of eternity as God's life. By 4-D is meant the fullness of time which is the same as the full term of a process or its maturation. In a very broad sense, then, we can speak of 4-D time as the omega of any process, while the stage of its evolution is properly called 3-D.[14] Thus

12. Cf. his book, *The Two-Edged Sword* (Milwaukee: Bruce, 1956), p. 190.

13. Albert Gelin, *The Key Concepts of the Old Testament,* trans. George Lamb (New York: Sheed & Ward, 1955), p. 36.

14. When we speak of our philosophy as 3-D instead of 4-D, it is because reality is in the 3-D stage in relation to its Omega which is 4-D. Cf. note on p. 109.

for a seed, the attainment of the fruit which is a rebirth to new being is, for it, 4-D. Any rebirth or new level of being with respect to the previous stage is termed 4-D. Hence, the attainment of life by matter, of consciousness by life, and of the supernatural by the rational are all 4-D levels, hence their "eternities," so to speak, in proportion to their degree of being.

If we locate 4-D within the ontological and epistemological structure of process that we outlined in the preceding section, it would be placed at the omega. In relation to it, the present is the place of 3-D or evolutionary time. Within this 3-D time is 2-D time, or the phenomenal time of our activities, and 1-D or mythical time is at alpha. 1-D time corresponds to the seed that is outside the ground and has not yet begun its process, hence possessed of no *real* time and therefore mythical; or, again, the foetus in the womb that has not yet begun its real life outside may be said to have mythical time; the unbaptized who is not yet reborn to the life of grace has unreal time, hence mythical time, in relation to the reality of the Christian life.

Having explained the notion of 4-D and located it within the 3-D framework, let us now situate the strict notion of eternity within the same framework.

From the Christian point of view, eternity is first applied to Christian time possessed by the mystical body; secondly, to the time of the second coming when the Church begins to live its life in heaven; and, thirdly, to the life of God himself. The term "eternity" in these cases is applied analogically, with God's eternity as the prime analogate. In the first use, the man who attains the life of grace is, in relation to his previous state, possessed of 4-D time or eternity. But this life of grace in its turn has its fullness or omega which is the life of glory. Hence, the life of glory is 4-D in relation to the life of grace. Now the life of God in himself is beyond human comprehension and properly should be termed 5-D, but in so far as we speak of it in human terms we necessarily grasp it in human terms, hence we speak of God's eternity as 4-D. We have to be aware, however, that to express God's eternity properly we must deny this appellation since 4-D as we know it is but a participation in God's eternity; but God does not participate in his own life; he is that life.

Coming back now to the previous objection that eternity is the place of being, not time, we answer that indeed eternity is the place of being, but in the 3-D framework eternity is equated with the fullness of time or 4-D. This answer is not satisfactory, however, since it will be objected that the essence of eternity is timelessness. The essence of time, on the other hand, is contingency. To say then that eternity is the fullness of time is the same as saying that it is the fullness of contingency, an appellation which is hardly applicable to God's life.

To show how eternity is the fullness of time, it is necessary to re-examine the 2-D premise that served as the basis for the 2-D notion that eternity is timelessness. According to Oscar Cullmann, eternity for the Greeks is atemporal, but for the Scriptures it is limitless time.[15] For the Greeks, eternity is qualitatively different from time; for the Hebrews, time and eternity are on the same plane. According to Greek thought, time is negative, it is a degradation as we noted earlier. With this view of time, the eternity of God must necessarily be conceived as qualitatively different from time. Christianity, which had to pour revelation into the Greek pattern of thought in order to convert the Greeks, began to speak of salvation as a liberation from time and to assert that to attain eternity is to be atemporal. In scholastic

15. *Christ and Time,* trans. F. V. Filson (Philadelphia: Westminster, 1950), see Chapter III. In the German original, Chapter III, "Zeit und Ewigkeit," p. 53.

theology eternity is identified with God's essence, for there could be no distinction in God. God does not *have* eternity, will, intellect, and so forth. Rather eternity, will, intellect are one with his essence. Thus within the pattern of Greek thought it is proper to say that God is eternity.

But today, with the revival of scriptural studies and the discovery of evolution, we have a new awareness of time as positive, oriented, creative and directed, and of biblical time as essentially positive and good.[16] Hence if we move now from the Greek pattern of thought to the Hebrew or 3-D pattern, where timelessness is death and limitless time is life, being and truth, then God has to be identified with limitless time. It is proper to say, therefore, that God is the fullness of time. This appellation would have been scandalous to the Greeks, but in the context of a history of salvation it is most proper and logical.

The Scriptures speak not about God's atemporality but about what came to be called his eternal procession. Procession implies movement, rather than lack of it as in the Greek notion of eternity. Hence procession is more properly grasped as the fullness of time. Fullness of time does not mean contingency, for when one has the fullness of time as in the case of a process that has reached its term, or *is* the fullness of time as the alpha and omega of all processes because he is the eternal procession, then there is no evolution or becoming—the true basis of finitude and contingency.

Exodus 3:14 has been traditionally interpreted atemporally. But modern exegesis guides us in understanding the real meaning of the statement, "I am who I am," by comparing it with other passages denoting God's description of himself. The Apocalypse was intended by its author to be

16. Tresmontant, *A Study of Hebrew Thought,* p. 27.

the fullness of the first books of Scripture, Genesis and Exodus. Thus the last book of the Bible explains the creator of Genesis and the "I am who I am" of Exodus: "I am the Alpha and the Omega, the beginning and the end, says the Lord God, who is and who was and who is coming, the Almighty" (1:8). Again: "And the four living creatures have each of them six wings, round and within they are full of eyes. And they do not rest day and night, saying, Holy, holy, holy, the Lord God almighty, who was, and who is, and who is coming" (5:8). Thus, in these passages, time is more apparent than timelessness. The mention of past, present and future together and simultaneously is not a declaration so much of timelessness as of the fullness of time.

If we call God's time four-dimensional (4-D), then our time in relation to his would be 3-D. This distinction explains the transcendence and otherness of God. He is in a totally different dimension. Thus, because God is on the level of 4-D he is totally other, utterly transcendent; but because he is the fullness of time, he is also totally immanent in 3-D time. In a very true sense, God is the ground of our being, more intimate to us than we are to ourselves, to use the words of St. Augustine. The Greek pattern of thought is able to explain God's transcendence by making God's eternity qualitatively different from time, but by equating eternity with timelessness it is unable to explain how God, whose essence is timelessness, could be in time. We believe that the efforts of John A. T. Robinson, Paul Tillich and Dietrich Bonhoeffer to make God immanent in time could best be helped by the conversion of the notion of eternity from timelessness to limitless time.

With the conversion of eternity into limitless time, the different parts of theology could be integrated as a history of salvation. Thus the Omega of the process is God as limitless time. In order to attain the Omega there has to be involvement in Christian time, which is redemptive time; this involvement is a must; outside it there is no growth towards the *pleroma Christi* where alone we are assured of a participation in God's eternity. The Christian attains redemptive time in the Church which is a mystical body; the whole Church attains fullness by experiencing, through the celebration of the liturgy, dying, rebirth, and growth in the seasons of Advent, Lent, Easter, and Pentecost. Thus Christian spirituality cannot be a flight from time, but only an immersion in time; time itself is salvific and sacred, for the very heart of revelation is the coming of Christ to redeem time. Time no longer leads to death but to life—eternal life, which is not timelessness but limitless time, a participation in the eternal procession where limitless novelty is always forthcoming.

CONVERSION OF THE PRINCIPLE OF INTELLIGIBILITY FROM THE RELATIVITY OF ESSENCE TO THE ABSOLUTENESS OF OMEGA

The question that may be uppermost in the mind of the reader at this point is whether a philosophy of process can give true unchanging knowledge. The fear is that a philosophy of process must be relativistic. It is precisely this threat of relativism which prevents many theologians from wholeheartedly accepting Teilhard's synthesis.[17] For would not theological truths suffer from relativism if formulated in the context of an evolutionary view of reality such as Teilhard's? It is, therefore, the search for intelligibility in the context of process that will occupy us here.

With regard to the requirements of intelligibility in general, we might note that for there to be knowledge at all,

17. A comment of Father Gustave Weigel, S.J., in his introduction to Tresmontant's book, *Pierre Teilhard de Chardin: His Thought*.

there must be something which is at least relatively permanent. A reality that is in complete flux is totally unknowable; it would not even be existent, since for anything to exist it must be something, that is, identifiable, and the basis of identifiability is some permanence in the thing. To say then that the essence of reality is precisely that it is flux is to utter nonsense. The result would be total chaos and complete skepticism.

In general there are two theories of knowledge, the first founded on reality as basically static, the second, on reality as basically becoming. Of the first, we can point to Platonism and Aristotelianism as examples. In the platonic framework, knowledge is possible because there are permanent, unchanging eternal forms; in the aristotelian-thomistic framework, knowledge is possible because there are essences or universals in things which are permanent and unchanging. But these explanations of knowledge, while able to show the possibility of human knowing, do not take into account the fact that reality is evolving. This inadequacy has been explained in the first part of our philosophy of process, namely, that the 2-D framework, whose principle of permanence is substance, precludes evolution. On the other hand, of those theories of knowledge that do take account of evolution, some go to the other extreme of denying all permanence, asserting that all reality is flux and then trying to devise some form of intuition by which to know this constantly changing flux which is possessed of no orientation or direction. An example of this is Bergson's philosophy. The problem, then, in the philosophy of process is to find a principle of permanence in an evolving universe and thus strike a happy mean between the two extremes mentioned above.

Let us begin our search by reflecting on the principle of intelligibility in 2-D. In 2-D it is claimed that there are essences in things, essence being defined as that which makes a thing what it is. Now, essences of finite things are a combination of two intelligible notes, one serving as form, the other as matter. These intelligible notes, we are told, which can be multiplied in different individuals of the same species, are eternal, unchanging, and supratemporal, in contradistinction to the sensible notes of the same given object which are contingent, accidental, and temporal (for example, size, weight, color, shape).

If we ask how intelligible notes are determined so that we can accord this object such and such an essence, the answer would be that the so-called intelligible notes are observed by means of an intellectual process of abstraction from temporality and the sensible notes of the object, and thus are found to be constantly present—not as a necessary property merely—but as constitutive, substantial principles of the thing. Thus, in the last analysis, it is really the aspect of permanence of a central characteristic of the object that determines what the essence of an object is. And the reason why such characteristics as size, weight and color are disqualified as candidates for essential or intelligible notes is because they are contingent, changeable and impermanent.

Judging the 2-D theory of knowledge, we can say in its favor that the so-called essence in things does indeed give us some knowledge of the thing since it is based on something that is permanent in the thing. But our objection to it is this. Can we say with absolute certainty that the essence we have derived by intellectual abstraction is really the essence of the thing? The answer would be in the affirmative if the object always gives the same presentation of itself whether in the past, in the present, or in the future.

But what assurance do we have that the object has always presented itself as it is now and will continue to present itself in the same way in the future? The 2-D answer would be that if the object presents itself differently in the future, such a presentation is either substantially different from its present form or merely accidentally so. If substantially different, the argument continues, then we have a different essence and we are no longer speaking of the former essence; if accidental, we have a true knowledge of the object because the essence is still the same. The immediate premise in this reasoning is that there are only two kinds of change—substantial and accidental, evolutionary change being classified as accidental. Hence, even if we accept evolution, claims the 2-D argument, essences of things are unaffected by it; the 2-D theory of knowledge remains intact, applicable and valid.

The more basic premise in the argument is that the world is taken as substantially finished; evolution, therefore, is unable to work any substantial damage to the 2-D universe. Having relegated evolution to the realm of the accidental, there is now assurance that it will not tamper with the essences of things; hence the 2-D conclusion that the intellect is ordained to, and is capable of, knowing the quiddity of sensible things. Our basic objection to all this, however, is the questionable validity of 2-D cosmology or world-view on which its epistemology is founded. The subjective certainty of the 2-D mind that its epistemology gives absolute knowledge is in fact based on an antiquated cosmology. Its claims to certainty are excessive once we accept the modern awareness that the world is not substantially finished, that it is still in process. From this modern awareness it follows that what we thought were unchanging essences are not really so but are merely temporary presentations of a given evolving process.

Let us show by further reflection that what 2-D epistemology calls essence is not really the essence of evolving reality. We will start by accepting the 2-D observation that the so-called essence of a given object is permanent and constitutive of the thing. What is not often realized, however, is that the observance of permanence is not absolute, but merely relative to the time scale used. Even if we observed a million individual cases within the time scale of a million years and found that invariably and constantly we kept seeing the same intelligible notes, we still could not conclude that these notes are the essence of the object. All we can conclude is that in these million cases and within the length of a million years this is what the objects observed present themselves to be. We cannot extrapolate and say absolutely and timelessly that this indeed is the essence. For in the context of an evolving universe, the presentation of the object that we see is not necessarily the object's essence. The only time we can say with absolute certainty that this is the essence of the given object is the time when the object is fully evolved, for it is only in this final stage that the final presentation and revelation of the object is attained. If we take evolution seriously, then as long as a given object is evolving, its present form can give only a probable basis for knowledge of what the object is.

Let us further develop the preceding observations by an analysis of a concrete process. Thus to represent something which is still evolving, let us take a seed. Suppose now that this particular seed takes a million years to germinate so that within that time no perceptible evolution in its form is observed; what we would then observe as its constant presentation is seedness. From this time scale all we can validly say is that seedness is what we know the thing by; we are not allowed to say unqualifiably that the object has seedness as its essence. To maintain that this is so is obviously false because seedness is not really its constant presentation in the total time scale of its evolution. Absolutely speaking, what identifies the seed is the kind of fruit it is. Of course, in the ordinary time scale of human existence we can identify what a given seed is by saying, for example, that it is an apple seed. The reason is that we know what its fruit is going to be. We are able to see the process attain its fruit and have seen the actual fruit; we have experience of it. But in the macrocosmic level we do not know the "fruit," so to speak, of the irreversible and unique process of evolution in which all things are involved and from which they take their ultimate meaning. Since this is so, neither can we know for certain the essences of things.

From the vantage point of 3-D we can see that 2-D epistemology which is based on essences and which has provided traditional philosophy and theology with the stability and security necessary for the formulation of metaphysical and theological truths, is upon deeper examination really relative, hence insecure.

Let us now try to show how an epistemology of process can give certain knowledge. From the epistemological structure of process outlined in the preceding chapter, we noted that the present is the region of becoming. Therefore it is the wrong place to look for a principle of permanence. The only place of permanence is at the omega, for this final stage of the process does not evolve. Hence the unchanging basis of knowledge of a given process is its omega. In relation to the other stages it is absolute because, being fully evolved, there is now absence of any relativity. To be fully evolved is the same as to be fully unfolded or revealed. Hence it is at the omega that the final form or presentation of being is achieved. This final presentation is what is called essence in 3-D.

Thus the philosophy of process does not deny essence, it merely relocates it. Instead of situating it behind phenomena in the present, it locates it in the future, at the omega of the process. But let us immediately add that this certain knowledge based on the omega is certain only in the context of the given process itself. In the context of the total process of the universe, this certain knowledge is still relative. This is so because processes are not autonomous and totally distinct from others. The universe is not accidentally assembled, each species or level having an absolute meaning in itself. In order to show that a philosophy of process is not relative but built on an absolute principle of intelligibility, we need to show the actual presence of this principle.

Let us start by recalling what we mentioned earlier, that processes are contained as stages of still larger processes and all processes are contained in the single evolutionary process of the universe. Thus, for example, on the macrocosmic level, there are four major processes: matter, vegetative life, sensitive life, self-conscious life. Within these four major processes are contained specific and individual processes. The certainty and meaning of these specific and individual processes are relative to the omega of the major process in which they are contained. Thus the meaning of this or that particular process is relative to the meaning and omega of the evolution of matter as a whole; or again, the evolution of this or that species of plant is dependent on the omega of the evolution of vegetative life as a whole, and so on. The four major processes just mentioned are not autonomous but are joined evolutionarily as stages of one single process. Hence, just as the seed as a process finds its omega and meaning in the full-grown plant, and the plant in the fruit, so matter as process finds its omega and meaning in vegetative life, vegetative life in its turn in sensitive life and sensitive life in man. Man, therefore, holds the meaning to the infrahuman levels of evolution. As he grasps himself, so he imposes this meaning on the lower levels.

But man is not his own omega. He is not the ultimate principle of intelligibility of the universe, contrary to the claim of rationalists and naturalists that man's meaning is in himself. Man has to get outside himself to attain his omega. This getting outside oneself, which even the Scriptures and the mystics tell us is the way to truth, is not really a going outside literally but a going within, a tending towards greater interiority and immanence. For in the context of process, the *within,* as Teilhard notes, is the omega of the process. To resort again to our example of the seed, it is the seed that is outside its real self, the fruit. Hence to get within itself it has to go outside itself. Similarly, man is outside himself; hence to possess his within, he has to go outside himself.

To say that man must go outside himself to find the ultimate truth about himself and the universe is the same as saying that reason-in-the-present must go outside itself and take the vantage point of the future. Reason-in-the-present cannot know the absolute omega for it is in a different dimension. Hence reason-in-the-present has to believe in reason-in-the-future, in order to put itself in the same dimension as the absolute omega. Great thinkers of the past like Augustine and Anselm saw that in order to understand, that is, to see the ultimate truth of reality, one has first to believe. This attitude of belief is the necessary methodological attitude toward the knowledge of ultimate truth. The next step is the search for the absolute omega as the ontological and epistemological basis of reality. Before we go into this search, however, let us study the procedure of others in establishing the ontological basis of their philosophies, in contrast.

Let us take the cartesian *cogito* and the thomistic intuition of being. For Descartes, the thinking self is both the methodological and ontological basis of his philosophy. Methodologically, no doubt, our point of entry into reality is the present, and specifically, the present self, as Descartes and Augustine before him correctly emphasized. The inadequacy of Descartes, however, is that he built his philosophy on this intuited self. The *cogito* is not as self-evident as it is purported to be. It may be evident to the intuition of common sense, but this intuition is delusive, for the thinking-self-in-the-present is still evolving; its existence is still hypothetical and hence not a secure ontological basis; furthermore, it is still a mystery to itself since it is not fully unfolded or revealed to itself; hence it is not an adequate epistemological basis for truth. Nor can ultimate truths be deduced from the self-in-the-present because this self has to go outside itself. Only the self-in-the-future can attain the absolute.

The inadequacy of thomistic ontology, it seems to me, is first of all that it locates being in the present, then devises the metaphysical separative judgment to intuit being-in-the-present, and finally, founds ontology on this so-called transcendental notion of being. Our objection to all this is that if reality is process, then the present is the region of becoming, not being. Being does not hide behind temporality; rather, it is located in the future. Hence, an ontology built on the present is literally one built on shifting sands.

If it is argued that the transcendental notion of being, since it is attained precisely by a metaphysical separation from time and temporality, is not founded on becoming, again we observe that there is no being in the present, only becoming, for if present reality were already being it would not be in process. But granted that one can intuit being in the present, other difficulties remain. Thus how can a notion outside time perform its function of integrating reality which is in time? Only a reality that is the fullness of time can integrate presently evolving reality. Furthermore, in the context of process, for a reality to be separated from time is to cease to be. Reality is one with the possession of time, the greatest reality being that which possesses the fullness of time, or rather, *is* the fullness of time.

Let us come back now to the search for the absolute omega.

We might note here that this search is a categorical imperative for man since he is the head of the evolutionary process; it is his mission to direct this process to its Omega. Human reason, however, does not have prophetic powers to know this Omega; nor does it have command and lordship over time to command it to yield its mystery. In such a situation, it would be absurd to impose on man a categorical imperative to tend towards an Omega whose knowledge is beyond the powers of reason-in-the-present to know. To escape the alternative of branding the universe absurd, there must be some revelation that will tell reason what this Omega is. Hence, the philosophy of process shows the need and propriety for revelation and the necessity to include it in a total theory of knowledge. We can see that revelation is really the highest form of knowledge; it gives absolute certainty, for its content is about the Omega and the true direction to follow, the proper practices and ritual to perform, the true organization in which we should unite ourselves to attain Omega.

According to reason enlightened by faith, the Omega of present reality is Christ. As the Scriptures say, Christ is the truth, the alpha and the omega of creation. Christ, then, as Omega, is the principle of intelligibility of the universe. Compared to others, this principle is not a mere concept or a transcendental notion but a concrete "universal" that has existence-value. As Teilhard notes:

> . . . Plato, Spinoza and Hegel were able to elaborate views which compete in amplitude with the perspectives of the Incarnation. Yet none of these metaphysical systems advanced beyond the limits of an ideology. Each in turn has perhaps brought light to men's minds, but without ever succeeding in begetting life. What to the eyes of a "naturalist" comprises the importance and the enigma of the Christian phenomenon is its existence-value and reality-value.[18]

18. *PH*, pp. 294-95.

To answer the fear of theologians that a philosophy of process is not a secure framework, we observe that because of its fixed and unchanging character, the Omega seems to be a valid principle of intelligibility.

A comment may be made at this point that the Omega as principle of intelligibility is really nothing more than the doctrine of final cause which for Aristotle is also accepted as one of the sources of knowledge of things. Our answer to this is that there is indeed a similarity; however, teleology as understood in Aristotle is not exactly what is meant by the omega in 3-D. In 2-D, the principle of intelligibility of a thing is its essence, for it is that which makes a thing what it is. The end as final cause is an extrinsic one, hence it does not contribute to the essential intelligibility of the thing.

By way of contrast, the end or omega in 3-D is not an extrinsic cause but most intrinsic, for the omega is the depth, the within, the fullness of being of process. Hence, when we say that the end is the principle of intelligibility in 3-D, we mean it not as final cause, but in the same sense that 2-D would say that the essence is the principle of intelligibility. In fact, as we noted earlier, the omega as the final presentation of process is really its essence. Hence in 3-D, the end or omega carries more weight than the end as understood in 2-D. In 3-D, without the end, the process is not only not revealed to itself, it ceases to exist. On the other hand, in 2-D, end or no end, substance not only has its own act of "to be" but possesses its matter and form.

The doctrine of end has tremendous practical importance in the modern ideological battle. Compared to the traditional view based on Aristotle, the communist view of the end as a utopia on earth has greater appeal to men today. Arguing from the theoretical presentation of the two doctrines alone, we can see that there is greater reason to involve oneself in time in the communist scheme of things because one's meaning and essence are to be found at the end. But if one is already possessed of one's meaning and substance, then what reason is there to involve oneself in time? If the thing that matters for present reality is at the end, then time acquires momentous value; but if it is already possessed, then time is of no consequence; logically, life becomes merely a time of waiting. Thus the traditional doctrine of final cause cannot give an adequate explanation for the new awareness that time is all-important.

Together with the problem of the principle of intelligibility, we should include here a brief treatment of a related problem, that of the principle of individuation and of class or group. In other words, how are processes distinguished from one another, and how are they grouped together? We will first treat of the questions in general, then specifically with regard to man.

In general we may say that processes are classed in groups by reason of a common omega. If the omega is proximate, then we have a "species," and if intermediate, then a "genus," and so forth. Conversely, processes ordered to different proximate omegas are specifically different, and to different intermediate omegas, generically different. In contrast to the 2-D notion of "universal" it might be noted that the bond that unites individual processes under a common omega is not merely conceptual but real—a common evolutionary origin and a common term. In fact it would seem that the actual foundation for "universals" is the common evolutionary origin and term which natural objects have, rather than a conceptual construct such as a common passive substrate called prime matter actuated by the same form—an explanation which does not seem to have any empirical basis.

With regard to individuation it may be explained that

processes are individuated by their own distinct relation to a "specific" omega, or again, by their different fruits or terms, since unique unions terminate in unique terms. Concretely, two processes may have the same specific "ground," but are individuated by their own "fruits."[19]

When we come to the level of personality, these general principles of individuation and classification are valid, broadly speaking. Thus what specifically distinguishes man from the infra-human level is a distinct Omega and omega. However, these omegas (O and o) are not just on the biological level, for man is much more than a biological animal, but on a level proportioned to man, hence a hyperpersonal Omega and a spiritual rebirth as "fruit" or omega. With regard to individuation, let us first study briefly the principle of individuation in 2-D.

According to aristotelian-thomistic philosophy, the principle of individuation is *materia quantitate signata* (matter signed by quantity). Form cannot be a principle of individuation because it is the common denominator, so to speak. In other words, it is that which specifies or places individuals in the same species, hence a principle of specification rather than of individuation. Consequently, matter has to be the principle of individuation. But how can matter (which is pure potency) have the power to individuate since all perfection comes from the form?

There is another objection to this 2-D principle when applied specifically to man. Personality is the deepest category and value in man. It is hard to believe that this uniqueness can be accounted for by a mere difference in material equipment. No doubt, Peter and John can be distinguished

19. To avoid confusion between the "ground" of a process and the term or "fruit" of the process let us designate the ground as Omega, and the term of a process as omega. Thus, a given seed, for example, has the soil for its Omega, and its fruit as its omega. Or, again, the "I" has the "Thou" for its Omega, while the fully evolved or reborn "I" is its omega.

by material quantifiers, so to speak, but this basis is nothing else than an explanation of the ordinary way we distinguish individuals. Distinction between persons, however, goes much deeper than the externals. Personality, which is the deepest reality in man, justifiably requires a deeper principle of uniqueness than the material and external ones; it requires a principle that is on its own level.

In 3-D, individuation on the level of personality is on the basis of union between the "I" and the "Thou." Recall what we said previously, that union differentiates. Furthermore, union is not merely accidental but essential, since in process existence itself is this union. This unitive existence between the "I" and the "Thou" is one of love. Hence the principle of individuation of personality is love. The more one loves, the more one becomes unique and personal and not merely an individual. Love touches the very core of the "I." God is an Absolute Thou precisely because he is love. He is the source of differentiation for all because it is by participation in this love that beings are multiplied. The objection may be brought up here that if human beings have one and the same Omega, how can they be individuated? This objection is really in our favor because it shows how individuals belong to the same species, that is, by the possession of a common Omega. Furthermore, since no union of love between a particular individual and the Omega of all is the same as any other, it follows that each "I" develops into a different personality.

CHAPTER VII

The Methodology of Process

This chapter will develop the methodological implications of the categories treated in the previous chapter.

CONVERSION IN THE NOTION OF TRUTH FROM CONTENT TO DIRECTION

Let us first set the background for this conversion. Since truth is convertible with being (reality), it follows that if reality is approached as process, truth, likewise, must be approached as process. In the preceding chapter we outlined the ontological and epistemological structure of process. It is the methodological implications of this structure that we will develop with respect to truth.

If we diagram truth as process it appears thus:

Past	Present	Future
Alpha————————————————————————————Omega		
seed—truth	developing	fullness
or untruth	truth	of truth

We are interested in the nature of developing truth, but before we study it, it is appropriate at this point to define more precisely the various significations of truth in the context of process. Truth in general is conformity of one with another. But we are not concerned here with what the 2-D tradition would call logical truth, that is, the conformity of the mind with reality. We are interested rather in the authenticity or inauthenticity of process itself, hence, with what we might call generically its existential truth, as opposed to conceptual or logical truth; we are not, however, taking the term in the phenomenological sense. The truth (or untruth) of process belongs to a category all its own. The closest it comes to being categorized in terms of 2-D is that it is ontological truth, insofar as this term points to the fact that the truth of process is in the extramental rather than the logical order. However, ontological truth in 2-D is the conformity of a thing with the mind of God. Since all natural things in the 2-D universe are finished, that is, possessed of their respective essences, they necessarily conform to the mind of God; hence they have ontological truth. But reality in process is still in quest of its essence, hence we cannot speak of it as having ontological truth in the 2-D sense.

We will attempt, then, to define the various significations of truth in the context of process. Let us recall the various conversions we have made with respect to the traditional notion of being, namely, that being is not an island but always has its other and that present reality is a becoming which is in quest of its essence and therefore oriented. From these conversions we will derive the various meanings of truth. Thus, we can speak of the truth of process as in the "other" or "Omega," because process tends to it in order *to be*. Let us then call the Omega the ontological truth of process. We believe this designation to be apt because the individual process has to "conform" to its "Other" (that is, be with its "other") in order to be and be true to itself.

There is another truth besides ontological truth, and that is the term of the process, designated as omega. That which is in process is still becoming; it is not yet being. Hence, with respect to its fullness, it is not yet true. Truth for it is attained when it is fully revealed to itself, as the fruit fully reveals the seed to itself. The conformity to the fuller self we designate as epistemological truth, and again, we believe the designation to be apt, because it is revelatory. While epistemological truth pertains to a being which is already at the omega point, there is another truth that corresponds to that which is still in process. Thus one that is tending in the right direction towards the Omega is true. We call this truth methodological truth, which is an apt designation also, because it literally means the correct road or way to the goal.

Corresponding to the truths just defined are their opposite untruths (or falsehoods). Thus a process that is either separated from its Omega or united to a false Omega is ontologically untrue. For example, a seed that is unplanted or dead, or a dead plant, or one planted in bad soil (false Omega) is ontologically untrue. To give an example in the Christian context, we might say that a person who is not in the state of grace, or follows false gods is ontologically untrue. Conversely, one who is in a state of grace, and believes in the true God, has the truth and we call this truth ontological truth. Coming next to the epistemological level, we observe, first, that just as epistemological truth is based on ontological truth, so epistemological untruth is based on ontological untruth. Hence a process that is ontologically untrue will necessarily be untrue epistemologically. For example, a process that is not revealed to itself, like a seed that does not germinate or a plant that is barren (hence without fruit or omega), is epistemologically untrue, and the reason is that the process was ontologically untrue to begin with.

Again, in the Christian context, one who is not reborn to the life of grace, and does not have any of the light of faith and revelation, or one unborn to the life of glory, is epistemologically untrue. Conversely, those who are born to these levels are epistemologically true, because they are revealed to themselves. The third untruth, methodological untruth, would pertain to a process that tends to the wrong direction or is on the wrong road, so to speak, because the end is not known, or one does not have the directions, or the dynamism of the process is false (for example, the dynamism of selfishness and egocentricity instead of the true dynamism of love). In the Christian context, one who does not *know* of the true God, or is not in possession of any of the truths of revelation or is blinded by passions is methodologically untrue.

Having given these definitions of truth, let us now develop the implications of methodological truth. Thus, truth, instead of being viewed as content, becomes direction. In 2-D, present reality has its essence, hence things have truth-content. The search for truth is the search for content. Knowledge is a content. But in 3-D, present reality does not have its essence yet. Hence there is no final or essential content. The search for truth is the search for direction. Knowledge is predictive. In science, which is the most positivistic of the disciplines, this character of knowledge is slowly being realized. Thus, as a well-known scientist observes:

> The aim of science is to foresee, and not, as has often been said, to understand. Science describes facts, objects and phenomena minutely, and tries to join them by what we call laws, so as to be able to predict events in the future. For instance, by studying the motions of the heavenly bodies, astronomy has succeeded in establishing laws which enable us to calculate the position of these bodies with respect to the earth in an unlimited future.[1]

If scientific knowledge is predictive in character, all the more is this character verified in philosophy and theology which deal with ultimate realities. Thus the aim of philosophical and theological syntheses and world-views is not

1. Pierre Lecomte du Noüy, *Human Destiny* (New York: Longmans Green & Co., Inc., 1947), pp. 13-14.

so much to understand as to foresee, to give meaning and direction to human endeavor.

The methodological notion of truth as direction rather than content is confirmed by the Scriptures. The Hebrew notion of truth is set in the context of the Hebrew view of man as a wayfarer. The very name Hebrew (*'abiru*) means traveller, wayfarer. Untruth is one with sin and sin is a going astray, a hitting off the mark. Thus Bruce Vawter[2] observes that "in the Hebrew Old Testament the word most commonly used for sin is *hattah,* 'to miss the mark,' and the mark missed is not necessarily a moral one. Proverbs 19:2 uses this verb of the hasty traveler who loses his way through inadvertence to road signs. . . ." Hence, for Hebrew thought (as opposed to hellenic), to lack truth is not so much to lack content or have the wrong content in the mind, but to have the wrong way, to miss the mark.

The notion of truth as direction restores to revelation its true and dynamic meaning. Thus revelation is not so much an idea to be contemplated, nor the Bible a book, nor the truths of faith a deposit—formulations used by scholastic thought to conform to a static world-view. Rather, revelation is an unchanging direction that points unerringly to the true way to the land of truth. The quintessence of revelation is none other than Christ. He is revelation. Now in the context of revelation as the way, the true direction, Christ appropriately said of himself that he is the way, the unerring way. Significantly, he also said that he is the truth and the life. In that single statement, "I am the way, the truth, and the life," is summed up the different 3-D significations of truth. Hence, as the true direction or way to eternal life, Christ is our methodological truth; as the "first fruit" or "first born" of those who enter eternal life he reveals the

2. Cf. his article, "Scriptural Meaning of 'sin'," *Theology Digest,* (autumn, 1962), p. 223.

truth of our rebirth, hence he is our epistemological truth. And finally, he is our ontological truth because we depend on him for existence—in him we breathe, move and have our being; he is the life.

The implication in all the scriptural formulations is that reality is in process. Man is on a journey, but he has lost his way. Therefore there is need for a guide. A pillar of light was given him in the desert, the light being a symbol of Christ. Later this light revealed itself as Christ, the light of the world, who will bring forth men from the darkness (of sin) to the light (faith) of the sons of God. Christ shows the way; he knows the way for he has been there with the Father. Revelation then, which is none other than Christ, is a sure guide to the land of truth. It is immutable—not as an idea, not as a content, but as a direction. The Scriptures also speak of revelation as a light. A light, yes, but one that increases the dim light of reason so that it can see the depths of the future and know where to go to attain its goal. Hence, revelation is not just a light to be contemplated, but a light for "scattering the darkness" before us.

If this is the character of revelation, then its theological formulation should conform to it—hence the need for a history of salvation, a process theology, not a "thinking theology" for contemplation. Greek thought achieved immutability for revelation by assimilating it to the realm of ideas, but did so at the expense of the immanence of revelation in history. To see revelation as the true, unerring direction toward God is the only way, it seems, to explain both the temporality and immutability of dogma. In 2-D an idea cannot evolve; process or direction unfolds.

CONVERSION FROM A SPECTATOR TO A SYMBOLIC INTELLECT

If truth lies in direction, once possessed of the right direction, one is possessed of methodological truth. But within this direction there are various levels of truth that have to be distinguished. Before making the distinctions, let us first establish these various levels. The direction towards the Omega has stages or dimensions, for union of process with its Omega culminates in growth and rebirth. Between stages there is a quantitative increase up to a critical point where a unique qualitative change takes place. This change is a "birth" into a new dimension of existence. The change is a "dying" from one level of existence in order to live to the new level. This new dimension is also a new manifestation or unfolding of being. The new stage in its turn becomes the starting point for the next higher stage of birth, unfolding and manifestation, and so on until the fullness of truth is reached at the omega point. The nearer one is to the omega the greater the revelation and unfolding, hence, the greater the level of truth reached.

Considering now the relation of the stages to one another, we observe that if the stages are *a, b, c,* then the stages are related to omega as the symbol is to its reality. By symbol we mean that the stage reached does not point to itself as the source and explanation of what it is, but to a higher level. Thus in the relation *a* and *b, a* is the symbol of *b* and, conversely, *b* is the reality of *a;* but *b* in relation to *c* is related as symbol to its reality. The higher is the reality of the lower because it manifests the lower to itself; it contains the truth of the lower. The lower has the function of pointing not to itself but to the higher where its truth is found. The reality of the total direction, however, is the omega. Thus the seed does not point to itself but to the forthcoming seedling. Hence it is a symbol of the seedling. Its meaning, purpose, and end are not to remain itself, to point to seedness as its true form, but to point to the seedling as its truth and form. The seedling in its turn is but a symbol of the full grown plant, since it does not have the true form. The full grown plant points to the forthcoming fruit. Thus, in the context of development, the present is always a symbol of the future.

Our use of the term symbol has nothing in common with the ordinary connotation of sign or symbol. The ordinary use of these terms is purely accidental and of human convention: an arrow pointing to a direction, a red traffic light, a flag, and so on. Nor do we use the term symbol in the sense of a platonic symbol which is mythical. For Plato the sensible world is a mere shadow, a reflection of the eternal world of pure forms. There is no reality to it. For us, it is the concretely existing but unfinished reality which is a symbol. Nor should our use be confused with the aristotelian-thomistic notion of sign. In this philosophy, the concept is a mental sign of the essence, the term an external sign of the concept. In no case within this philosophy, however, is an extramental reality a symbol of another in its very being and nature. Thus smoke is a sign of fire. But smoke has its own meaning independently of fire; its significative aspect is accidental to its meaning.

In 3-D, we are speaking of extramental realities whose whole meaning and existence is precisely to be a symbol. Thus the seed is a symbol of the fruit. This is its whole purpose and existence. We cannot think of the seed without logically thinking of the fruit. Logically cut off the fruit, and the seed has no meaning in and for itself. The difficulty in the 2-D mind in perceiving the existence of symbols is that for it, reality is finished. Hence it can only have content or form which refers to itself and not to another. If it refers to another, it does so only metaphorically or allegorically. But for us present reality is unfinished, therefore objects, facts, historical events which are one with the progressively-being-created-reality are symbols. The present order of things is but a symbol of the fuller unfolding and revelation of being.

Another way of contrasting the 2-D formalistic view and

the 3-D symbolic view of reality is to observe that the former sees things as "set forth" while the latter sees the same things as "drawn towards." The former sees things against the background of the past from which they have emerged, and in this sense "set forth." The latter, in contrast, sees things in the context of the future where the weight of being is. Hence present reality is essentially seen as "drawn-towards-the-future," hence symbolic.

With present reality as symbol rather than form, the intellect takes on a different function and object. In 2-D, the intellect has traditionally been held to have the "form" or quiddity of sensible things as its object. First it abstracts these forms, then it lists, categorizes, classifies and systematizes them, and finally it contemplates them conceptually. In terms of function, the 2-D intellect is a mere recorder and accountant of reality; in terms of end it is a spectator. In 3-D, on the other hand, the objects of the intellect are symbols. Since symbols point to the future for their meaning, the very ordination of the intellect is towards the future and not narrow containment in the present. In terms of function, the 3-D intellect is a gatherer of symbols. In terms of end, it is prophetic, predictive, believing, or imaginative, depending on the dimension of the future to which it is ordered. Thus the higher function of reason is not so much to see as to foresee, not so much to conceptualize as to predict, and it should appropriately be named after this higher function. In fact in the context of science, as we noted earlier, the facts, objects, phenomena that science deals with are not so much concepts to be understood as symbols for the prediction of future events.

In the 2-D rationalistic tradition, reason is identified with the conceptual and objective, while the imagination is equated with the subjective and animal part of man. But in

3-D, imagination is an inherent structure of developing reason, in fact a deeper part than the so-called conceptual reason which attains only the present, because imagination can attain a portion of the future. We are speaking here, of course, of creative imagination and not of the activity that produces phantasms which, being pictorial, are really part of the spectator or seeing intellect. In the context of reason as a gatherer of symbols, imagination has a role in the interpretation of these symbols in terms of the future. If we consider the great discoveries of the world, we find that it is creative imagination which has produced them. The production of the first tools, the invention of the first wheel, the discovery of Galileo, were all due to great imagination. Traditionally, the ideal scientist and philosopher was supposedly the perfectly rational, objective, uncommitted, emotionless individual. But we realize today that this view is a construct valid only for a finished universe in which everything is given—in which there is nothing to imagine. In 3-D, imagination is for the future, as memory is for the past.

But the future that imagination reaches refers only to the present life. With regard to absolute realities—God and human destiny—a deeper part of reason alone can attain them, namely, the level of faith, hope and love, which, however, tradition commonly attributes to the will. To the hellenic tradition, the will is a faculty distinct from the intellect because they are specified by different objects, the intellect by truth, and the will by the good. This distinction however is quite tenuous, for if being, the good, and truth are convertible, then they should be attained equally by both will and intellect. Empirically, it is difficult to prove that the will does not also attain being and truth, unless of course we identify truth with the conceptual. Then indeed the will does not attain conceptual truth. But experience shows that the "heart" has its "reasons" which conceptual reason cannot fathom. An act of love reaches the truth more surely than conceptual reason and attains a greater depth of it. Acts of belief, hope and love are nonconceptual but not necessarily irrational. In fact, they are the deepest signs of rationality.

In 3-D, as in Hebrew thought, will and intellect are not divided. There is just the conscious human act which remembers, sees, believes, loves, hopes, imagines. All these aspects of the act are diversified by the temporal dimension to which they are ordained, remembering with respect to the past, seeing with respect to the present, imagining, believing, hoping, loving with respect to the future. All these aspects are rational. That part of reason that is concerned with the future necessarily becomes imaginative, believing, hoping or loving. The difficulty in the 2-D view of reason is that in identifying the rational with the conceptual, believing, imagining, loving and hoping become irrational, or to use a euphemism, nonrational. As a result, we have the historical battle between the intellectualists and the voluntarists as to which faculty grasps reality better, which faculty grasps God more fundamentally in the beatific vision, and so on. In 3-D, the issue is a false one because reason is not identified with the conceptual, the will with the nonconceptual. There are not two faculties but only one—reason. But reason in 3-D is not understood in the narrow sense of 2-D as purely conceptual. Reason is a process. In so far as it is ordained to the past, it remembers, to the present, it sees, and to the future, it wills (believes, hopes, loves).

We might note too that the existentialist's categories of *angst,* boredom, care, fidelity are all future categories of reason, hence, to reason-in-the-present or conceptual reason they are irrational. The norm by which we judge the superiority of the several acts of reason is the degree to which they reach the future. According to this norm the acts of faith, hope and love are the highest acts of reason. In making these acts reason is reborn, hence able to see what reason-in-the-present (conceptual reason) cannot see. Incidentally, to propose love as the deepest dynamism of being is not to be voluntaristic but to be highly rational, since love is the highest act of reason, able to reach what conceptual reason cannot reach—the absolute Omega.

Following from our conversion of the intellect from a spectator to a searcher for symbols is a corollary, namely, that the intellect is not so much a faculty of timelessness as of time. Since forms or essences are not outside time but are relocated at the omega point, the intellect does not have to withdraw from time to attain truth; rather, it must immerse itself in time. A condition for the fulfillment of its primary task of searching for true symbols is knowledge of the times, of the course of events, in order that it may guide reality to the fullness of time, being and truth in the future. Since the end is all important in 3-D, while only incidental in 2-D, the task of the intellect is a serious and weighty one. It must be able to see the signs or symbols along the way. It is not enough that it be possessed of the right direction; this is but to possess initial truth. The more important task is to continue in it. To do so, one must watch for signs along the way.

The conversion in the dynamism of the intellect from the timeless to time, however, cannot but affect other areas of philosophy. The real difficulty in introducing a new concept into a system is not the introduction itself, which is easy enough, but the work of harmonizing it with other parts of the whole. But such an attempt is not without its compensations, too, for the attempt may throw a new light on other areas. The specific difficulty we are confronted with is that if the intellect is a faculty for time, then how are we going to show the immortality of the soul? We do not have the space here to treat the problem at length, hence a more complete treatment of reason in relation to immortality will have to be undertaken at a future date. But a brief treatment of the problem is sufficient and necessary here to show the unity of 3-D philosophy.

Let us first review the 2-D proof of immortality based on the immaterial nature of the intellect. Immortality, like eternity, is conceived in 2-D as timeless, once having been achieved. The effort then in 2-D is directed to showing that there is a principle in us that tends to the timeless. This is shown by demonstrating that if there is a capacity for the timeless, then the source of this capacity must therefore be immortal. This capacity is shown to be the intellect insofar as it knows universals which, supposedly free from the conditions of matter, are timeless. Now, in judging this proof, we recall what we noted earlier, that the term "universal" is really just another name for the common evolutionary origin and term of a group. In other words, the basis for similarity in natural objects is really evolutionary unity. Furthermore, the capacity of the intellect to unify all individuals, past, present, future, and in all places, under, say, the name "cat," is not so much a capacity for timelessness as for the fullness of time.

Much ado is made about the difference between animal and human knowing insofar as a brute has only material phantasms while man has rational concepts. But this distinction is quite hard to prove from experience. What we can prove as a clear distinction between animal and human knowing, however, is that among all the animals, man alone is able to foresee, an ability which includes prediction or forecast, belief, hope, guidance, direction. Brutes can attain the past and present, but man alone can attain the future. But for 2-D philosophy, the significance of this difference is missed, or rather, ignored, because knowledge is conceived as essentially pictorial, patterned after sight. Hence the difference between animal and human knowing has been sought in terms of a difference in "seeing."

In terms of process, however, this capacity for foreseeing is significant for it is an indication of man's capacity for immortality. Now, immortality in 3-D is not timelessness but the fullness of time or limitless time. The capacity of reason to unify past, present and future is a capacity for limitless time, hence an indication of man's immortality. Truly may we say that the intellect is a divine faculty *(capax Dei)* because the intellect, being a faculty for limitless time, has a capacity for God who is the fullness of time. But we add here that only through reason's act of faith which attains the absolute future can reason attain God.

The 3-D view of present reality as symbolic and of the intellect as a searcher for true symbols, hence predictive and prophetic, is confirmed by the Scriptures. In Israelitic history, the main event was yet to come. The present gave signs of it. Hence the people had to read the signs of the present. This methodological approach to the present can be seen from a few Scriptural passages:

> From the figtree learn this parable: when its shoots become tender, and when its leaves grow, you know that summer is near. Likewise, when you see all these things, you will know that (the event) is near at hand, before the very gates (Mt 24:32; Mk 13:28; Lk 21:29).
>
> Come evening, you say: tomorrow will be fine for the sky is dark red; and in the morning: today there will be storm for the sky is dark red. You can distinguish the aspects of the sky, but the signs of the time, you cannot (Mt 16:2).
>
> When you see a cloud coming up in the west, you say at

once: here comes rain, and so it is. And when you feel the
south wind blowing, you say: we will have hot weather. . . .
How is it then that you do not recognize the times that are
upon you? (Lk 12:56).

We note from these passages that the people were reproached
for not recognizing the signs of the time. To distinguish the
true signs was not an easy matter, however, for there were
other gods besides Yahweh, each god having his own
prophet. Furthermore, even the signs of the true God kept
evolving in order to mark the direction and stage of Israel's
growth. To have the correct sign was vital to Israel, for the
sign was a saving act, a sacramental one. Without it, Israel
could not be redeemed. The correct sign was the one Yahweh gave at that present stage and not the one he had given
in the past. To help Israel recognize the correct signs, Yahweh sent his prophets. The prophets were the "philosophers"
and "theologians" at that time, not because they possessed
unchanging ideas or timeless dogmas but because they
possessed the true direction and knew how to read the signs
of the time. This ability was attributed to greater vision. The
intellect was thought of as a light to see ahead. The people
followed the prophets as guides precisely because, being
closer to God who is Light, they had a more powerful light,
hence could see farther ahead than the ordinary man. The
function of the prophet is described very well in the following passage:

It is characteristic of biblical history that those who carry it
forward are made aware of its *direction* through the teachings of the prophets. The prophet, the *nabi,* is someone who
understands the "sense" of history, what it means and
whither it moves. We can understand the "meaning" of a
historical event only if we can see what it forebodes. A historical event is a *sign* only in so far as one may read in it
what will come of it, just as we can foretell, when the bud
appears, that the flower will follow. It is not because of

some extrinsic relationship, but very simply because the former actually does produce the latter. The *nabi* is aware of God's creative action and understands those "phases" of it which regard man especially. In this he is like the farmer who knows the "time" of the maturation of his crops. "The king turned to the wise men who had knowledge of the times" (Est 1:13). "A knowledge of the times to determine what Israel should do" (1 Chron 12:33).[3]

The 3-D methodological approach to truth has tremendous significance for ecumenical unity, for it would seem that part of the issue is epistemological. All members of the Judaeo-Christian tradition trace their respective "types" and symbols (*symbolum Fidei* or Creeds) to the Old or New Testament. In this sense the symbols are all true. But while all these symbols point to, and are derived from, one and the same authentic history of salvation, the difference among the denominations is that one is holding on to the types or symbols of one stage of that history while another denomination is at another stage and sees only the types and symbols of that stage. Concretely, the Christians believe that in the present dispensation, Christ is the type—the symbol and revelation of the Father. The old covenant with its symbols is past. This is not to say that to stand with the old covenant is totally false. As a matter of fact, since the whole evolutionary process has one common Omega, which is the truth of the single process, all stages in this process participate in this truth. But the law of salvation history is growth.

To be is to grow. In order to grow, however, one has to have the proper sacramental symbol with its attendant ritual and laws and organization. For just as to be a grown man one has to put away the things of a child (psychological framework, activities, interests, and so on), as St. Paul well observes, so for the *qahal Yahweh* to grow it must adopt

3. Tresmontant, *A Study of Hebrew Thought*, p. 27.

proper organizational framework, ritual, laws and so forth, corresponding to its stage of growth. It cannot be pointed out as a sign of authenticity that one's denominational history has outlasted all others, for a stunted growth can also go on surviving. The true sign of authenticity is vital growth.

The application of the methodology of truth might also help Christian renewal within Roman Catholicism. The Church is a growing mystical body. But there are some who still look at the Church statically, who believe that it is the task of the modern world to adapt itself to the Church and not of the Church to adapt to the modern world, that renewal must be on the part of the world, not the Church. What these Church leaders, whose sincerity is unquestioned, are actually doing is freezing the Church in a given stage of its growth, absolutizing this stage and using the formulations of this stage—its philosophy and theology—as absolute norms for judging what is right and wrong. Hence, what are needed today are true prophets, those who have a feeling for the times, those with a sense of history. Such a man was Pope John XXIII. The norm of thinking with the Church in order to be authentic is a valid norm but quite unworkable until we have determined what stage of its growth the Church is in. This is the hardest part of the task of renewal, for the existence of true prophets to tell us what that stage is is no assurance that the Church will listen to what they say.

From the point of view of Christian apologetics, if non-Christians do not see and believe in our symbols, it is perhaps because reason is not in the proper dimension, or is outside the Christian dimension. Just as the seed must die to its vantage point to be able to see what the seedling sees, so, we believe, reason must die to its norms and criteria to enter the dimension of faith. The lower stage cannot use its norms and criteria to judge the higher; rather it is the higher that judges the lower because the reality of the lower is the higher; the higher possesses the truth of the lower. And in the total context, it is the Omega that judges all dimensions and stages. For this reason, Christ as Omega is the judge; and Christians who participate in Christ are said by the Scriptures to judge the world, to sit in judgment with Christ. Rationalism, to our mind, is like an ungerminated seed; it does not see what the seedling sees. It must be reborn to faith in order to see. It has some truth, this is not to be denied, but its mistake is to absolutize its truth, using it as the absolute criterion for judgment.

CONVERSION IN THE PRINCIPLE OF VERIFICATION FROM IDENTITY TO PARADOX

A problem that has been left unanswered in the preceding section is how to read symbols and thus follow the right direction. How are we to determine what symbols correspond to which stage? What are we to expect of the future from a given symbol, granting it is true? How can we trace the continuity of a given process starting from either direction? These are some of the questions that need to be answered. Hence our problem here is the search for a principle of verification. Needless to say, the knowledge of this principle is a necessary condition for the understanding of reality as a process.

The 3-D principle of verification can best be seen from the background of 2-D. Hence let us start with the 2-D principle of verification. In a 2-D world populated by substances that are specified and individuated, things point to themselves for their meaning. Hence things are what they are. To say then that a thing is what it is, is to state the principle of identity—the 2-D principle of verification. But in a 3-D world, present reality is not what it is since it is still in quest of its being and essence. We cannot say then that a thing is what it is. The 3-D world, consequently, is not governed by the principle of identity. The paradoxical statement that a thing is not what it is, is true in the 3-D world. Hence the principle of verification in 3-D is paradox.

Let us develop the similarities and differences between these two principles. Since in 2-D, the concept is a sign of the essence, the principle of identity that applies to essence also applies to the mental world. Consequently, both 2-D ontology and logic are governed by the principle of identity, or in its negative form, by the principle of non-contradiction. Likewise, the principle of paradox holds true in both the extramental and the logical world of 3-D, since a symbol is a sign of presently evolving reality.

In 2-D there is either substantial or accidental change. In the former, the effect in the mental world is a change in the formality of the concept; in the latter, the concept is essentially the same. In the context of 3-D, an evolving process is grasped by symbols. Thus one and the same process is grasped by different presentations. Aristotelian logic does not make this distinction. For example, the terms "infant," "boy," "youth," and "man" point to substantially different realities that coexist extramentally. As concepts they are essentially different, having different formalities. In process, the terms point to different levels which take their meaning from their position and place in the process.

Aristotelian logic does not and cannot provide for the evolution of a concept, for such a logic would not then conform to a static universe, populated by finished essences. Hence, the concept "boy" cannot give rise to the concept "youth," or the concept "youth" to the concept "man." In 2-D, concepts may be univocal, analogical, or equivocal, but never evolutionary. These divisions of the concept are based on a cosmology that sees each species as being directly made or created rather than as evolving from other species. Hence, even analogical concepts are based on a static hierarchy of beings in which the lower participates in the lowest dimension of existence of the one directly above it; this participation, however, does not take place in time but is built in by the maker. There is no historical or evolutionary continuity in the hierarchy. In the context of process, on the other hand, "boy" evolves towards "youth" because we do not take them in their formalities but in their presentations.

The principle of identity of concepts based on the same formality is inapplicable in the context of process. According to this principle, two concepts with the same formal notes point to one and the same reality, and to different realities if the essential notes are different. If we apply this principle in the context of process we fall into what we might call the fallacy of dualism. In other words, we see two distinct orders or entities where there is really only one. To give a familiar example, "seed" and "fruit" have different formalities but point to one and the same reality in the context of process.

Of course, we will never make the mistake of dualism in the example given above because the time scale is short enough for us to verify actually the continuity of the seed and the fruit. But in the immense time scales which do not allow us to actually see the continuity of the process, one could very well fall into the fallacy of dualism. To see continuity properly, one must be able to detect the continuity of apparently contradictory stages. Hence, the principle that will help us see the true logic of evolution or process is the principle of paradox. Thus in the context of process, to verify whether b is the same reality as a, or to put it another way, whether a is the germinal presentation of b one must not look for the formality of b at a. To say that a is b only when they are identical is to fall into the fallacy we mentioned. Rather, one must be prepared to look for a *non-b* at stage a. In terms of aristotelian logic this is a fallacy because it violates the principle of non-contradiction. In 3-D, however, one must not see the form of an oak at the stage alpha but precisely a non-oak form, namely, an acorn. To look for a miniature oak is to fail in the search. By the principle of paradox then, if the given reality is *a* at alpha, then its truth is a *non-a* at omega, and conversely, if it takes the form *b* at omega, at alpha it is *non-b*.

To understand better the principle of paradox and its tremendous importance in the understanding of reality, let us apply it concretely. Thus an application of the principle is in the understanding of the macrocosmic process of evolution itself. Without this principle we cannot understand Teilhard's insight that somehow matter is not only pre-life but also pre-conscious. This lack of understanding is the cause for the derogatory label of panpsychism which many have attached to Teilhard's evolutionary view. Teilhard is interpreted to mean that the table in front of me is not only possessed of life and sensation but is somehow conscious. The question is then asked in shocked disbelief how the table, or a stone for that matter, can be said to feel and think. Thus Teilhard's assertions, it is claimed, have no basis at all in experience. The difficulty here is that the objector is trying to grasp with his 2-D logic a world that does not conform to it.

Given the 2-D framework, let us see how a 2-D logician would interpret the statement that the lower levels of being participate in consciousness possessed by the higher. First of all he gets a definition of consciousness from the higher where it is perfectly verified. He then takes this definition along and goes about looking for the same formality at the lower levels. If he finds the same formality, he then concludes that consciousness is present analogically; if not, then there is only equivocation. Now such a procedure is perfectly valid given the 2-D cosmology of direct creation of each distinct level of being. The fallacy, however, is in applying this methodology to an evolving world. We are not saying that the 2-D logician does not believe in evolution, for he very well may. The point is that while believing in evolution, he tries to understand it in terms of 2-D logic and methodology. Thus a modern man who may no longer subscribe to the antiquated cosmology of 2-D may nevertheless hold on to the logic derived from it, unconscious that its basis is precisely the cosmology he has consciously rejected.

In the 3-D cosmological framework, the 2-D logical procedure of verification just will not do. In verifying whether a given reality evolved from the lower, one cannot start with a definition of it based on this self-same evolved stage and then go looking for some formality in the lower stages and expect to find it there. It may well be there, but our method has precluded our ability to see it. Thus, to use a previous example in the effort to be clear (even if it is at the risk of repetitiousness), to find the oak in the lower stages one must not look for a miniature oak, otherwise we could never see and accept that the acorn is indeed the oak. One must be prepared to surrender the formality of the higher—in fact, to deny logically its formal presence in the lower—if one wants to see properly. To see the oak in the acorn one must see a non-tree. To persist in looking for a miniature tree at the lower level is an invalid procedure, for this would be to deny the very condition we started with, namely, that there is an evolution. In other words, if one persists in looking for the same formality at the beginning as at the end, one is actually implying that there was no process or evolution. The very premise of 2-D logic is that the universe is static. Hence if we use it as an instrument of verification, no matter how sincere and open-minded we are, we cannot understand the evolutionary view of Teilhard, for sincerity is not enough to enable us to see. A valid methodological instrument is necessary.

If we start with the premise that there is an evolution, then by the law of paradox, one must look for qualitative changes at lower levels, different from those found at the higher. Of course, even the 2-D mind would not fall into the mistake of looking for a miniature oak tree at the beginning of the process of the evolution of an oak; it looks for the seed; but when it comes to the macrocosmic level it is unable to apply the same procedure. The reason may be that it is not aware that the previous example is actually governed by a new principle. It goes on in the belief that its principle of identity is universally applicable.

Armed with the principle of paradox it might be possible to see the presence of consciousness at the lower levels of the evolutionary process. The presupposition in all this, of course, is that our universe is an evolving one, therefore that all things in it emerge by way of evolution. Consciousness which has emerged later on in the evolutionary process must therefore somehow be found at the lower stages.

To verify its presence at the beginning it is easier to go to the next lower stage, that is, to that directly below the conscious stage; there the continuity is easier to detect. At the next lower stage then, by the law of paradox, one should not look for consciousness as self-consciousness, but as infra-consciousness, that is, a consciousness that is not self-conscious. Such a stage is verified by the presence of the sensible level. To reverse the process, if we start at the level of the sensible and verify its presence at the higher, we should look for the supra-sensible which would be self-consciousness or rationality. But going back now to the sensible level and working down, we should logically look for the infra-sensible, and that would be represented by vegetative life. Below life would be infra-life or non-life which is matter. Thus the evolution of consciousness postulates that the alpha be matter, for just as to be able to see the oak at the alpha stage one has to see a non-oak, so to see consciousness at alpha one has to see non-consciousness, and that would logically be matter.

But a warning must be given here, namely, that the antithetical "non-" has to be understood in the context of process. For outside this framework it can also be said that a stone is a non-oak. In the context of process, however, a non-oak is that which can evolve into an oak; expressed affirmatively, the non-oak is a pre-oak, and this would apply to the acorn in a way which cannot be applied to the stone. Similarly, to speak of matter as non-consciousness is not to say that it is totally inert and outside the line of evolution leading to consciousness, the way a stone is outside the line that leads to the oak tree, but, if one were to speak affirmatively, it is to say that matter is pre-conscious the way an acorn is a pre-oak. But in saying this we cannot emphasize often enough that we are not then saying that matter is a thinking substance, that all reality is thought or panpsychic.

In spite of this effort at intellectual understanding, we are still left with incredulity as to how matter could have evolved into consciousness. Before the immensities and perpetual wonders of nature, this incredulity is a natural one. The phenomenon of growth of a tiny seed to a giant tree, of an almost microscopic ovum to a full grown man, are among the greatest wonders of nature. If in the time scale of at most a century the imagination and sense experience find it hard to believe the evolutionary continuity of many things, so dissimilar are the beginning and the end result, except that we are able actually to verify their continuity, how much more is this so in the time scale of a billion years or more where a century is but the tick of a clock, where the phenomenon is beyond the imagination and sense, beyond actual verification. Just as there are realities in the realm of space that completely stagger the imagination but which we nevertheless find acceptable, like "infinite" distances and infinitesimal particles, so there are comparable realities in the realm of historical and evolutionary time. To use the 2-D framework of the senses in these instances to determine what is possible or not is to be naïve.

The use of the principle of paradox to show and reveal the evolutionary or historical continuity of things and events that are often beyond a single man's life-span (and hence beyond his actual experience) is again confirmed by the Scriptures. This principle, used by both the Old Testament prophets and the New Testament evangelists, goes by the name of biblical typology. The Jews always thought of their relation to Yahweh in terms of the central and all-pervading idea of the covenant, conceived as a marriage between Yahweh and Israel.

The main event of the divine message whose fulfillment Israel was chosen to bring about in cooperation with Yahweh, was the coming of the promised one, the first born and first fruit of those who shall be saved. A necessary condition for the successful fulfillment of the promise was the fidelity of Israel, that she follow the right path, that is, maintain union with Yahweh. To this end, Yahweh sent as types and symbols historic events and personages that pointed out for Israel the direction toward the promised Omega as each new stage in Israel's growth and purification was reached. Recognition and acceptance of the typological significance of these events and persons was important for the individual Israelite, for each type deepened the salvific meaning of the original message and thus carried it forward sacramentally toward its true fulfillment.

But there were many who would not accept the new

dimension as prolonging and fulfilling the old. Instead they measured the new by the old, not realizing that for continuity the new type must necessarily negate the old. This inveterate blindness, noted by Christ himself when he said that there were some who saw and understood the symbols and some who did not, was ironically visited on the chosen people when Christ, the antitype for whom the whole long and painful history of Israel prepared, was not recognized; when instead of the antitype, the types that had meaning and salvific power only because they pointed to the antitype, were preferred.

The superficial testimony of common sense logic, which demands that for a thing to remain the same through a given time span it has to retain its form, is so deeply ingrained that the more profound and paradoxical truth is missed: that for a thing to remain in being and hence be the same, it has to change. If a seed remained the same then it would not really remain, that is, exist, for its being is a being-towards-death. Change is the law of permanence, and hence of being. It is easy enough to see that a seed has to die to be reborn, but many, including Christians, cannot see the principle implied in it repeated at higher levels of reality even though none other than Christ himself taught the principle by using the very same example of the seed that has to die in order to be reborn to explain the paradox of the Christian life: that in order to truly live, a man has to die. The inability to apply this principle is a common trait of those possessed of the hellenic complex. We noted this in the reluctance felt by otherwise sincere Christians toward Church renewal and reformulation of the Christian message, which in fact are imperative if the Church is to remain the same—that is, continue being vital to itself and to the world.

The inability to think paradoxically is also, at bottom, the reason for the continuing difference and unresolved conflict between rationalists and non-rationalists concerning the principle of verification, especially as it applies to the validity of philosophic syntheses or world-views. Specifically, the question concerns the norm by which we judge the validity of a synthesis. We have indirectly touched on this question previously, but let us bring the problem into focus here.

The rationalistic attitude of empiricism, realism and positivism lays down as a criterion of validity that a philosophic synthesis must stick to the facts. To go beyond the facts or to make assumptions is to weaken the value of one's synthesis. The ideal is a presuppositionless philosophy. Hence, the aim in the past was to prove the evidence of one's philosophic starting point. Once this was established, it was believed that the conclusions would necessarily be true. Another methodological demand was that the investigator be totally objective and rational.

The premises in the rationalistic attitude are, first, that the meaning of reality is given in the present and can be attained because reality is essentially finished; and, second, that reason is precisely ordered to attain this meaning and can attain it since God does not create a nature in vain. Given these premises, which are derived from a static world-view, it follows that there is no room for assumptions. Under these conditions, philosophic synthesis cannot but be presuppositionless and has to proceed from pure objective reason alone. Consequently, the presence of elements of assumption is "used as a ground for criticism and condemnation of the opposition; for it is constantly pointed out that the assumptions of a certain thinker are the basis for the limitations, and in time, the final rejection of his philosophy."[4] An example of the application of this criterion is to be

4. Harold A. Durfee, "An Unresolved Conflict Between Realism and Existentialism," *Proceedings* of the Georgetown University Philosophy Club, (1958-59), pp. 10-11.

found in an objection to Teilhard's philosophy: "that teil-hardian views are mostly assumptions, are entirely unproved, and not worthy of acceptance as a serious philosophy."[5]

Evaluating the rationalistic norms, we find that histori-cally the ideal of a presuppositionless philosophy has not been achieved. The judgment of Durfee is that "the histori-cal attempts at a presuppositionless philosophy have failed, the possibility of such a philosophy is a misleading notion, and the attempts to achieve such best be abandoned for more fruitful philosophical pursuits."[6] And as regards the demand to approach reality from pure objective reason alone, not even science, which is supposedly the most objective of the disciplines, proceeds this way in practice. As Teilhard notes:

> During the last fifty years or so, the investigations of science have proved beyond all doubt that there is no fact which exists in pure isolation, but that every experience, however objective it may seem, inevitably becomes enveloped in a complex of assumptions as soon as the scientist attempts to explain it. But while this aura of subjective interpretation may remain imperceptible where the field of observation is limited, it is bound to become practically dominant as soon as the field of vision extends to the whole.[7]

The basic inadequacy in the rationalistic attitude proceeds from the inability to look at present reality paradoxically. The first paradox is that the present is not what it is; the second is that reason-in-the-present does not have the capac-ity to attain all the facts, even if all the facts were given. We have explained these paradoxes previously. The implica-tion from these is that the present cannot be a judge of what is true or false because it does not have all the facts. The present (both knower and known) is half-evolved, half-true, half-present to itself. It is the future that rightly judges the present.

5. Michael Stock, O.P., *op. cit.,* p. A 12. Cf. p. 94 above.
6. Durfee, *op. cit.,* pp. 10-11.
7. *PH,* p. 30.

In the attempt at synthesis, it is inadequate to stick only to present facts because the present is not synthesized, its principle of integration being the future. Hence to be objective, the synthesizer has to take the vantage point of the future, but this is the same as saying that he has to be prophetic, to postulate, assume, interpret, predict. True empiricism is based on fullness of being and facts, but the fullness of being and of facts is in the future. The rationalistic attitude is really a false empiricism because it judges without sufficient facts. Again, the true empirical attitude is respect for facts, but it is not by being "empirical," "realistic," or "positivistic," in the traditional sense of these terms, that we show proper respect for facts. In fact, it is to be disrespectful to reality to accept only present facts, absolutizing them, when the present is merely a symbol of what it will be. Proper respect for the present, hence true empiricism, is to view it as a symbol, to foresee in it what the future will be, hence, to use it relatively, not absolutely.

Two men can have the same facts, but what makes one of them a great scientist, philosopher, or theologian, while the other remains mediocre, is the ability to predict from the facts, to make the correct assumptions. It is this creative ability that extends the frontiers of knowledge.[8]

The rationalistic attitude is part of the larger hellenic complex which is ptolemaic in structure, organizing everything about the present as center and as the region of being. Idealism, realism, empiricism, positivism, are, it would seem, the ultimate unfolding of the hellenic complex which stems from Plato and Aristotle and which sees being as that which is. As Heidegger well notes, this tradition, which is the dominant one in the Western world, is unable to see the paradox

8. Unhappily for education, however, it is the false empirical attitude that rules the schools, insisting on information and the ability to give it back as the basis of excellence, rather than on originality and creativity.

or riddle of reality—that "being" is not what it is. Hence to explain the present, one necessarily has to assume what it will be. Synthesis, then, of its very nature, is assumptive and predictive. Paradoxically, it is when reason is assuming, predicting, believing, that it is most rational.

We have delayed long on the principle of paradox because it is this principle that we will apply in trying to bridge the duality between nature and supernature, a duality established by the principle of identity.

SEMANTICS: CONVERSION FROM THE LITERAL TO THE SYMBOLIC

After the analysis of the ontological, epistemological and methodological structure of the 3-D world, our next and last step (which in no way implies that our treatment of the philosophy and the problems connected with it is complete) is to analyze briefly its semantic structure. Again, to effect the transition to the 3-D semantic structure, let us start with the 2-D.

The hellenic mind accepts as a matter of course the time-honored distinction between the literal and the metaphorical and their respective spheres of application. Thus a poet is expected, for example, to be metaphorical; a scientist, philosopher, or theologian, on the other hand, to be literal. One may be allowed the use of analogy and metaphor in arguments but such arguments do not have strict probative value. To express objective truth, literal expression is used.

But many today are uneasy about the traditional aristotelian distinctions and the over-emphasis on the literal. For example, T. A. Goudge believes that the emphasis on the literal as the means of scientific expression is antiquated. Thus he says:

Another linguistic feature of a growing discipline is that its practitioners, in searching for ways of expressing new facts and of stating new conclusions, frequently mingle figurative and nonfigurative forms of speech. This is a perfectly respectable procedure, since the notion that only literal language ought to be permitted in scientific discussion is antiquated. Plenty of things can be said effectively in science (and philosophy) by means of metaphors and analogies.[9]

Part of the uneasiness with regard to traditional semantic theory could be the increasing influence of the evolutionary mentality on modern man. T. A. Goudge makes the point that there is a language peculiar to evolutionary theory and that by paying heed to the linguistic formulations of evolutionists we escape conceptual pitfalls.[10] It is necessary, therefore, to indicate the respective spheres of application of 2-D and 3-D semantics.

The foundation for the distinction between literal and metaphorical may be illustrated by an example. Thus in the statement, "Peter is a man," the term "man" is predicated of Peter univocally and literally because Peter has the essence or intrinsic characteristics of a man; but in the statement, "Peter is a lion," the term "lion" is predicated analogically and metaphorically because Peter is not really a lion. Now this traditional distinction between the literal and the metaphorical does not apply in the 3-D framework. Let us take, for example, the statement, "The acorn is really an oak," in the sense that the acorn will become an oak. We cannot say that the acorn is *now* a full grown oak, hence the statement cannot be literal, a literal statement being one founded on present facts or qualities possessed by the subject. Nor can we say that it is metaphorical, for the full grown oak is germinally, hence, really, in the acorn, while in metaphor the character attributed to the subject is in no way intrinsic

9. *Op. cit.*, p. 15.
10. *Loc. cit.*

to the subject. Nor can we say that the statement is analogical, for the formality of the term "oak" is totally distinct from the formality of the term "acorn." The terms are equivocal. From this simple analysis we see that the literal-metaphorical distinction has limited scope, applicable to static realities but unable to deal with evolving and historical ones. It is valid only within the ordinary time-scale of everyday life where we see forms that are permanent. In this context, since a given substance has only one form, the attribution of another form to it can only be metaphorical.

In the semantics of process, however, the statement that the acorn is an oak is not a literal or even a metaphorical statement but a symbolic one. By symbol, we recall, is meant that the lower stages in a process point to the higher stages for their meaning. Hence, in the diagrammatic structure of process: alpha, beta, omega, to say that alpha is omega is to make a symbolic statement. The verb "is" in the statement is not only copulative in an evolutionary sense but has the structure of futurity as well.

On the other hand, to say that alpha is alpha is not only a tautological statement but a false one, for by the principle of paradox alpha is not really alpha since its truth and being are on the higher level. Furthermore, the subject alpha is in process of evolution; it does not perdure, hence we cannot say that alpha is really alpha. It is only in a static framework or in the context of a very small time-scale in which the evolution of alpha is not seen that the statement has any significance.

Going to the next stage of the process, beta, it would likewise be false to make it the foundation of a literal statement because it is also a stage of becoming. Hence, to say that beta is beta is to say that it is identical with itself, it is finished, which it is not. To make a relatively true statement in stage alpha or beta, one must say that alpha is beta or that beta is omega, for the truth of the lower is in the higher. In other words, the fact of alpha is beta since alpha comes to its conclusion at beta. But beta in its turn has its truth in omega, hence although relative to alpha it is true, in relation to omega it is still only relatively true, its full certainty being at omega.

Only at the omega do we have a literal statement because only the omega is fully being, fully true. It is a perduring and permanent subject. Relative to the previous stages there is no contingency in it, no uncertainty, because it has arrived. All chances of the process failing are gone. Hence one can be literal about it. It is what it is. Only at the omega is the principle of identity applicable. To say that omega is omega is not a tautological statement as it is in a static framework; in 3-D the statement is meaningful. It means that the process has arrived. It is here. What was becoming is now being, or what was absent to itself is now present to itself. It is. But in a context in which everything comes forth an adult the statement is meaningless.

Before the final stage of omega all statements are symbolic. The first characteristic of symbolic statements is relativity. The reason is obvious. The present is not the region of being and truth, but of becoming. Hence all statements based on becoming are relative. Only at the omega do we have absolute statements. In terms of mood, symbolic statements are in the subjunctive, while the literal statement about the omega is in the indicative. The symbolic statement, since its ontological basis is unfinished reality, has inherent in it mere probability, doubt, fear, that the process may not arrive. Hence such statements about the present are provisionary and hypothetical and are properly expressed in the subjunctive mood. The literal statement, on the other hand, is based on the indubitable fact that the process has arrived. All fear, uncertainty and doubt are absent. There is only the serene and peaceful possession of truth. Hence the statement is in the indicative mood.

Another distinction of the more profound nature of the omega is that the omega is properly the concept or word; it can be uttered, while the symbol is silent, it listens.[11] The omega is properly a concept because it is conceived, that is, it is reborn. Having the concept, the omega can utter it, hence it is *the* word of the given process. Because it is *be*-ing, it can stand up in the name of the previous stages and say, "I am." The symbol, on the other hand, does not possess the word but rather tends toward it to participate in it, and in so doing it can possess a name. The symbol does not possess the word because it does not have the concept, and it does not have the concept because it does not have its own truth and being. Not possessing the concept, the symbol cannot utter the word. Hence the symbol is silent. Before the omega, it assumes a kneeling posture of silent adoration. It attains to truth, not by seeing, but by listening.

Teilhard's synthesis in *The Phenomenon of Man* confirms the semantics of 3-D. Thus in the teilhardian view the macrocosmic process up to man has the stages of matter, vegetative life, sensitive life and rational life; man is the omega of the process, and as such, is able to speak. Being the head, he is endowed with reason; hence he is able to form the concept and thus utter the word. He is the word of material creation —its spokesman. He it is who gives names to creation as the Scriptures say. Again, the possession of the fullness of being and of truth (in relation to the lower levels), hence of certainty, is significantly expressed by man's erect posture—the

11. Our use of the term "word" or "concept" has no similarity to the Greek notion which is synonymous with *idea*. The "word" is not a universal; it is being itself in so far as it fully reveals and unfolds itself for others. Hence, being as revealing is appropriately called "word" or "truth." Being is a living "word" or living "truth."

posture of the indicative mood. The stages previous to man do not possess the word. This explains their silence. Being merely symbols, they point to where the word is. Their truth and meaning are in man's head—his reason. Hence the whole long process of evolution towards man was aptly characterized by Teilhard as a process of cephalization.

The Scriptures also confirm the semantics of 3-D. Thus all the symbols in the Old Testament point to Christ. Christ is the *Word,* the *divinum verbum.* Since Christ is the Omega of the whole macrocosmic process, man in relation to this Omega is but a symbol, an image of God. Before this Omega, man does not have the word. It is Christ as Omega that gives a "name" to man. It is in Christ's name that man is baptized, and baptism is the giving of a name. Baptism, too, is our initiation into faith which is truth, being and life. Man's meaning is not in himself but in the Word; thus he tends to the Word—the living Word—to attain truth, being and life. Before the Word, man is silent, receptive. Hence he listens to revelation which unveils the Word. Before revelation or faith man's reason is silent because it does not have the Word; only by faith do we possess the Word. Not having the Word, reason does not have the truth, and not having the truth, reason cannot sit in judgment on truth itself.

Lack of appreciation for the semantics of process is responsible for the confusion of many of Teilhard's critics. Teilhard is accused of being metaphorical, poetic, mystical. For example, the statement that matter is pre-conscious is considered semantically confusing. But Teilhard was not confused in his own mind, nor was he being poetic and metaphorical; he was dead serious. The 2-D mind, however, would reason thus: If Teilhard was serious then he was literal, but he cannot be so naïve to mean that matter *is* conscious, hence the most charitable explanation would be that he was being metaphorical. But then we could not accept

Teilhard's synthesis seriously either. The truth is that Teilhard was being neither literal nor metaphorical. We cannot get clarification from Teilhard as to how his statement is to be understood since, first, he is no longer with us, and, secondly, he was not a professional philosopher and thus able to characterize with precision the nature of his terminology. Nevertheless, it is true that his statement is valid in the context of process. It is a symbolic statement in much the same way that the statement, "The acorn is an oak," is symbolic.

Again, the teilhardian statement that all reality is Christian because it terminates in Christ-Omega is considered mystical. Far from it. Here Teilhard was being literal, for recall that the omega point is the region of the literal statement. To use the example of the seed again, we notice that when we want to identify the seed we modify it by telling what fruit it is, thus *apple* seed, *apple* seedling, *apple* plant; but with regard to the fruit we do not say *apple* apple, but simply apple. The fruit needs no modifier; it can stand by itself, revelatory of itself, pointing only to itself. But the seed needs to be qualified; it needs to be related essentially to the fruit to be intelligible. It is the term or "fruit" that specifies the lower stages of the process, and this specification is not metaphorical but most literal. Hence, for Teilhard, since the Omega of the macrocosmic process is Christ, he specifies the lower stages literally.

To avoid semantic confusion, it is well to remember that the nature of one's universe determines one's universe of discourse. Since the 3-D universe is different from that of 2-D, 3-D has its own norms for judging the truth and value of expressions. In 3-D present reality is symbolic of the future, hence the truest linguistic expression of it is the symbolic rather than the literal. Therefore when 3-D writers use symbolic language to describe the 3-D world, they are not being metaphorical or poetic or mystical, but, paradoxically, most literal in the sense of being most serious, for they are expressing the exact nature of reality as presently evolving. On the other hand, to be literal (as opposed to symbolic) about the present is to be false because one cannot be categorical or absolute about the present. When the Old Testament writers used water, air, fire, stone, land and even man himself symbolically and typologically, their approach to reality was not pre-logical, nor was their expression primitive and unscientific; rather, it was most profound and "scientific."

Let us keep the linguistic norms of the 2-D world to itself. The 2-D world is the world of common sense, a ptolemaic world. Its time-scale is small, thus precluding evolution. Consequently, the present is seen statically, populated by permanent and enduring forms. Hence, according to the principle that the nature of one's universe dictates the manner of expression, the 2-D world requires literal expression because forms are precise, objective and pointing only to themselves. To be symbolic about such a world is to be subjective because there is no basis for symbolism on the part of reality.

If we compare the adequacy of conceptual and symbolic expression, the difference is ultimately the adequacy of the 2-D or 3-D framework to grasp reality. Since we consider the 3-D framework to be more adequate, it will be from its context that we compare them. Thus the concept evacuates reality of its mystery while the symbol restores it. The reason is that the concept does not point to the future which is the region of mystery; the symbol does. It follows from this too that the symbol is able to express levels of meaning which the concept cannot, hence the symbol is richer and fuller in signification and is better able to express the many-sidedness of reality.

The symbol may be likened to a stone dropped in water. It has multiple references in different areas and depths; the concept, on the other hand, may be likened to a stone dropped on soft ground. It makes an impression, it makes a definition, but only on the area upon which it rests. Again, the symbol as half-revealing, half-concealing, can express the paradoxical nature of the present as half-present, half-absent which the literal conceptual expression cannot. Especially is the symbol most apt in expressing the paradoxical nature of the sacraments. For example, saving grace which destroys sin and gives life is best expressed by the symbol of water which paradoxically destroys and saves. Conceptual expression in terms of matter and form cannot express the paradox. Another difference is that the concept touches the objective and universal while the symbol touches the subjective and the unique.

In other words, conceptual language takes the I-It pattern while symbolic language takes the I-Thou. Symbolic language is the appropriate language of encounter, hence of subjectivity. The mystics, for example John of the Cross, Bernard of Clairvaux, Teresa of Avila, Blessed John Ruysbroeck, tell us that as one comes in contact with the Absolute Thou all discursive reasoning ceases. And when they try to express this divine experience, it is always in symbols derived mostly from the Song of Solomon. The liturgy of the Church, which is our means of contact with the divine, is also highly symbolic. And revelation, which is a history of the encounter between God and man, is conveyed in terms of types and symbols.[12] One is able to symbolize God, but one cannot conceptualize him. Thus the symbol is able to reach the nonconceptual, which the concept obviously cannot.

12. If revelation as an I-Thou encounter is best expressed symbolically, should not theology, which explains this encounter, be symbolic rather than conceptual?

PART THREE

Application of the Philosophy of Process

CHAPTER VIII

Man and Grace

The primary purpose of this third and last part is the attempt to show how the supernatural could be truly immanent, first, specifically in man, and second, in creation in general. The scholastic formulation of the immanence of the supernatural which we examined in the beginning of this study did not seem to be satisfactory, for it presented us with an apparent dilemma: the transcendence of the supernatural is safeguarded only by sacrificing its immanence—which must be equally safeguarded. To show both the transcendence and the immanence of the supernatural, a more adequate philosophical framework seems to be needed. Hence we proposed in the second part a philosophy of process which we believe to be intrinsic to the teilhardian world-view and which we consider to be more adequate. It is within the framework of this philosophy that we shall undertake to situate the supernatural, applying its categories to see whether we can come up with a satisfactory formulation.

The application of the categories of process will be attempted in two main areas:

A. The specific problem of the relation between man and grace;

B. The general problem of the relation between creation and the incarnation.

In each area we will give: 1) a philosophic analysis;
2) a scriptural verification.

In determining the relation between two things, say, A and
B, there are two possible methods to follow. The first is to
start with a definition of A and then view B in relation to A.
The second is to start the opposite way, namely, ask what
B is and then define A's relation to B. The traditional scholastic solution of the problem of grace followed the first
method, namely, starting with a definition of man in terms
of his human nature. It then related grace to human nature.
From the point of view of method, the advantage in starting
with man, it may be claimed, is that we start with what is
more known to us in order to arrive at the less known. This
is a typical statement of aristotelian method.

The disadvantage to this approach, however, is that grace
is then tailored to fit a concept of man that is limited to his
human nature. It could very well be that one might arrive at
a correct formulation of the relation between the two terms,
but this would only be accidental. This disadvantage, however, seemed inconsequential to the scholastics who believed
not only that the truths of reason do not contradict the truths
of faith, but also that the truths of reason are synonymous
with the truths of scholastic philosophy. In this particular
instance, they believed that the essence of man was as
Scholasticism formulated it, for they believed that the
scholastic method of abstraction really reached the essences
of things. Hence scholastics believed that, at least methodologically, it did not matter whether one approached the
problem of the supernatural from the side of grace or from
the side of nature.

Furthermore, there were other compelling reasons that
persuaded the scholastics to relate grace to man in terms of

his human nature. Although the scholastics had a concept of personality as a rational supposit, they would never have dreamed of relating grace to it. In the framework of their philosophy, personality (although a singular) was, for purposes of science or knowledge, treated as a particular. Since the scholastic theologians were dealing with theological science, the true foundation for it had to be a universal.[1] For this reason, grace was related to the universal, human nature. It was believed that in this way objective truth would be attained.

The approach to man in terms of his human nature has been unquestioned in orthodox Scholasticism. Extrinsic factors confirmed the approach, such as the polemic against Protestantism which championed the personal approach to God. Another was the constant and solemn reiteration by those in authority that aristotelian-thomistic philosophy is perennially valid and true, together with the strong paternal and authoritarian rule exercised by the hierarchy on any creative departures from traditional formulations.

We do not have the aforementioned philosophic presuppositions and extrinsic reasons to determine our approach. Methodologically, we start with the requirements of grace itself. They will determine our approach to man.

Although grace is not as well "known" to us *(quoad nos)* as man is, yet in itself *(quoad se)* it is more certain than our philosophical concepts of man, for there is a common teaching about it in the Scriptures and its certainty is of a higher order, that of revealed truth. While man is nearer to us in the sense of being perceptible, observable, yet no one philosophic formulation of what man is can enjoy any claim to certainty since there are many views of what man is. Hence,

1. As Joseph de Finance, S.J., observes, "for St. Thomas as for Aristotle, scientific knowledge deals only with the universal; truth is found only in what is true for all." See his article, "Being and Subjectivity," *Cross Currents,* 6 (1956), p. 163.

by the first method, the solution to the problem of grace is only as valid as one's philosophic view of man.

Let us start with grace then. The first truth about grace which must be upheld is that it is the highest perfection of man. Methodologically, this truth requires that for it to have any significance at all, it must have an ontological counterpart in the deepest part of man. On this requirement the scholastics were methodologically correct since for them human nature was the deepest part of man. We can still ask, however, whether indeed human nature is the deepest part of man, for modern man, unencumbered by medieval philosophy, is more inclined to the belief that the deepest in man is his subjectivity. On this question even some thomists side with the moderns. Let us quote at length from them to show that the approach to man from the side of his nature does not reach his deepest part and that therefore we have to look for another approach.

Thus Robert Johann, S.J., observes that the approach to man in terms of his human nature reaches only being-as-object and not being-as-subject.[2] And Joseph de Finance, S.J., explains that being for the scholastics, thomists included, is the order of objects, and that the subject enters into the domain of being only insofar as it is capable of being transformed into an object. In its intimate depths, in the abyss of its incommunicable and ineffable subjectivity, the subject constitutes a domain into which the metaphysician—specialist of being that he is—cannot enter.[3] Again, he observes that "when traditional philosophy did treat of the individual, it speculated about it as an object and

2. Cf. his paper, "Toward a Philosophy of Subjectivity," read at the Twentieth Annual Convention of the Jesuit Philosophical Association, (1958).

3. De Finance, *op. cit.*, p. 163.

expressed itself in terms proper to an object. The subjectivity hidden within remained outside of its horizon."[4] Johann reflects on the reason for the scholastics' objective approach to man:

> Having started with a philosophic interpretation of the external world, a philosophy of objects, it was natural to prolong this approach to being-as-object when they [scholastics] came to man. It was natural, I say, but the point is it was also justified. For man is a kind of being, knowable therefore as object, just as much as is a tree or stone. And just as the *existence* of a tree (unknowable anyway in its positive originality) is only instrumental to the analysis of *what* it is, the analysis proceeding from the structure of the manifestations to the *structure* of its source (what has these [empirical] properties has such and such a [metempirical] structure), so also with the existence of man.[5]

Before we can appreciate Johann's critique of the objective approach as applied to man, let us first hear from him a description of an object:

> [It] may be described in general as that which can properly be abstractly or conceptually; it is that which confronts thought and presents itself as not depending on the one thinking for its intelligible content. It is the universally valid-for-all, including not only universal essences but also singulars, insofar precisely as these are apprehended merely as concrete realizations of such essences. Thus, for example, Marcel describes the object as whatever can be known "scientifically"—where science is equivalent to detached, impersonal thought—and lends itself to technical manipulation and control. The object is thus what can be grasped not merely as independent of my inner life but as isolatable in a sense from its existential context, as circumscribable and determinable in its constitutive notes.[6]

Johann next describes how being-as-object is grasped:

4. *Ibid.,* p. 164.
5. Johann, *op. cit.,* p. 19.
6. *Ibid.,* p. 12.

To be able to be grasped adequately in the manner described above, a being must be impersonal, not an "I" or a "you" but an "it." This is not to deny that it may also be personal. A man as well as a stone may be apprehended as an object. It simply means that to apprehend being as object is to apprehend it as thing. . . . The impersonal, since it is deprived of any true initiative, is not a giver, but the given. . . . It exists, to be sure; it is there. But its existence has no depth, is absorbed, as it were, in the pattern it actualizes, in the face it presents to all comers. Since there is nothing in it transcending its actual determinations, it is wholly and adequately known when these are known. Because these determinations are that by which it is formally distinguished from what surrounds it (including the knower), the impersonal allows itself to be isolated and circumscribed (i.e., conceptually defined) without falsification. Finally, with nothing within that resists such circumscription, it has nothing to resist possession, manipulation and control by others.[7]

He then shows the inadequacy of this general approach when applied to man:

In the analysis of man as object, existence is no more than the *givenness* of a certain *kind* of essence and does not enter as a determining factor in understanding what kind. Since the *givenness* of essence is contingent, whereas science seeks the necessary, that givenness can be "bracketed" without detriment to the analysis. It can, I say, so long as one is interested in man only from the side of essence. That such has been, for all intents and purposes, the sole interest of the scholastic (Thomistic included) philosophy of man, is, I submit, unquestionable. The fact that in man, who is admittedly knowable as object, we have an altogether new revelation of being—a revelation in which alone and for the first time being presents itself precisely in its originality as subject—is either discarded as irrelevant and unimportant (which indeed it is for an analysis of man as object), or it is reduced to being simply a special attribute of this kind of being. When the scholastic mind meets the person, how

7. *Loc. cit.*

does it seek to understand him? Not in terms of his unique exercise of existence, but simply in terms of the structure according to which that existence is exercised. The person is simply a certain kind of supposit, rational as opposed to non-rational. Viewed thus from the outside, the subject is not only conceptualized but strictly "objectified."[8]

We have in these passages an excellent and perceptive observation of the inadequacies of the approach to being-as-object. From Johann's observations we realize that it does not reach the depth of being. The person in its originality as subject is discarded as irrelevant, or made simply an attribute, hence peripheral. The object is independent of the inner life; as impersonal it is all surface, no depth. Thus if these are the characteristics of being-as-object, one wonders whether grace as the highest perfection of man is properly founded on the deepest level if it is related to human nature.

The next step in our negative approach of showing the inadequacy of relating grace to human nature is to apply a second methodological norm—the nature of grace itself. This methodological norm, I believe, will help us to relate grace to man properly. In asking what grace is we are not interested in the traditional theological formulations of it, for such formulations are influenced precisely by the philosophic category used by the theologian. Thus we cannot start with the notion that grace is an accidental extrinsic (or intrinsic) determination of human nature elevating man to the supernatural life. This is an aristotelian-thomistic view of grace. Let us take instead the meaning which revelation itself uses to explain grace to the common man, to whom, after all, revelation is directed.

Grace in Greek is *charis* which means love. For Christians, God is love, and the central teaching of Jesus is that we are to love. Love is the most distinctive, original and profound

8. *Ibid.*, p. 19.

trait of Christianity. Thus the essential aspect of grace cannot but be love; for this reason, grace is aptly identified with love. For the Christian, to have grace is to have both the love of God and the capacity to love him in return; the absence of grace is the same as the absence of love for God. In the context of love, then, grace is God's offer of divine love to the creature; it is also the divine call to a union of love (Eph 4:24; 2 Tim 1:9; Rom 8:26, 30). This basic understanding of grace is all we need for an operational definition.

The essential characteristic of grace as love can help us derive the correct procedure in relating grace to man. Thus, if grace is God's offer of love, God's divine call to loving union, then it must be addressed to that part of man which can respond to love. Love is an inter-personal union of two unique beings; it is based precisely on uniqueness, not on what is objective and universal. Hence, grace is addressed to the personal, for only the person can respond to a call of love; only the person has depth, uniqueness.

Has human nature the characteristics necessary to relate it to grace as love? We gather from Father Johann's observations that it does not. First, the epistemological approach to man as his human nature precludes the subjective and personal. The approach to being-as-object attains the impersonal, not an "I" or a "you" but an "it." Johann is careful to note that human nature may also be personal; however, the way this personal nature is apprehended is to grasp it, not as personal, but as *thing*. Secondly, human nature as the object of the approach presents only the surface of being, hence accessible to all comers. It exists, to be sure, but its existence has no depth.

It is not only the way human nature is apprehended and its impersonal character, but also its dynamism of act and potency which convince us that grace as love could not be related to it. We noted in the second part of this study that the dynamism of act and potency rests ultimately on the hellenic view of nature as a self-subsistent, autonomous being, possessed of natural powers to achieve its own end. It is in potency towards that end, actualizing its potencies by the reception of secondary acts. For the reception of these perfective acts, it is fitted with operational potencies whose dynamism is that of act and potency. This dynamism of act and potency is one of receiving rather than giving. It thus deprives man of any true initiative—which is a prerequisite for love. To love, one has to give of oneself, to sacrifice, surrender. Hence, man must be fitted with an outward dynamism, not an egocentric one.

Furthermore, grace as love has for its purpose the unification of the individual with the people of God. But, as may be gathered from history, a dynamism of act and potency results in individualism, not only in spirituality but in theological formulation as well. Thus, instead of the *koinonia* of the Scriptures and an awareness of our communion in the mystical body, we had the emphasis on individual salvation —the salvation of souls. In line with this individualistic view, theology in its formulation was also individualistic: grace, original sin, the last things, God—all were related to nature as center—a ptolemaic form of spirituality. Communal service like the liturgy waned, while the individual devotion of adoration of the blessed sacrament flourished. Instead of an emphasis on communion with the members of the mystical body for growth in grace, growth was in the amassing of graces for the individual soul as its perfection and ornament—a practice whose abuse was the trading in indulgences.

With regard to the theological formulation of grace, the dynamism of act and potency determined the methodological procedure. Since the dynamism was self-centered, all perfective acts were related to nature as center. Grace, being a perfective act, was consequently related to it. Specifically, grace was said to be received by nature as its supernatural entitative perfection in the accidental order. Generically, it was placed under the category of the good as perfective of man. Under such a category, grace was desirable only as a certain specific determination, a communicable perfection, capable of being appropriated by the subject and of fulfilling its needs. Grace considered as unique and as a gift from the Absolute Thou was ignored, unappreciated by this dynamism interested only in the objective and specific. Grace was thus considered not as a good in itself but as that by which something else was made good. It became a relative accidental good.

The view of good as perfective, rather than as something loved in and for itself, was the ordinary viewpoint from which St. Thomas considered grace. This point of view was maintained in his later works where the good was most consistently presented as perfective, as principle of actuation, as object of desire. And even when St. Thomas treated of love, his treatment was a perfect example of an objectification of it.[9] In the *Prima Secundae* where a short treatise on beatitude as man's ultimate end is found, God is considered not as an end to be loved directly for himself, but rather as an object of desire, or more precisely, as that whose "acquisition, possession, use or fruition" is desired.[10] Even recent studies on love by scholastics like Rousselot, Simonin, Gilson, and Geiger approach love from the outside.[11] That Scholasticism confused the dynamism of love for that of desire or of act and potency may be gathered from the

9. Robert O. Johann, S.J., *The Meaning of Love* (Newman, 1965), p. 7. Cf. *De Mal.* 1,2c; *ST* 1,5 1 ad a; 5c, etc.

10. *Ibid.*, p. 57.

11. *Ibid.*, p. 7.

opinion of three authors.[12] Thus Anders Nygren's thesis is that the Christian *agape* is totally different from the Greek *eros* and that it was in contact with Greek philosophy that we lost the Christian *agape*. John Burnaby observes that in Augustine, *eros* and *agape* were confused, and that St. Thomas' notion of love is simply a borrowing from the crude individualism of Aristotle. And Martin D'Arcy notes that in the middle ages, the problem of the relation between *eros* and *agape* took the form of finding a way to reconcile the gospel command to love God with our whole heart and with our whole strength with the movement of human desire which ends in the self.

We conclude that from the requirements of grace as love, grace cannot be related to human nature, first, because human nature is impersonal and, secondly, because its dynamism of act and potency precludes the proper grasp and formulation of grace as love.

The third and last methodological step in showing that grace is truly immanent in man is to locate it at the very core or center of man's deepest level. Thus, it is not sufficient merely to relate grace to the deepest level of man; one must also show that it is central to this level. With regard to this requirement, the scholastic formulations have not been successful. They have not been able to show that grace is central to human nature. We explained this in the chapter on moderate intrinsicalism. The closest one can locate grace in nature is to make it the innermost type of accident; nevertheless, it remains an accident, so that man is intelligible apart from grace. Grace is not and cannot be a constitutive part of nature. Thus immanence is not fully explained.

---

12. Anders Nygren, *Agape and Eros,* trans. A. G. Hebert (New York: Macmillan, 1932-39); John Burnaby, *Amor Dei* (London: Hodder & Stoughton, 1938), p. 269; Martin D'Arcy, *The Mind and Heart of Love* (New York: H. Holt & Co., 1947), p. 85.

After this negative task of showing the inadequacy of the "nature" approach, let us now take the positive task of showing the greater adequacy of the personality approach. Is personality the deepest level in man? It would seem that it is not because it is particular, contingent, subjective, hence on the level of the phenomenal, while human nature is on the level of the metaphysical. But if we move now into the 3-D framework, does personality assume a different value altogether? To answer this, it may be helpful to review the 3-D framework as a general background and then situate man as process in it.

In 3-D, the perfection of being-as-process is in the other. Hence, being is never alone; it is not an island, or, to speak more philosophically, it is not like the Greek notion of nature whose dynamism of act and potency seems to segregate being from others. According to that notion, the degree of perfection is measured in terms of greater definition (understood as a cutting off), resulting in the proud isolation and self-sufficiency of being. In 3-D, however, being is always humble because it always needs its "other"; it never becomes fully itself by being alone, but attains itself and lives for itself fully only when it lives for the "other." In so giving itself, it dies, but this death is not a total loss, rather it is the recovery of self at a higher dimension. Thus self is found in the "other," in the very process of giving itself up.

We used the analogy of a seed to show the ontology of being-as-process. Thus the seed arrives at a fuller self only when it dies to its aloneness, giving itself to its ground, and thus being reborn to a new level of life and existence. In being alone, its death ceases to be a rebirth. Thus being has need of its ground. The more it unites itself with the ground the more it grows in fullness. Union with the ground does not annihilate being; it differentiates it. With this ontology of being, we noted that being is fitted with a proper dynamism to enable it to give itself—that dynamism being love.

At the level of man, the generic category of being-and-its-ground takes on a more specific form. It becomes a conscious relation, an inter-personal relation of "I" and "Thou" whose dynamism is that of inter-personal love. We might note at this point that to affirm the 3-D view of man is not necessarily to deny the 2-D view. Thus nature with its dynamism of act and potency is not denied. Eating, studying to get knowledge, engaging in business to acquire profits, working to buy a home or a car, are all activities that are governed by the dynamism of act and potency. This is not denied. What is denied, however, is that the act of love could be assimilated to these activities. We believe that the nature-activity category derived from a very small time-scale can be assimilated into the category of process derived from a wider time-scale.

At the deeper level of 3-D, man as process takes on the categories of birth and death (commitment, immolation, sacrifice, suffering, hope, faith, and so on), all of which can be summed up in the category and dynamism of love. In 2-D, the categories of birth and death are ignored, "bracketed," since being for 2-D is that which is between them. They are the limits of being. Since being is confined to the present, the depth of being is that which is behind the phenomena. The essence is grasped by abstraction. But for 3-D, this is but a superficial grasp of reality. All we grasp is being-as-object—the form that is seen as frozen within the small time-scale of 2-D. In 3-D, the depth of being is in the future —in the omega and Omega, and that depth is attained by an act of love, or rather, by a life of love.

It is also through the act of love, which in 3-D is the highest level of rationality, that the "I" grasps itself in its depths, for one achieves oneself only in the act of giving oneself to the Other. The more the "I" gives, the more it attains deeper levels of self. It is at death that the "I" is able to grasp itself fully, for as long as it lives, it never fully gives itself. The highest act of love is sacrifice or a form of "dying," and the more immanent it is the deeper the act of love. And the deeper the love, the deeper the union with the Absolute Thou. Through this union, the new "I" is born and revealed to itself in its innermost being; it also attains the fullness of freedom and truth.

A 2-D objection to the approach to man in terms of I-Thou is that it is subjectivistic; it is claimed that personality is no true basis for objective certainty. The answer to this objection has been explained generically in our treatment of the epistemological structure of process. Specifically, we may note that personality as a process has a definite structure (an alpha, beta, omega and Omega) which can be analyzed and is true for all. Concretely, the categories of personality are birth, growth, death (rebirth), its dynamism is that of love, and its Omega, the Thou. Methodologically, the process is one of dying to be reborn; ontologically, the structure of the "I" is feminine—it gives birth to the new "I"; epistemologically, the process is a self-revelation; ethically, the process is from slavery to freedom. The "I," contrary to traditional beliefs, is not undefinable. It is defined by relating it to the Absolute Thou; it is individuated by the depth of union forged between itself and the Absolute Thou.

We noted earlier that the 3-D view of man as process is confirmed by the Scriptures. Thus the categories of birth and death are the principal categories. On them are built the central mysteries of Christian faith: the incarnation and the redemption. The incarnation is seen as an act of love which reaches its consummation and fullness on Calvary. In that act of dying, Christ was most one with his Father.

The view that the depth of man is in his personality is a

modern awareness. Thus the existentialists show that it is not in the abstract, conceptualizable human nature that man's depth is to be found but in his concreteness and temporality. Many of them, including neo-thomists, personalists and psychologists, implicitly or explicitly use the I-Thou category, so importantly emphasized and developed by Martin Buber,[13] who attributes the source for this category to his study and translation of the Scriptures.

Johann gives a very penetrating epistemological analysis of the greater depth of the I-Thou (being-as-subject) approach to being as against the I-It (being-as-object) approach:

> [Being-as-subject] is being as experienced from within, i.e., not according to its objective surface, a certain sum of determinations by which it is conceptually definable, but in itself as a unique subsistent, an original center and source of free initiative. It is being as *self*; the "I" of which I am conscious and which, though identical with me, still transcends all my actual determinations and presents itself as a sort of inexhaustible source; or again, the "you," turned towards

13. According to Maurice Friedman in his book, *Martin Buber,* (Chicago University, 1955), Chapter 21: "The psychological significance of the I-Thou relation was recognized, independently of Buber, in Ferdinand Ebner's *Das Wort und die geistigen Realitaten.* Insanity, writes Ebner, is the end product of . . . the complete closedness of the I to the Thou. It is a spiritual condition in which neither the word nor love is any longer able to reach the individual. The irrationality of the insane man lies in the fact that he talks past men and is unable to speak to a concrete Thou. The world has become for him the projection of his I, not just theoretically, as in idealism, but practically, and for this reason he can only speak to a fictitious Thou." Again, Friedman notes, (*loc. cit.*): "A number of European psychologists and psychoanalysts . . . have recognized the importance of Buber's I-Thou philosophy for psychology." Friedman also notes that "a significant confirmation of Buber's attitude towards psychotherapy is found in the recent developments in the 'client-centered' therapy of Dr. Carl R. Rogers and the University of Chicago Counseling Center." In *Client-Centered Therapy* (1951), Dr. Rogers states that the role of the counsellor . . . is an active acceptance of the client as a person of worth for whom the counsellor has real respect." Friedman concludes that Rogers makes use of Buber's concept of I-Thou relation when he says that "once there is complete unity, then there is, to use Buber's phrase, a real 'I-Thou' relationship."

me and engaging me in a dialogue, knowable only in relation to me as freely responding to my initiative and therefore itself seized as a unique source ever capable of new manifestations, new revelations. The subject is therefore a sort of subsistent, self-revealing plenitude, open to itself (or to another) not as a pure datum capable of being isolated and determined by a collection of attributes, but attainable only in the act by which it affirms itself.[14]

Johann notes that outside the I-Thou relation, the depth of the self is not grasped:

To seek to know the "you" apart from the activity of dialogue is immediately to change him into a "he," to make him an object at least to this extent that he becomes for us a mere individual instance of certain abstract determinations which his very selfhood reduced to a characteristic common to all men.[15]

He further observes that even the attribution of personality to human nature is not a knowledge of man as a person:

The finite person is of course formally determined, shares in a certain specific nature, indeed in rationality. But to be known simply in terms of this nature is not to be known properly as a person, but only in the measure that the person is also a thing and can be conceived in the manner proper to a thing. Even the attribution of personality to a being known to be rational is not a knowledge of this being as person, i.e., in his personality. On the contrary, it is precisely to reduce him, at least by the mode of our knowledge, to the level of thing, the potential substrate of various conceptually known or knowable determinations of which personality, logically consequent upon rationality, happens to be one. "Person" instead of being "you" or "I" unique and ineffable, attainable only through direct encounter, becomes a predicate equally attributable to all rational creatures.[16]

14. Cf. *Twentieth Annual Convention of JPA* (1958), p. 13.
15. *Op. cit.*, p. 14.
16. *Loc. cit.*

Johann also shows that personality is a deeper category than nature as manifested by its deeper dynamism of love compared to nature's dynamism of act and potency.[17] Thus he observes that the dynamism of act and potency looks to the outside. It is a dimension of exteriority, a teleology situated on the plane of the relative and based on the passive synthesis of act with potency. It consists in the quest of the potential for what it lacks, of nature for its completion. In virtue of this drive, man looks out upon the world that surrounds him and seeks to appropriate what he needs—first of all, what he needs for physical survival, but also and hardly with less urgency, whatever may contribute to his natural perfection. He desires, therefore, not merely food and clothing and shelter, but over and above these, all the fruits of civilized life—cultivation of mind, refinement of tastes, his basic share in the common patrimony of society, and indeed of the whole human achievement of reason and virtue.

But there is the deeper level of personality with its dynamism of love. Johann continues: this dimension is one of interiority, based on man's participation in the eternal presence of being to itself and achieved through the inwardness of consciousness; it looks to the progressive fathoming by the finite self of the unique value, the unique Self in whom he actually participates. It is a structure of finality situated on the plane of the absolute—a drive, not to possession or the appropriation of impersonal goods, but to communion, the communion of act with Act, of a person with the source of all personality, of being with itself.

In the teilhardian synthesis we can find a profound explanation of personality as the depth of reality. Teilhard shows that the end of the macrocosmic process, whose dynamism

17. *The Meaning of Love,* pp. 69-70.

is that of love, is an I-Thou relation. He first describes the emergence of the personal:

> With the advent of the power of reflection (an essentially elemental property, at any rate to begin with) everything is changed, and we now perceive that under the more striking reality of the collective transformations a secret progress has been going on parallel to individualisation. The more highly each phylum became charged with psychism, the more it tended to "granulate." The animal grew in value in relation to the species. Finally at the level of man the phenomenon is precipitated and takes definitive shape. With the "person," endowed by "personalisation" with an indefinite power of elemental evolution, the branch ceases to bear, as an anonymous whole, the exclusive promises for the future. The cell has become a "someone." After the grain of matter, the grain of life; and now at last we see constituted the *grain of thought*.[18]

Teilhard concludes that we thus reach the personalisation of the individual by the "hominisation" of the whole group.[19] But, says Teilhard, because of our obsession with the impersonal, and the hellenic tendency to analyze, we have neglected to give due place to the person and the forces of personalisation.[20] For traditional thought, he continues, the supreme reality has to be impersonal to be universal and to span the infinitesimal and the immense, so that at the world's Omega lies the impersonal.[21] The "I" or ego is seen as a blemish. And with the trend towards the collective and the universal as the most real and most lasting in the world, the ego (which is located in the opposite direction, at the antipodes of the impersonal all) is conceived of as diminishing and eliminating itself; it is an ephemeral property; a prison from which we must try to escape.

18. *PH*, p. 173.
19. *PH*, p. 174.
20. *Ibid.*, p. 257.
21. *Ibid.*, p. 258.

But if evolution is an ascent towards consciousness, then it should culminate forwards in some sort of supreme consciousness, for it is only by hyper-reflection—that is to say hyper-personalisation—that thought can extrapolate itself. The Omega is the end point of this process of hyper-personalisation. It is the hyper-personal, the hyper-universal.[22] Far from being mutually exclusive, the universal and personal (that is to say, the "centered") grow in the same direction and culminate simultaneously in each other. It is therefore a mistake to look for the extension of our being or of the noosphere in the impersonal. The future-universal could not be anything else but the hyper-personal—at the Omega point.

From these considerations, we can for several reasons draw the conclusion concerning the first methodological requirement of grace: that personality is a deeper category than human nature. Broadly, we can say that the 3-D category of personality is deeper than the 2-D category of nature because the 3-D framework is deeper than that of 2-D, substance being assimilated into process. Specifically, we can say that if the future is the depth of reality or the region of the metaphysical, then the "I" which has the dimension of the future is deeper than human nature, which, being timeless, has no future dimension.

Again, if the Absolute Thou is the deepest level of reality, then the "I" which alone attains it must be deeper than human nature. And since the "Thou" is obviously subjective, it follows that the subjective "I" is deeper than objective nature. Furthermore, a man's depth is not in what he has in common with others but precisely in his uniqueness. That I have a human nature merely shows the specific type of being I am; it separates me from other specific types. But what makes me me is not my nature but my personality. And

22. *Ibid.*, p. 260.

lastly, it is by the continued process of love that a being unfolds and reveals its innermost depths. The dynamism of love is properly related to personality rather than to nature.

The second methodological norm requires that for the explanation of grace as love, it must be related to a category that explains and facilitates love. We showed that the category of human nature cannot explain grace as love because nature does not have the dynamism of love. Clearly that which can respond to a call of love is the person, since its dynamism is that of love. Hence grace as love demands that it be related to personality. Furthermore, the dynamism of love, which is a bond of union at the deepest level of being, assures us that grace can be united with personality at the deepest level and thus be shown to be truly immanent. As Teilhard de Chardin profoundly observes, love is the radial energy of the universe, the *within* of things.[23] And even from common experience, Teilhard observes that love is indeed a deep bond of being:

> Love alone is capable of uniting living beings in such a way as to complete and fulfill them, for it alone takes them and joins them by what is deepest in themselves. This is a fact of daily experience. At what moment do lovers come into the most complete possession of themselves if not when they say they are lost in each other?[24]

Love not only unites beings at the deepest level, it deepens and universalizes being. Again, as Teilhard notes:

> In trying to separate itself as much as possible from others, the element individualises itself; but in doing so it becomes retrograde and seeks to drag the world backwards towards the plurality and into matter. In fact it diminishes itself and loses itself. To be fully ourselves it is in the opposite direc-

23. *Ibid.*, p. 264.
24. *Ibid.*, p. 265.

tion, in the direction of convergence with all the rest, that we must advance—towards the "other." The goal of ourselves, the acme of our originality, is not our individuality but our person; and according to the evolutionary structure of the world, we can only find our person by uniting together. There is no mind without synthesis. The same law holds good from top to bottom. The true ego grows in inverse proportion to "egoism." Like the Omega which attracts it, the element only becomes personal when it universalises itself.[25]

By relating grace to personality we have already achieved for grace a greater degree of immanence than could be had by relating it to nature. But even this degree of immanence is insufficient unless it can be shown that the "I" is intrinsically ordained to grace, that is, that the "I" is ontologically structured for grace as its one and only and hence all-important end without which the "I" is unintelligible—and whose rejection would involve loss for the fullness of time. In other words, the third methodological requirement of grace demands that grace be located at the very core of personality itself. We recall that in this regard the orthodox scholastic theories have not been successful. They could not make grace the very substance of nature. The most they could do was to make it an intrinsic accident.

Can we say that the "I" is intrinsically ordained to grace? Let us approach this problem through a general study of the ordination of a being to its end. The ordination of a being to its end is explained differently by the 2-D and 3-D frameworks. Thus in 2-D, the intrinsic ordination of a being to its end means that the being is formally structured for that end. If the end is rational, then the being in question must be essentially rational in order to be proportioned to that end. Furthermore, it is fitted with operational potencies or powers capable of attaining that end. And lastly, the given

25. *Ibid.*, p. 263.

being is unintelligible apart from that end because its very essence is formally structured for that end. Intrinsic ordination means, therefore, formal, epistemological and methodological (operational) structuring of nature for its end.

As a concrete example of structuring in 3-D which will help us to understand better the structuring of the "I" towards the "Thou" let us again study the relation of the seed to its ground. We observe that the seed has existence only in union with the ground. Apart from the ground, it is a being-towards-death. Hence in the very depths and totality of its being the seed is structured for the ground. Morphologically, or ontologically, so to speak, the cotyledons, plumule, radicle, seed coat, and so on, are all structured for union with the ground. A pebble, on the other hand, though planted or buried in the ground and watered, obviously will not grow because it is not structured for the ground. Again, a pebble can be thought of apart from the ground, but a seed cannot. Intrinsic to the very definition of the seed is its relation to the ground. And physiologically, or methodologically, so to speak, the seed is structured towards the ground because its dynamism is towards the ground. It is able to give birth to new life, thanks to the ground (soil, moisture, air, light). There is a feminine-masculine relation, so to speak, between the seed and the ground which the pebble and the ground do not possess.

What is generally true of the being-and-its-ground relation is true in a most special way of the I-Thou relation at the inter-personal level. Thus the "I" is in all senses of the term structured towards the "Thou." In its very ontological structure it is a being-towards-the-Thou. Hence its definition includes an intrinsic relation to the "Thou" and cannot be conceived apart from it. The "I" was not created in and for itself, ordained to an end apart from the "Thou" and then ordained to the "Thou" only as an after-thought. Rather, its whole being, logically, physically and ontologically, is structured towards the "Thou." The "I" cannot give birth to the new "I" alone. The necessary condition for the "I" being reborn is that it be structured for the "Thou" the way a seed is structured for the ground.

The difference in structuring in 2-D and in 3-D is that nature, being substantial, has already an existence of its own, while the "I" tends towards the "Thou" for its existence. Again, nature is already in possession of its essence; the "I" on the other hand tends to the "Thou" in quest of its essence. A greater difference is that in 2-D the structuring of being for its end is not unique, but merely specific and objective. The reason for this, as Johann pointed out, is that the relation of nature towards the end is impersonal, an I-It relation. Hence, any "It" will do as long as it meets the specifications of the being in potency. In 3-D, however, since the end is unique, it requires a unique structuring of the "I."

If we ask which of the two types of structuring of a being towards its end is more precise and more profound we find that there are reasons for saying that the structuring of the "I" towards the "Thou" is more precise and more profound than the structuring of nature towards its end. Union at the deeper level of personality obviously requires a more profound and more precise ordination than at the less profound level of nature. Furthermore, the structuring of two unique terms requires greater care because of the closer fit, so to speak, than is required at a specific level. And lastly, structuring in the actual, existential order requires greater precision that in the ideal order. Thus it is easier to fit a peg into a hole in the mind than in the actual order. So, too, nature, which does not have to have to tend towards the end except accidentally because it already has its act of "to be" and essence, does not require as precise an ordination to the end as the "I," which must actually tend towards the end for its existence and meaning.

If the structuring of the "I" towards the human Thou is

deeper than that of nature towards its end, then the structuring of the "I" towards the Absolute Thou must be the deepest since God is the absolutely unique. The condition for the rebirth of the new being in man—the "new Adam"—is that man give of himself completely to the Absolute Thou. Hence, to be able to give himself, he must be structured in his very depths for God.

Let us now deal with the structuring of man towards grace, man's omega. Grace would be the new life attained by the "I" in union with the Absolute Thou, in much the same way that the seed attains new life in union with its ground. Continuing the comparison, the "I" would be like a barren seed apart from the "Thou," hence, a being-towards-death. The "I" does not have existence of its own apart from grace—if we understand existence here as being-towards-life. Thus, the "I" is ontologically and concretely structured towards grace, as the seed is towards its new life. Just as rebirth is intrinsic to the meaning of the seed, so man's intrinsic meaning cannot be thought of apart from the new life in grace. And just as to fail to tend towards the new life is death for the seed, so the failure to tend towards the new life in grace can justifiably be seen as eternal death for the "I." Just as the center and core of the seed, the whole purpose of its existence, is to carry the germ of life in it, so in the very core of man is the ordination to divine life. This ordination is the very "substance," so to speak, of the "I." No deeper structuring could be had for the "I" than this. It is thus that grace is made immanent in 3-D.

But at this point we come face to face with the central problem of the supernatural—the reconciliation of the immanence and transcendence of grace. It is easy enough to locate the supernatural at the very core of man and thus explain how grace is man's highest perfection. But it would seem that we have attained this formulation at the expense of the equally important aspect of grace which must be defended at all cost—the transcendence and gratuity of grace. Furthermore, it would seem that in stressing that the ordination of man to grace is deeper in 3-D than in 2-D, we have compounded our problem, for it follows that we have also correspondingly increased man's exigency for grace; thus it seems that we have all the more degraded the supernatural, making it completely natural; as a result we have not explained the supernatural, we have abolished it.

The first step in the attempt at reconciliation is a study of the main difficulties related to the second truth about grace —its gratuity and transcendence. First of all it has to be taken as an incontrovertible fact that man has no claim or exigency for the supernatural, for if he had the supernatural would cease to be gratuitous. But now a second implication seems to follow from this, namely, that if man has no exigency for the supernatural, neither is he intrinsically ordained to it, in which case grace is not really immanent to man. The basic premise here is that intrinsic ordination to an end means necessarily and absolutely an exigency for that end. And if one has an exigency for an end, then it cannot be supranatural, that is, above nature; it must be natural if nature is inconceivable apart from it. The scholastic argument is expressed in the following passage:

> Whatever may be the diversities of opinion among theologians, the supernatural must retain the character which its very name indicates and which the documents of the Church attribute to it: "perfectionem quae naturalem superet." But an end, without which a nature is inconceivable, cannot be an end which surpasses this nature; such an end is natural to it. It is the end which is due it, and which God owes to Himself to give to it. It is an end strictly exacted by nature, even though we must all hold that human nature, on its side, could have no strict exigency for it; deprived of the

means to tend toward this unique end, nature would be in a violent, abnormal and disordered state, and all of its movements would be deordinate.[26]

This argument is, in substance, the one we stated above, except that the minor is stated first. The major is worded differently but is, in effect, the same. Thus it says that an end without which a nature is inconceivable is an end that is due that nature. This is the same as saying that an end to which nature is intrinsically ordained is due that nature or, to put it another way, nature has an exigency for it. Now the reason given for the exigency of nature is that deprived of the end, nature would be in a disordered state. Hence, God owes it to himself to give it. In another passage of the same article, the basis for the exigency of nature is further developed:

> For, a nature is an essence which either finds rest in a good which is proportioned to it, or is in pursuit of such a good. It would be a contradiction to admit a nature of this kind without putting within its reach the only good for which it is made. There is no exigency more acute, whether for a created nature or for its Creator, than to avoid contradiction, especially when the contradiction would be found in the very core of a reasonable being.[27]

Thus a deeper reason is given for the exigency of nature to attain its natural end, namely, that it is an exigency on the part of God to avoid contradiction—in this case, the contradiction of creating a nature without putting within its reach the only good for which it is made.

From the passages above we gather these principles: nature has an exigency to its unique end; that unique end is natural; God owes it to himself to give that end. A philosophical basis for these principles is given:

26. Philip J. Donnelly, S.J., "Discussions on the Supernatural Order," *Theological Studies*, 9 (1948), pp. 236.
27. *Ibid.*, p. 237.

But, if by "nature strictly delimited" is understood an essence, which is well defined, having its proper laws, its natural resources, and an end corresponding to these natural means, then such a nature is one of those possibles which have their foundation in the divine essence and in the eternal reasons which constitute the absolutely necessary and unchangeable knowledge of God.[28]

This passage contains the basic aristotelian notion of nature —the ultimate starting point and explanation for the philosophic principles that govern scholastic thinking concerning the relation of grace to man. Since this notion of nature is founded "in the divine essence and eternal reasons which constitute the absolutely necessary and unchangeable knowledge of God," the implication is that the scholastic principles derivable from nature are absolutely true and unchangeable. Consequently, if these scholastic principles are used in the formulation of the relation between nature and grace, the formulation is likewise absolutely true and unchangeable.

However absolute and final the impression given by the previous piece of scholastic reasoning may be, it is nevertheless just to qualify and delimit its validity to the aristotelian framework alone—until it is shown that this framework is an absolute and true expression of the actual universe, and that God actually had an aristotelian universe in mind when creating the world. In short, it may be asked whether the real God thinks in an aristotelian way. Does he think in terms of natures? Of course, our notion of God is derived from and influenced by our framework. But is this framework adequate?

The aristotelian universe of the medieval Christian was one in which each being was thought to be able to attain its end by its own powers. God was imagined as an aristotelian

28. *Ibid.*, p. 239.

God in so far as he planned each being or nature to be a little universe, self-sufficient in the attainment of its end. Given this philosophic view of the universe, it would be impossible to refute the scholastic arguments stated above. Once we say that a nature is uniquely ordained to an end, then that end is due it, for God cannot create a nature in vain. In the aristotelian universe, intrinsic ordination to the supernatural is a contradiction.

The first step in showing how intrinsic ordination and gratuity are not necessarily contradictories is to question the conclusion that intrinsic ordination necessarily means exigency. Is it possible to show that intrinsic ordination to an end does not necessarily mean exigency for that end? The first negative task is to question the aristotelian concept of nature, and to question the concept is ultimately to question the adequacy of the framework. Aristotelian philosophy is so logical, so harmonious in all its parts, that we cannot question one part without ultimately questioning the whole.[29]

In the aristotelian universe, the basic relation among natures is that of justice or exigency. Everything is defined in terms of it. Thus a given nature has an exigency—ontological for non-personal beings, moral for personal beings—which is also called a right. The juridicism of aristotelian philosophy partly influenced the extreme juridical outlook of the medieval Christian. The redemption, the greatest example of love, was formulated in terms of justice; the Church, the bride of Christ, was seen as an impersonal, juridical structure; moral theology, which was supposed to

29. In this study, we could have gone directly to the questioning of aristotelian philosophical principles, but we doubt whether this would have resulted in any dialogue at all with those who hold that the aristotelian framework is absolute and who know no other semantic than that derived from it. Hence, the establishment of the philosophy of process as an alternative to aristotelian philosophy was a necessary step, for at bottom, the problem of the supernatural is a philosophic one. In particular, the conversion to be made is from a framework of justice to one of love.

explain Christ's one law of love, was nothing but a treatise on justice, and grace was defined as a perfection which was beyond nature's right or exigency.

The teilhardian universe, on the other hand, is based on love. Its framework is a framework of love. As Teilhard says, love (not in its popular sentimental meaning but in its full reality as the propensity to unite, the affinity of being with being) is not peculiar to man but is found on all levels of reality.[30] The philosophy of process takes account of this insight by saying that being is not an island (nature) but being-with-another, and that its dynamism is that of love.

As a general answer, then, to the scholastic dictum that intrinsic ordination means exigency, we can say that the I-Thou relation is in the context not of justice but of love; that the "I" is not an aristotelian nature, hence what is predicable of an aristotelian nature is not necessarily predicable of the "I."

By analyzing the I-Thou framework we will discover whether it is possible to establish the contradictory assertion that intrinsic ordination does not mean exigency.

In the context of love, the "I" is not able to attain its end by its own natural resources and capabilities; it is not self-sufficient, hence it is not a nature. The "I" is a being-towards-the-other. Its end is union, so that its very ontological structure and finality requires the need for an "other." The end is impossible of attainment by the "I" alone, for true love requires two terms. This is not self-love such as a nature would have for itself. In this situation of true love, God does not have to create the "I" self-sufficient; in fact, if he did, it would not need the Other. For God could not create the "I" self-sufficient if the universe he has in mind is one of love, for the "I" which is ordered for love

30. *PH*, p. 264.

would then be unable to love. It would be in a disordered, disorientated state. And we could very well borrow the scholastic observation that "there is no exigency more acute, whether for a created nature or for its Creator, than to avoid contradiction, especially when the contradiction would be found in the very core of a reasonable being." But if God did create the "I" self-sufficient, then it is an aristotelian nature and, to avoid contradiction in himself and in the creature, he would have to put it in an aristotelian universe.

But even in a universe of love, it may be objected, God cannot create a nature in vain. Hence, to create the "I" without giving it the powers to attain its end is to create it in vain. To this objection it may be answered that it is not necessarily against God's wisdom if he does not give self-sufficiency to the "I" as long as he places self-sufficiency in the unity of "I" and "Thou." In the context of love, the latter condition is the case. Love is in the totality. Hence the members are impelled by the law of love to unite and thus attain self-sufficiency. The sharp and deep contrast between the aristotelian universe and the teilhardian one is that in the former, self-sufficiency is placed in the individual—in the "I" alone; in the latter, self-sufficiency is in the I-Thou. The former is a universe of "mine" and "thine"; the latter is a "we" universe.

Those trained in Scholasticism will find it difficult to grasp the view that God need not create the "I" self-sufficient as long as they view this statement in the context of the aristotelian universe. That universe, many think, is absolute, self-sufficient, able to integrate even the framework of love within it; and in that context the statement we made is contradictory.

But if we accept the validity of the framework of love, then we should be prepared for the paradoxical conclusion that what it is to create a creature in vain in an aristotelian universe is precisely to create a creature properly in the teilhardian universe. If God ordains the "I" towards love, he could not also create it self-sufficient, as an aristotelian nature. In fact, to create the "I" in vain is to create it an aristotelian nature, or, what comes to the same thing, place it in an aristotelian universe. The "I" would be frustrated if, being intrinsically ordained towards the "Thou," it were given the dynamism of act and potency, or created wounded in its ability to love, hence with a dynamism of hate.

Original sin precisely is a wounding of the inherent dynamism of love. Love is now turned upon man's own self and becomes self-love. Hence, truly was the first sin a sin of pride, whatever be the specific act performed. The result was that the "we" relationship was destroyed, man idolized himself, and proclaimed that he could go it alone. Cain went at it by killing Abel, and so on. God's Incarnation was precisely to restore the "I-Thou" or "We" relation. Grace is a gift that heals the wound of original sin by enabling men to love. It is indeed love that makes the world go round; it is the foundation of being, and not the self-sufficiency of nature. In fact, it is when man relies on himself alone that he destroys the world. We have but to look around us to see how disordered the world is without love. We know the havoc created in the very depths of the individual by pride. Hence, the "exigency" on God's part to create the "I" insufficient in itself (that is, as needing another) is greater than the exigency in an aristotelian universe to create a nature self-sufficient. God created the real universe from love and out of love because he is love. Hence, he would be creating it in vain if he created it self-sufficient, if it were based on a businesslike and juridical arrangement of mine and thine. To create a world without love is to create a hell.

From the context of love we can draw as a first conclusion that if the "I" by itself is not self-sufficient, being unable to attain alone the end to which it is intrinsically ordained, then the end transcends its sole powers. Grace, then, as the one and only end of man, is transcendent. It is supra-natural in the sense that it is beyond the natural capabilities of man alone. The assertion that once one assigns to nature a uniquely possible end, this end is *ipso facto* natural, while true in 2-D, is false in 3-D. In 3-D, no being attains its end naturally, that is, by its own powers alone. In 3-D, the end is always transcendental. Therefore, just because we assign to man grace as his unique end to which he is intrinsically ordained does not make grace natural (in the sense of being within man's natural powers), nor do we abolish or degrade it; it remains transcendental.

The second conclusion is that in the context of love, the "I" has no exigency for the end to which it is intrinsically ordained. There is no claim on the part of the "I" for the "Thou," since the union is freely entered upon by both. The "Thou" calls freely and the "I" responds freely. The only means by which the "I" can attain its end is a union of love. Hence, by the law of love justice is excluded. If there is any exigency at all, it is the exigency that there be no exigency (claim or due), for this would be the death of love. Thus the "I" waits on the good pleasure of the "Thou" and hopes for his coming. The attiude of the "I" is one of full surrender and complete abandonment. The "Thou," on his side, is not coerced into union. If he gives himself it is out of love. Thus gratuity is of the essence of the relationship of love. In other words, love necessarily requires freedom to give oneself to the other; gratuity or gift-giving is intrinsic to the I-Thou relation; it is its condition, its nourishment.

Our conclusion then from the preceding analysis is that the "I" does not demand grace as a right or claim. The "I" waits, hopes, prays for it, and listens to the call of love. Grace is freely given by the Absolute Thou; this is the only way grace could be given, if we are to stay within the framework of love. Hence the framework of love safeguards the gratuity of grace; it demands that it be gratuitous. We do not destroy the gratuity of grace therefore, but enhance it. On the other hand, to situate grace in the context of nature which is ordained to its end as something due would be to destroy the gratuity of grace, to degrade it. For gratuity would be meaningless to a nature whose dynamism is that of act and potency (egoistic); nature does not understand what gratuity is; all it understands is the language of justice. Furthermore, to re-structure nature for a gratuitous end is to destroy nature also. Grace would no longer be a perfection of nature, but its destruction.

We go even farther in our conclusion to assert that intrinsic ordination does not mean exigency; on the contrary, intrinsic ordination is a condition *sine qua non* of gratuity. Let us show this by taking the relation of man and woman in marriage as an example. For there to be love at the conscious level, both partners have to be persons. This is the first degree of ordination. There can be no gratuity or love between a man and a stone, or even an animal, because there could be no free gift of self to the "other." One has to be conscious of one's being as a self to be able to love and give oneself in love. The second degree of ordination on the part of the I-feminine is that it be structured to receive the free gift of love of the Thou-masculine. Women are structured physically, physiologically and emotionally to give birth to new life and attain the fullness of femininity in motherhood. Thus a necessary condition for love is the intrinsic ordination of woman to man, not only at the physical level but at the spiritual as well. What is true at the level of human relationships is incomparably more true at the level of the relationship between the human "I" and the Absolute Thou. To receive grace, which is the unique gift of love given by God who is love, the "I" must be uniquely structured for it. Hence, the gratuity of divine love demands that man be structured in his innermost depths for it.

To conclude this philosophical reflection on the problem of man and grace, we submit the tentative conclusion that it seems possible to reconcile intrinsic ordination and gratuity in the context of I-Thou. However, there are still areas to be explored and objections to be solved before we can arrive at a surer position. These unexplored areas and unsolved objections will be treated in their proper places.[31] Right now the next step is to go to the Scriptures to see whether they confirm our use of the I-Thou framework for the understanding of grace, for if not, then our attempt is abortive and we need not go further.

THEOLOGICAL CONFIRMATION

Some may object to our having started our investigation with philosophical considerations. The problem of the supernatural, some will assert, is mainly theological and therefore its solution must be drawn from theological data. In a sense this objection is valid, but in practice it is not possible. For, try as we may, we cannot approach scriptural data without some presupposed mental pattern. What data to choose, what categories we consider important are influenced by our epistemological presuppositions—as has been only too well demonstrated by the practice of scholastic theology which approached Scripture with aristotelian categories. Our own view is that Scripture has a dynamic and functional view of things and, if so, then its own mental pattern has to be adapted to understand its language and message. Because of

31. An important question, for example, is whether it is necessary to affirm the concrete possibility of pure nature to explain the gratuity of grace.

its affinity to the mental pattern found in the Scriptures, the philosophy of process, we believe, can help us in the correct choice and emphasis of ideas in the Bible.

Before we can appreciate the force of our scriptural confirmation and not consider it purely metaphorical, hence of no scientific value, it is necessary to speak briefly about the Hebrew epistemological pattern of thought. We hear the oft repeated remark that the Scriptures are pre-logical, the implication being that Greek thought is logical. Modern thinkers, however, whose mental pattern has evolved from the timeless and abstract to the temporal and concrete, from the impersonal and objective to the personal and subjective, are slowly beginning to realize that just because the Hebrew mental pattern is earlier than the Greek, it is not necessarily more primitive.

Let us not judge the concrete mode of expression as inferior to the abstract, for to the Hebrew the concrete did not have the same inferior value it had for the Greeks. For the Hebrew, the concrete is not the equivalent of sense knowledge, hence pre-logical, while the universal alone is logical. In terms of Hebrew typology, the concrete singular is a symbol of transcendental realities and participates in the power of that which it symbolizes; it is not a sign which points to something different and in which it does not participate at all and which often is metaphorical; it is much more than a universal which can point only to itself. Thus the concrete carried more epistemological significance for the Hebrew mind than either sense knowledge or abstract knowledge of universals. When we go to the Scriptures, therefore, it is bad methodology to look for abstract ideas, because Hebrew thought expressed itself in the symbolic and the concrete.

Let us see how the concrete individual gives knowledge

of more than itself. The concrete individual embodies the type.[32] A type is not an abstraction. As Sigmund Mowinckel says: "In certain instances and in special circumstances, the personality of the people is entirely concentrated in the person of an individual. Above all, in the king, chief, the representative of the people, and then especially when he takes the place of the people in such a culminating act as religious cult. Then he is not only a representative in the modern sense of the word, but the entire people is in him, and he is in the people."[33] For example, "under the image of the golden head of the statue (Dan 2:36-38), collective Babylonia is not personified but represented concretely in Nabuchodonosor who is the typical embodiment of everything Babylonian. The people of the saints of the most high are not personified (Dan 7: 27), but portrayed in their supreme representative, the Messias, under the figure of the son of man (Dan 7:13)."[34]

Le Frois adds that "the same concrete manner of portraying a collective runs throughout the Apocalypse. John writes to the seven Churches (Apoc 2-3). Why just seven? Why omit important commercial centers along the same commercial route, such as Hierapolis, Thalles, Magnesia? Because seven symbolizes totality. . . . Hence the letters are intended for individual Churches as well as for the entire Church." Le Frois further observes that "the harlot is another collective (Apoc 17-18). It symbolizes not merely pagan Rome, but the sum total of all such world centers inimical to God. Yet this collective is portrayed in its typical individual pagan world-center, Rome, dressed up symbolically as 'Babylon.' "[35]

32. Cf. Bernard Le Frois, *Woman Clothed With the Sun* (Rome: Urbis Catholicus, 1954), p. 252.
33. Quoted from Le Frois, *op. cit.*, p. 252.
34. Le Frois, *op. cit.*, p. 253.
35. *Loc. cit.*

With the above short note on the proper epistemological approach to the Hebrew mind, let us now go to the Scriptures to seek confirmation for man's intrinsic ordination to God.[36] Right away, to pose the question by asking whether the Scriptures give an answer on the relation between human nature and divine nature would be a faulty procedure because the Scriptures have no abstract concept of nature. For Hebrew thought, man was always a person. Even a people is not seen as "humanity"—an abstract notion that is typically Greek, but as a "corporate" personality.[37] The correct procedure is to look for concrete expressions of the relation between man and God. Thus we find that man in relation to God is represented concretely by Israel. Israel is the symbol of the total human collectivity. As a concrete personality, Israel is a type embodying all humanity. Having determined how man is portrayed, we next see how the Scriptures describe the relation between Yahweh and Israel and from this description and its implications, we discover the truth of man's ordination to God. This conclusion is true not only for Israel as a people but for each Israelite; and because Israel is a type of all humanity, what is true for Israel is true for all humanity collectively and singly. The historical events that happened to Israel in the nation's relation with Yahweh are recapitulated in the spiritual life of every Christian.

36. We do not deny the Greek influence in Scripture, but in its totality, the Scriptures are basically Hebrew in epistemological pattern. In fact, even in the New Testament where we would expect the Greek influence to be greatest, Gregory Dix has this to say: "If there is any 'process' observable in the Gospels it is a process of 'translation' rather than one of 'adaptation.' Strictly speaking, there is no more 'Hellenic' *thought* in them (so far as we can discover) than there was in Jesus Himself. We have to recognize this fact. The Gospels present purely Syriac, not Hellenic, *ideas,* even though they are written in Greek, and for a Greek and Gentile public." See his *Jew and Greek* (Westminster: Dacre Press, 1955), p. 4.

37. Cf. W. Robinson, "The Hebrew Conception of Corporate Personality," *Beiheft zur ZAW,* 66 (1936), 49-62. See also, C. Lattey, "Vicarious Solidarity," *Vetus Testamentum,* 1 (1951), 269.

If we start with the Old Testament we find that the relation between Yahweh and Israel is summed up in the concrete image of the covenant. This image is not a passing one. It is the deep abiding ontological framework of revelation from which we can with confidence and certainty deduce the nature of the relation between God and man. Thus David Stanley, S.J., says, "the OT [Old Testament] view was that the covenant was primary in God's self-revelation to Israel. This point of departure of OT religion was, historically speaking, summed up in the dictum, 'You shall be my people, and I will be your God' (Jer 31:33; Ex 19:5)."[38] While scholastic theology would give primacy to the treatise on creation, the Old Testament considers it secondary, both historically and theologically, to the covenant-idea. So fundamental to both the Old and New Testaments is the idea of the covenant that Walther Eichrodt has built the whole structure of his Old Testament theology on the idea of Yahweh as the covenant God.[39] Karl Barth starts his *Church Dogmatics* with the covenant plan of God as the internal basis of creation, and creation as the external basis of the covenant.[40] And it is precisely from the idea of the covenant that Martin Buber derived his I-Thou philosophy.[41] Thus it is clear that the covenant is the central concrete image given us by the Bible for deriving the true relation between man and God.

But we must study the meaning of the image of the covenant if we are to arrive at specific determinations of the

38. Cf. his article, "The New Testament Doctrine of Baptism; An Essay in Biblical Theology," *Theological Studies,* 18 (1957), p. 179.

39. Norman H. Snaith, *The Distinctive Ideas of the Old Testament* (Westminster, 1946), p. 135.

40. Cf. Edmund Jacob, *Theology of the Old Testament,* trans. A. W. Heathcote and P. J. Allcock (London: Hodder & Stoughton, 1958), p. 136.

41. Maurice Friedman, *op. cit.,* p. 257.

nature of the God-man relation. Let us trace the development in meaning of the notion of the covenant to its evolved form as a conjugal relation. The biblical doctrine of marriage is intimately linked to the unfolding of the history of salvation.[42] Where marriage is concerned, this history has three essential chapters: the periods of Eden, of the old covenant, and of the new covenant.

By the sin of Adam and Eve, the marriage or covenant relationship was broken, resulting in the forgetfulness by men of the nature of their relation to God. God recovered and renewed the covenant with Abraham (Gen 15:18); then he made a covenant with his people Israel at Sinai, (Ex 19:5; 24:7, 8, etc.). Here the relation is conceived as a father-son relationship, an image that is also developed, but with ever-increasing insight the prophets speak of the covenant union of God and his people in the imagery of marriage (Hos 2:14; 51:4-8; Is 54:5; 61:10; 62:1-5; Jer 2:2; 3:22; 31:32, etc.). The infidelities of the people were compared to adultery (Jer 3:1 ff.; Ezek 16:23; Hos 1-3, etc.). Thus "the married state became, in the corpus of the prophetic tradition, the most frequent image of the covenant relation of Yahweh with his people."[43]

The conjugal relation spoken of by the prophets was perfected in the new covenant. In the epistle to the Ephesians, St. Paul speaks of the Church as the bride of Christ. Paul explicitly relates the union between Christ and the Church to that between husband and wife. In fact, the union of Christ and the Church is the exemplar for the proper union between man and wife (Eph 5:22-33).

What is true of Israel or the Church as a whole is true of

---

42. Cf. J. J. Von Allmen, ed., *The Vocabulary of the Bible* (London: Lutterworth Press, 1958), pp. 253-256.
43. Edmund Jacob, *op. cit.*, p. 250.

the individual Israelite and the individual Christian. Thus the Israelite saw himself as forming a covenant with Yahweh. What is applied to Israel as a whole he saw as applicable to himself personally. The same holds true for the individual Christian. Thus Christian baptism is seen as the act by which one is born into the covenant. It is a rebirth, a new life in Christ—the life of grace. This union with Christ is seen as an espousal. Paul uses the figure of the espousal in describing baptism: "Christ loved the Church and handed himself over for her, that he might sanctify her by cleansing her with the bath of water, accompanied by the word, in order to bring the Church to himself in all beauty, without flaw or wrinkle or anything of the kind, but to be consecrated and faultless" (Eph 5:25-27). And again: "I experience a divine jealousy with regard to you, since I betrothed you to a single spouse: I presented you, as a pure virgin, to Christ" (2 Cor 11:2). Paul is speaking here not only to the whole Church, but to each individual Christian.

And just as Paul used the figure of espousal, so we find the early Fathers of the Church using the same image to describe baptism. Thus in the *Procatecheses,* Cyril of Jerusalem applies passages of the Song of Solomon that refer to the bride to the catechumens, following St. Paul's practice of alluding to the Old Testament. St. Ambrose, Gregory of Nyssa and St. Augustine likewise speak of baptism as a marriage.[44] Baptism as a nuptial union is found in Tertullian for the first time: "When the soul comes to the faith, recreated of water and the Holy Spirit by its second birth, it is received by the Holy Spirit. The flesh accompanies the soul in this wedding with the Spirit. O blessed marriage, if it allows no adultery."[45] The same idea is found in Origen: "Christ is

44. Cf. complete passages from Jean Daniélou's book, *The Bible and the Liturgy* (Notre Dame: University of Notre Dame Press, 1956), pp. 191-207.
45. *Ibid.,* p. 192.

called the bridegroom of the soul, whom the soul espouses
when she comes to the faith."[46] In the fourth century, Didymus the Blind writes: "In the baptismal pool, he who made
our soul takes it for his bride."[47] These few but representative citations from writings in the early Church are sufficient
to show the common imagery as regards the relation between
man and Christ.[48]

Thus from our cursory study of the category of the covenant we derive the obvious conclusion that it is an interpersonal relation, understood both as a father-son relationship and, later, as a conjugal one. As a conjugal relation it
is evident that the covenant is based not on justice but on
love.[49] As Kittel observes: "Hosea clearly recognizes the
flowing forth of divine love at the heart of the election of
Israel and the Covenant. When he represents Jahwe as a
man wooing an unworthy woman in defiance of convention,
law and reason, he makes it clear that he understands that
no legal forms or guarantees can adequately set forth God's
relationship to his people (Hos 3:1)."[50] And in the new

46. *Loc. cit.*
47. *Loc. cit.*
48. C. G. Jung confirms from his life-long work with peoples of both
sexes and of different religions and cultures the scriptural view of man
as feminine in relation to the divine. He has found that the level of what
he calls the collective unconscious—a region which is the basis for the
unity of man—invariably yields the same symbols, for which reason he
called these symbols archetypal symbols. These symbols are the feminine
symbol and the child symbol—which symbols, he explains, signify the
deep desire of the soul to give birth to something new—to be delivered
of a child, a desire of the soul for what he calls "individuation." Cf. his
Psychology and Religion (Yale, 1938), pp. 1-77; cf. also Ira Progoff,
Jung's Psychology and Social Meaning (New York: Julian Press, 1953),
pp. 90-93; 194-97; 208-213.

49. As Albert Gelin notes, it is not simply a pact nor does it simply
come into the category of a *do ut des* contract. See his book, *The Key
Concepts of the Old Testament,* trans. George Lamb (New York: Sheed
& Ward, 1955), p. 37.

50. Cf. Gerhard Kittel, *Bible Key Words*: Love, trans. Gottfried Quell
& Ethelbert Stauffer, (London: Adam & Charles Black, 1949), p. 17.

covenant, the relation between Christ and the members of his body is love.

It is from the nature of the conjugal relation that the Scriptures describe the closeness of the union between man and God, and hence, the nature of the ordination of man to God. From common experience and reason it is obvious that the greater the union, the greater the ordination and *vice versa*—the greater the ordination, the closer the union. Now to show the closest type of relation, the Scriptures use the category of love, and appropriately so, since the bond and essence of the highest type of unity, that of the Trinity, is love. It will be noted too that the Scriptures select not just any type of love, but the highest human type—conjugal love. This love is deeper than parental love, as Genesis (2:22-24) implies:

> This rib, which he had taken out of Adam, the Lord God formed into a woman; and when he brought her to Adam, Adam said, Here, at last, is bone that comes from mine, flesh that comes from mine; it shall be called Woman, this thing that was taken out of Man. That is why a man is destined to leave father and mother, and cling to his wife instead, so that the two become one flesh.[51]

Whatever be the value of the imagery as to the origin of woman, the important message being conveyed here is the priority of conjugal love over parental love. To show this, the imagery of origin is given, namely, that the masculine-feminine relation is closer than the parental relation through physical generation.

We will be unable to appreciate the depth of this ordination of man to God spoken of in Scripture if we fail to realize that the conjugal imagery is merely a symbol of the transcendental reality—a much deeper union that transcends human comprehension. St. Paul implies this when he says,

51. Cited by Matthew 19:5; 1 Corinthians 6:16; Ephesians 5:31.

echoing the words of Genesis: "That is why a man will leave his father and mother and will cling to his wife, and the two will become one flesh. Yes, those words are a high mystery, and I am applying them here to Christ and his Church" (Eph 5:31-32).

To those of us who are possessed of scholastic categories, the deepest type of union between the Church and Christ, between man and God, does not have much significance because the imagery on the union of masculine and feminine is purely superficial, accidental. In this view, the basic identity of persons is in terms of identity of human natures. Sex is purely accidental. This is true at the impersonal level. But at the deeper level of inter-personal union the masculine-feminine polarity is the guarantee of the deepest type of ordination resulting in the deepest and closest type of union, graphically described by the Scriptures as two becoming one flesh. Whatever be the objective truth of the imagery, at least the symbolic meaning is intended to convey the idea that the ordination of man to God is not merely accidental and extrinsic but an ordination at the very depths of man's being. This interpretation is correct if the Hebrews understood it this way, for the fundamental meaning of a scriptural text must be based on the meaning intended by the Hebrew authors.

That this is the meaning the Hebrews put into it can be gathered from their view of sex. Thus for Hebrew thought, "the masculine and feminine polarity touches human existence in its very nature, with the result that one *is* a man or *is* a woman in the very essence of one's person; sex is constitutive of what we are; that the man and the woman are made for each other."[52] Therefore when the prophets revealed that the relationship between Yahweh and Israel

52. *Vocabulary of the Bible,* p. 253.

was like that of a marriage, or when Paul said that the relation between Christ and his Church was a bridegroom-spouse relation, they were not being metaphorical; they meant in a very real but symbolic sense that just as woman was made for man—physically, physiologically, psychologically—so man is intrinsically structured for God. This structuring is constitutive of man; it touches his existence in its very nature, in the very essence of his person, the way sex, to the Hebrews, "touches human existence in its very nature," "in the very essence of one's person," and is "constitutive of what we are."

The Scriptures go even further. Thus, just as woman came from the rib of Adam, so man came from God. But this imagery is not to be taken pantheistically, for as woman is distinct from man, so man is distinct from God. This symbolism is recapitulated and fulfilled on Calvary when from the side of Christ issued forth the Church, the bride of Christ. Thus the two examples explain one another, showing the closest type of ordination between man and God. Another way in which the Scriptures speak of the close ordination between man and God is to say that man is the image of God: "So God made man in his own image, made him in the image of God" (Gen 1:27), or again: "When God created human kind, he made them in his own image," (Gen 5:1; 9:6). St. Paul deepens the imagery between man as image and God as the reality by showing that the image is feminine in relation to the reality which is masculine. Thus he notes that just as man is God's image, the pride (glory) of his creation, so the wife is the pride (glory) or image of the husband (1 Cor 11:7). Woman is thus a perpetual symbol given by God to remind and teach us of man's true relation to him.

Let us now try to deduce more specifically the nature of this intrinsic ordination. Already we can gather from the imagery of man as "feminine" before God that ontologically, epistemologically, and methodologically, man is intrinsically ordained to God. From the masculine-feminine relation we can also deduce that outside this conjugal relation the feminine is barren. For the Israelites, it was a sign of God's anger when a woman was barren and a sign of God's love when she gave birth to many. With this background, the Israelite viewed himself as nothing outside the covenant relation with God:

> For the Israelites, the covenant relationship conceived under the analogy of marriage is a bond stronger than death. For the Israelites, one is born of a covenant and into a covenant, and wherever one moves in life, one makes a covenant. . . . If the covenant were dissolved existence would fall to pieces, because no soul can live an isolated life. It not only means that it cannot get along without the assistance of others; it is in direct conflict with its essence to be something apart. It can only exist as a link of a whole, and it cannot work and act without working in connection with other souls and through them. Therefore annihilation of the covenant would not only be the ruin of society, but the dissolution of each individual soul.[53]

This passage is an excellent summary of the Hebrew worldview, a view with which the philosophy of process of the teilhardian universe perfectly conforms. Thus being is a being-towards-others. The individual soul or the "I" cannot exist apart; no soul can live an isolated life; it is in direct conflict with its essence to be something apart. It cannot work and act without working in connection with others and through them. Hence, the "I" is not self-sufficient. From the passage we can deduce that man is absolutely unthinkable apart from the covenant: his existence apart from it is unthinkable; his meaning can only be derived in relation to it.

53. Pedersen, *op. cit.*, p. 308ff.

The fact should be pointed out that the reason the Scriptures are so insistent about the importance of the category of the covenant is that without it, it would be impossible to think properly of our true relation to God, and without that understanding, life and action suffer. Thus without the category of the covenant it would be impossible to see that man is intrinsically ordained to grace, that without it man is not only unthinkable but without "substance" or existence. And without these truths the essence of Christianity cannot be properly presented; rather, an extreme spiritual tension is produced in the Christian life.

The advent of Aristotelianism, of course, lost for us the category of the covenant in formal scholastic thought and formulation. Without this category, Scholasticism arrived at just the opposite conclusions: that man is not intrinsically ordained to the supernatural, that man is both thinkable and able to exist apart from it. For in its place, Scholasticism presented us with an uncovenanted world, a natural world that has meaning and existence apart from the supernatural and a natural end to which it is intrinsically ordained. Scholasticism starts with this uncovenanted world and then relates the supernatural to it, when the obvious and abundant testimony of Scripture is that the real world is a covenanted one. Instead of an I-Thou context, it has substituted an I-It one.

In order to clarify the nature of man's ordination to God, St. Paul uses, in addition to the feminine-masculine category, the imagery of a body and its head. He says that Christ is the head and the Church, the body, which means very much the same thing as the johannine image of the vine and the branches. In all these images it is clear that just as the body is nothing without the head, nor the branches without the vine, so we are nothing apart from Christ. We were made for Christ, structured for him.

The intrinsic ordination of man towards God is true, not only for this life but for all eternity, hence it is not only on earth that man is unthinkable apart from grace but for all eternity. Thus according to Prat, the aim of the epistle to the Ephesians is to explain the supreme mystery or secret design conceived by God from all eternity and realized in the gospel to save all men without distinction by uniting them with Christ by a bond so intimate that they form in him only one mystical body.[54] In other words, it is a union sung about by the prophets and of which the Song of Solomon is the magnificent epithalamium. The covenant union is going to go on. It will be solemnized in heaven: "I saw the New Jerusalem coming down from heaven, prepared as a bride adorned for her husband" (Apoc 21:2), and there will be an eschatological wedding procession and feast (Mt 22).

In spite of the intrinsic ordination of man to the covenant, the same category of the covenant nevertheless shows that there is no exigency on the part of man to demand God's covenant-love or on the part of God to give it. The call of Yahweh or Christ is free; he is not coerced; furthermore, he exercises the initiative. Man cannot enter the covenant alone; it transcends his powers. As Christ says: Nobody comes to the Father except through me; I am the way, the truth and the life; without me you can do nothing, etc. Yahweh exercises the initiative: "Who but I came upon thee [Israel], as I passed on my way? And already thou wert ripe for love; cloak of mine should be thrown about thee, to hide thy shame; my troth I plighted to thee, the Lord God says, and thou wert mine" (Ezek 16:8; cf. Hosea 2). It was Yahweh who led Israel out into the desert and there betrothed her; this was her election. Henceforth Yahweh tells Israel: "You

54. Ferdinand Prat, *The Theology of St. Paul I,* trans. from 11th French ed. by John L. Stoddard (London: Burns, Oates & Washbourne, Ltd., 1926-27), p. 508.

shall be my people, and I will be your God" (Jer 31:33; Ex 19:5).

In the new covenant it was Christ who elected the Church: "Christ loved the Church and handed himself over to her, that he might sanctify her by cleansing her with the bath of water, accompanied by the word, in order to bring the Church to himself in all beauty, without flaw or wrinkle or anything of the kind" (Eph 5:25-27). This new covenant election is but a recapitulation and fulfillment of the election of Israel by Yahweh: "And I swore an oath to you and entered into a covenant with you . . . So you became mine. Then I bathed you with water and washed your blood from you, and I anointed you with oil" (Ezek 16:8-9). We conclude from these passages that the supernatural gift of God's elective love is not only something man cannot claim as his due, but something beyond his sole powers to attain. Hence, though the supernatural is intrinsic or immanent, it is also transcendent.

Summarizing the results of our scriptural examination, we can safely conclude that by relating man to God in terms of the category of the covenant in which man is feminine in relation to God, it is possible to affirm man's intrinsic ordination to God and to see that this union is the closest one available on earth. On the other hand, by relating man as nature to God as divine nature, we arrive at just the reverse conclusion, namely, that the ordination and union are not substantial but accidental. Within the scholastic framework, the ordination of nature to its natural end is closer, more intrinsic, than the ordination of man to the supernatural. The natural end is located within the constitutive part of nature while man's supernatural end (which is his one and only end, *de facto*) is situated exteriorly to man's essence so that man can exist apart from it, be understood without it, and have substantial or essential perfection apart from it. But these conclusions seem to be radically out of harmony with the data of Scripture.

If man's union with God is the closest type of union possible for a finite being, then why call it an accidental union? The drive of any being is to attain to the closest union possible, because in union is its preservation and salvation. What justification from within the law of my being would I have to tend towards a union which is purely accidental? How can God effectively achieve his plan for the redemption of all reality by union with Christ in grace if this union is not the deepest type of union imprinted in the core of man's being? To say that this supernatural union is accidental is to imply that there is a closer type—the substantial. Of course, we could not speak of the supernatural union between God and man as substantial, else we fall into pantheism. But what this means is that we do not have within Scholasticism the categories to show that the God-man relation is the exemplar, the ideal of all finite union.

The substance-accident type of union is a category derived from the material world of sense experience. The mistake with respect to our problem is to assimilate inter-personal union to the type of union found at the material level. Within the scholastic framework, the closest type of union for a being on earth is the union of two substantial principles (prime matter and form) to form a complete substance. But this so-called substantial union is the lowest type of union really, if the minimum requirement for true union is the preservation of identity. Beings unite precisely for the purpose of attaining fuller differentiation, unfolding and possession of self, hence for the enhancement of their identity. Without differentiation, there is no true union.

From all the examples we see, a being tends to unite in order to preserve and extend its own being, reproduce its own type. Even at the molecular level this is true. As we ascend to greater degrees of immanence, greater union results in greater differentiation: asexual found mostly in plant life; sexual mostly in the higher forms of animal life. But in the so-called substantial union (for example, assimilation of food, burning of wood, or sugar in solution) the beings in question do not possess even a minimum degree of immanence at least to preserve their identities, let alone to attain some degree of differentiation. Hence, substantial union, so-called, is not true union but the destruction of union and should not be held up as the ideal of union.

The higher we ascend the evolutionary ladder, the more immanent the love energy becomes and the greater the union —and so, too, the greater the differentiation—until generation ultimately culminates in a someone, a person. Hence union at the highest level results in the fullness of identity. All infra-human reality tended towards the personal, for it is precisely through participation in man that the lower levels attain a measure of identity. Revelation supports the view that inter-personal union is the highest type since it shows that in the Trinity, the exemplar of all unions and of which man is the image, the infinite degree of immanence which results in an infinite degree of union produces by generation or procession subsistent personalities.

To show, then, how the supernatural union of man and God in grace is the highest type of union, it would be false to assimilate it into the impersonal categories of substantial and accidental. This would be to distort it, to devaluate it by saying that it is accidental. If the norm for union is that of love, then supernatural union, being the highest type of love, is the closest. By the same token, the so-called accidental union of, say, people gathered at a bus depot, is no union at all, for the minimum requirement for true union, a modicum of love, is absent; nor is the so-called substantial union of two things a union because it is totally impersonal: a pseudo-union which does not touch the immanent center of being at all.

Hence to say that grace as the life of union with God touches the innermost center of the "I" is not to say that it is a substantial union. This would be to reduce the union to the level of the impersonal and to ignore the significance of immanence in union. We can say that the higher the immanence, the less the possibility for substantial union; this does not mean the lessening of union but the increase in one's capability for union, a greater ordination of one to the "other." Hence, grace as the most immanent reality touches the very core of the "I"; God is present in the innermost depths, more intimate to me than I am to myself in St. Augustine's phrase.

Our conclusion is, therefore, that man is unintelligible apart from the covenant and that therefore he is intrinsically ordained to the covenant-love which is grace. It is also apparent that God is free in sharing his covenant-love with the creature. But at this point, we come up with a persistent and formidable problem. Is God really free if he has to fulfill the intrinsic ordination to grace in the creature? Our answer to this question in the philosophical part is that in the context of love, the very meaning of the "I" demands that the Absolute Thou give his covenant-love freely, otherwise we destroy the very context of love, the very meaning of the "I."

This answer may well be true on the part of the "I," but the Absolute Thou is also the creator of the "I," a situation which is obviously not true in the case of a finite "thou." While it is true, therefore, that the finite "thou" is totally free to give of his love, it is not necessarily true in the case of the Absolute Thou. For as creator of the finite "I" he cannot really refuse grace, presupposing the intrinsic ordination of the "I" to grace, since this would be to create the "I" in vain. God is forced to give of his love, so to speak. Hence grace is not really given freely. The answer to this problem is already implied in our scriptural study of the covenant, but its full answer is to be found in the incarnation itself.

CHAPTER IX

Evolution and the Incarnation

PHILOSOPHIC ANALYSIS

In one sense the specific problem of the relation between man and grace is part of the general problem of the relation of all created reality to the supernatural. But in another sense, since man is the evolutionary fulfillment of created reality apart from the incarnation, the specific problem really comprehends the general, and the solution proposed there is also valid here—which is why we treated man and grace first.

While the first problem may be of direct interest mainly to theology and philosophy, this second one addresses itself to the sciences as well. To appreciate the bombshell which *The Phenomenon of Man* dropped into our world of systematization and formulation, let us briefly outline the structure of that world. Basically it is dualistic. There are two distinct and autonomous orders: the order of nature and that of supernature. In the first order we have reason, philosophy, the sciences; in the second we place religion, faith, theology and revelation. Man himself is split down the middle, living a dual life in his thought and in his actions. In his daily life he is naturalistic, rationalistic and empiricistic; on Sundays he is idealistic, transcendental and supernatural. Thus we have two worlds, each one self-enclosed, self-sufficient, self-intelligible. Our society is built on this basic principle of dualism, resulting in the separation of Church and State.

Even theology is infected with this dualism. In the systematizations of theology there are two distinct orders: that of creation and that of redemption. Each of these orders is complete and autonomous. The creative act produced a substantially finished world of essences; this world is called the natural order. The supernatural order is outside the natural; it is not the fruit or consequence of creation. True, the scholastics admit that grace too is created, but this creation is considered redemptive and not to be confused with the creation of the world which is considered cosmological.

After the creation of the natural order (the priority being not necessarily temporal but logical) the supernatural order is then related to it. Judging this view purely from the logical standpoint, the supernatural is really external to the natural order. As Berdyaev comments, "the natural order according to the Aristotelian and Thomist conception is not penetrated by divine forces; it lives according to its own laws, and is only subject to the organized action of external grace."[1] This comment of Berdyaev is also applicable to creation taken as an evolutionary process. The supernatural is external to the evolutionary process. By external we mean that the supernatural is not a constitutive part of it. Evolution is not intrinsically ordained to the supernatural.

Even with the discovery of evolution, the traditional dualistic world-view lived on unscathed in the mind of Western man. In the dualistic schema, evolution was confined to the natural order. The scientists considered it a natural process; the theologians in their turn simply considered it as a new view of the origin or creation of the universe. It did not have any redemptive or supernatural implications. Thus tradi-

1. Nicholas Berdyaev, *Freedom and Spirit* (New York: Scribner's Sons, 1935), p. 352.

tional thought went on secure and content in the adequacy and validity of the dualistic world-view.

But then came *The Phenomenon of Man* which had for its central message the view that evolution tends towards the incarnation as its completion, fulfillment and Omega. Now this view raises questions of far-reaching implications whose ultimate effect may be the shaking of the foundations on which Western thought is built. For this reason alone the book is in the order of the first magnitude. Thus if evolution tends towards the incarnation, it would seem that science and theology are one, that science leads to adoration, as Teilhard says. But more important than this implication is another, that there is only one order, that therefore our dualistic world-view on which we have built Western thought is really a myth, much like the ptolemaic view of the physical universe.

While the view of Teilhard has won many adherents, it has also aroused bitter critics because it attacks comfortable ways of thought and questions basic premises. From sincere objectors proceed two basic objections. The first one denies the teilhardian synthesis from the point of view of method. The argument is that the result of any work is as valid as the method. But Teilhard mixes the scientific, philosophic, theological, and even adds the mystical and poetic to arrive at his view. Hence, the view is held to be suspect and of little worth.[2]

The second objection prescinds from the method, but objects to the result from the point of view of basic presuppositions. Thus it argues that evolution as a natural process cannot attain the incarnation. The incarnation is in the supernatural order; evolution, in the natural. The end of

2. I try to justify Teilhard's method in my doctoral dissertation entitled, *A Critique of the Methodology of The Phenomenon of Man* (Georgetown University, 1962).

evolution cannot but be a natural one. The scientists and philosophers cannot accept Teilhard's view because of their basic presupposition that nature is autonomous, containing within itself all the powers and forces to evolve itself and having its own proper methods—scientific and philosophic —by which it can be known. Evolution, they conclude, is a purely natural process. The theologians, for their part, cannot accept the view. They, like their brother scientists and philosophers, accept the premise that evolution is a natural process. Therefore it cannot attain the incarnation as its natural fruit. How can what is natural attain the supernatural? And granting that it does, the result would be to destroy the character of the incarnation as supernatural, that is, as gratuitous and transcendent.

Among the devotees of Teilhard there is a general way followed in justifying his view. First, they too, like the critics described above, start with the dualistic context. Secondly, they make a distinction between the cosmic Christ and the redemptive Christ. The cosmic Christ pertains to the cosmological order; the redemptive to the supernatural. The problem for Teilhard according to these people becomes that of relating the cosmic Christ to evolution. With regard to this procedure, it may be objected that it is difficult to justify the distinction either from the writings of Teilhard or from the epistles of St. Paul. We cannot base it on St. Paul for he did not have a dualistic view of reality. Nor on Teilhard, because he has not made an adequate distinction between a cosmic and redemptive Christ. In fact, it would seem that for Teilhard, Christ is the Christ of the Eucharist, the redemptive Christ. But apart from this problem, we can still ask the theoretical question whether evolution *can* tend to the incarnation as its supernatural end. To my mind, this is the most important question raised by Teilhard's view, a question which, unfortunately, he has not answered. But the answer to it has tremendous implications for Christian renewal and for Western culture in general.

Reviewing the reasons against the possibility of evolution attaining the supernatural we find that they are philosophic and theological. Philosophically, the objection is that the lower (natural) cannot attain the higher (supernatural); theologically, the objection is that such a view endangers the gratuity and transcendence of the supernatural. Both of these objections proceed from the same basic premise— evolution is a natural process.

To start our investigation, let us take the methodological attitude of not taking sides. Let us approach the problem without any presuppositions, such as for example that evolution is natural or supernatural. Let us start with the fact: evolution is a process. Our question then becomes: what is the nature or meaning of this process? Common sense itself will tell us that a process is known by its issue or fruit. For example, we are given a seed and we do not know what it is. To discover what it is, one has to wait to see its fruit. Thus to know the meaning of the process one has to go to the stage of fullness where the process is fully revealed. But what is the fruit or omega of evolution? This is where there is disagreement. But let us follow the methodology and epistemology of process. First, we lay out the stages of the process, which are known by their unique qualitative changes. We come up with the following:

matter——plant life——animal life——man——incarnation

Right away we object to putting the incarnation in line with the evolutionary process. But why? Is it because it is beyond reason? But "the Christian fact stands before us. It has its place among the other realities of the world."[3] Shall

3. *PH*, p. 292.

we say then that evolution stops with man? But as most scientists and philosophers agree, man as an existent, as a historical being, is not finished. He is open and still in process. As Teilhard says, "man is not the centre of the universe as once we thought in our simplicity, but something much more wonderful—the arrow pointing the way to final unification of the world in terms of life. Man alone constitutes the last-born, the freshest, the most complicated, the most subtle of all the successive layers of life."[4] From his study of evolution Teilhard has shown that evolution tends towards personalization and immanence. Matter tended towards the immanence of life, life in its turn tended to a greater degree of immanence in consciousness. In accordance with the law of complexification, the very many centers of consciousness are now complexifying, unifying and tending towards a unique center of personalization, the hyperpersonal, the universal, the omega—the incarnation.

The naturalistic view of man admits that man is still in process but refuses to accept the incarnation as the omega of the process. To man is assigned a purely natural history where civilization and culture keep on improving till we have a utopia on earth. But by the law of process this is a false assumption. A historical process that does not tend to a unique event of a higher dimension, that is, supra-historical, is no process but a pure quantitative increase. There is no example of a process which does not at a certain critical point evolve to a new and qualitatively different level from the preceding stage. Thus man is either in process or not. If he is, then we cannot assimilate his process to the example of a seed that keeps on growing bigger and bigger till it reaches an infinite size we call utopia. This is no process.

If a thing is really in process, then after a quantitative increase there comes a critical point when a unique qualita-

4. *Ibid.*, p. 223, 36.

tive change occurs, where A becomes non-A and where non-A is supra-A. This is illustrated on the macrocosmic level of evolution itself. First we had matter which evolved towards life. Now life is uniquely and qualitatively different from purely material processes. Life dominates and organizes matter. It is a higher level of being—animate being. Hence it is "supra"-matter, or supra-natural, if we take matter as the natural level. Life in its turn evolved to a critical point where consciousness was born. Conscious, rational life is a higher level than vegetative and sensitive life. By his reason man dominates all lower forms of life and matter itself. By his reason man is a historical being. Hence, man by his reason is supra-natural relative to the infra-human forms. Thus in all these cases of process, there is a unique event that is qualitatively different, one that is of a higher dimension than the preceding.

We would expect, therefore, that if man is in process, there would be a point in human history where a unique event takes place, an event that is supra-human and supra-historical: where the birth, life and death of this unique event are all miraculous, giving birth to the hyper-personal, the universal. This conclusion presumes the basic principle of process: in order for a thing to remain itself, it has to become different. This principle is well explained by Teilhard. Speaking of the evolution of life towards consciousness, he says:

> Life, being an ascent of consciousness, could not continue to advance indefinitely along its line without transforming itself in depth. It had, we said, like all growing magnitudes in the world, to become different so as to remain itself.[5]

What is true for life is true for consciousness, as Teilhard goes on to show.

5. *PH*, p. 166.

Besides the deep-rootedness of our dualistic view, one of the main reasons, it seems to me, for our reluctance to admit the possibility of evolution tending towards the incarnation as its omega is a false methodology. We say evolution is a natural process because we are judging evolution by considering only a part of the total process. But to know the nature of the process, we must await its completion. We cannot tell from the germinal stage of nature, nor even from its present capacity, what its full powers are. If nature were given as substantially complete in the beginning, then what we see of it in the beginning and at any point in time is the true revelation of itself. But nature does not come forth an adult. The fallacy in prejudging nature as natural is in identifying nature with its partial presentation. But if we judge what a process is by its omega, then perhaps we can see that evolution is a supernatural process.

But immediately scholastic theologians would object to this conclusion. How can evolution attain the incarnation? This would be to make the supernatural natural. The difficulty here is in the aristotelian principle that nature attains its end by its own powers alone. We believe that we have sufficiently explained the inadequacy of this principle. Evolution, like all processes, needs its ground. God is not a prime mover that makes a world and leaves it to shift for itself. Nor is God merely preserving the world in existence. God is creating even now, and evolution is God's creativity expressed in time.[6] Process does not proceed from the universe any more than germination, growth, flowering and fruitfulness proceed from the seed alone. There is need of a ground in which it more fundamentally grows, matures—which brings its being to fullness. Hence God is more fundamentally the cause of the incarnation. Thus evolution does not attain the incarnation alone. Hence, the incarnation is

6. *PH*, p. 86.

transcendent, gratuitous, supernatural. Christ is not a natural fruit of the process if by this is meant that evolution attains it by its own powers alone.

With regard to the other philosophical and theological objections that proceed from the aristotelian view of the universe, we can say in general that they do not affect the teilhardian view because it is precisely the aristotelian framework that is being brought into question. Thus the objection that to say evolution is intrinsically ordained to the incarnation is to say evolution has an exigency for it, can be answered by saying that we have to look at the universe in the framework of love. In this context, intrinsic ordination does not mean exigency; in fact, it is the *conditio sine qua non* of gratuity.

It may be difficult, however, to see evolution in the framework of love. This is so if we exclude man when thinking of evolution in relation to the incarnation. But to exclude man would be false since man is not only part of evolution but the Omega of the infra-human levels. Hence if love is found in man, then we must expect to find it at the lower levels in its inchoate form as an affinity of being to unite.[7] With this ontological meaning of love, it is possible to see the universe in the framework of love. Furthermore, it is in man and through him that the infra-human levels actually attain the incarnation. Man is the "I" of evolution. Now if man does not have an exigency for the incarnation, neither do the lower levels. We can also conclude that if man is not self-sufficient to attain the incarnation, neither are the lower levels.

Another objection is that if the whole evolutionary process is insufficient to attain its unique end, which in this case is claimed to be the incarnation, then God would be creating the evolutionary process in vain. Again we answer that

7. *PH*, p. 264.

the universe is not like an aristotelian nature. God's purpose is to create a universe whose sufficiency is in union. The dynamism of evolution is precisely the drive to union in the incarnation to attain sufficiency and redemption.

Finally, the objection is raised that if incarnation be the unique end of evolution, then God has to give this end, hence the incarnation is not gratuitous. But we answer that in the context of love, uniqueness of the end is the necessary condition for gratuity. In short, intrinsic ordination to the incarnation does not mean exigency on the part of the evolutionary process, nor does it mean that it is within the natural powers of evolution to attain, nor that God is forced to give it.

SCRIPTURAL VERIFICATION

We want to verify that creation is indeed a process that tends towards the incarnation as its fruit. To show this it is not sufficient to point out merely that the incarnation chronologically followed creation, which is perfectly obvious. Rather, we must show that the incarnation was already somehow present in creation, that creation is not a distinct, independent and autonomous order which is self-intelligible and able to attain a natural end by its own powers. In short, we want to verify that indeed there is only one order, the supernatural order. Our procedure will be to study three scriptural categories: creation, the covenant, and baptism. Does scripture apply these categories equally to creation and the incarnation? If so, are they applied in a real and not merely metaphorical way?

1. *Creation.* What is the meaning of creation? Is it purely cosmological as opposed to the soteriological (redemptive)? Are there two distinct divine acts, one which is purely cosmological, the other soteriological so that from the first

we have creation and from the second, the incarnation-redemption? To this question scholastic theology would answer in the affirmative, while the Bible would answer in the negative. Thus David Stanley contrasts the scholastic and the Biblical view:

> The logical structure of Scholastic theology has assigned to the treatise on creation a place which has led us to regard that divine activity as cosmological rather than soteriological. Accordingly, it comes as something of a surprise to find a theologian like Paul describing Christ's redemptive work as a "new creation" (2 Cor 5:17). At best, we think it an arresting metaphor expressive of the novelty of the Christian order.[8]

One would understandably ask scholastic theology where it got its insight that creation is purely cosmological since the source is clearly not the Bible. In this matter, Scholasticism follows Aristotle. True, scholasticism derived the idea of *creatio ex nihilo* ultimately from the Scriptures, but not the idea that creation is an instantaneous act issuing forth into a finished world of natures able to attain their ends by their sole powers. With this view of creation the chance of understanding the biblical view that the incarnation-redemption is God's greatest act of creation is slim. To save the aristotelian view, the biblical view has to be interpreted as an arresting metaphor.

From the aristotelian-thomistic standpoint, creation and redemption are two distinct orders because they possess two distinct formalities. It would be improper then to apply the concept of creation in a literal sense to the redemption. Hence the only valid explanation according to aristotelian logic is that the language of Scripture in this case is metaphorical.

From the logic of process, however, it is possible to see

8. D. Stanley, *op. cit.*, p. 179.

that in a true sense creation is part of the redemptive process if somehow it is redemptive. But aristotelian logic would consider this a fallacy, because its presupposition is that creation is complete and finished, hence in essence it is non-redemptive. It is perfectly neutral. The supernatural is not of its essence. The only way it can see creation as redemptive is to see formal notes of that concept verified in creation, namely, that creation is salvific and efficacious unto eternal life, the way belief in Christ's incarnation is salvific. By this logic, a concept cannot evolve in such a way that what is salvific in form at omega is non-salvific at alpha.

To determine whether creation is somehow redemptive, it is better methodology to look for verification in the Scriptures rather than in a given philosophy. What did the Israelites think of creation? For the Israelites, creation was the first of a long series of saving acts of God. For the New Testament, these saving acts culminated in the incarnation as fruit and consequence. When they imply that creation was in some sense redemptive, they do not mean that it is already fully efficacious, fully fruitful for eternal life. One has to see their concepts as evolving. There is an alpha and omega to a concept for them: that is, a germinal stage at which the concept is not yet fully what it is, and a stage at which it is fully what it is.

The hellenic mentality is wholly opposed to this dynamic and concrete view of reality since knowledge for it lies in the unchanging. It finds it difficult to see truth as evolving and to understand a semantics that is based on this dynamic view of truth. But with the philosophy of process, it may be possible to understand the semantics of Scripture. Thus, for Paul, the incarnation is the fullness of the process of creation. And creation is the seed of redemption. Christ is called the "first fruit" or the "first born." To understand the basis of this appellation, let us resort to the example of the seed in evolution. In this process, we specify the stages by the fruit: thus apple seed, apple seedling, apple plant, but not apple apple. Using this example, we should similarly understand that when the New Testament sees creation as already redemptive it does not mean that it is redemptive in the same way as the incarnation any more than when we specify the seed by its fruit we mean to say that it is already fruitful.

Creation is salvific insofar as it is part of a salvific process and is thus specified by the Omega of the process, but at the stage of alpha we would necessarily expect the process to be non-salvific, for what need of a process if creation were already salvific the way the incarnation is? It is important to note that the use of the word "salvific" or "fruitful" can have two meanings. Thus the term "non-fruitful" could apply both to the seed and to a pebble, but in different senses. In the first instance it means that "non-fruitful" and "fruitful" refer to one and the same reality except that "non-fruitful" is the seed stage of the process. It means too that the "non-fruitful" is intrinsically ordained or structured towards the "fruitful." In the second, "non-fruitful" and "fruitful" refer to two different things which are extrinsic to one another and autonomous. Thus, to speak of creation as redemptive or salvific is the same as to say a seed is fruitful as compared to a pebble which is unfruitful, but not in the sense that it is fruitful as compared to the fruit. Compared to the fruit, the seed is non-fruitful, but not in the sense that a pebble is non-fruitful.

But according to aristotelian logic, "fruitful" and "non-fruitful" could not belong to the same reality nor could the "fruitful" be derived from the "non-fruitful." They are not in the same line; being contraries, one is outside the other. *Nemo dat quod non habet,* hence the "non-fruitful" cannot bring forth the "fruitful." This is a perfect logic for a timeless world, but inoperative in a historical, evolving context. Applied to our world, the result could only be a dualistic view according to which creation is of its very essence non-salvific.

Instead of seeing creation in relation to the incarnation as a seed in relation to its fruit, the scholastic mind, imbued as it is with the hellenic static and timeless mentality, sees it as a pebble which is essentially distinct from the fruit. Thus for it creation is non-salvific the way a pebble is non-fruitful. It is not intrinsically ordained to the incarnation; there is no Christ-line that leads from creation to its fruit, the incarnation. And if we insist that creation is salvific in order to emphasize its intrinsic ordination to the incarnation, the scholastic can understand this to mean only that creation is salvific in the same sense as the incarnation. Since obviously creation is not salvific in this sense, he concludes that creation is essentially non-salvific. It is purely cosmological, and only extrinsically ordained to the incarnation. But if this is so, then the incarnation is really outside the interest of our world no matter how much it is claimed that it pertains to this world. If creation is like a pebble in relation to the fruit, then no matter how strongly it is insisted that the fruit is somehow related to the pebble, words will not change facts. The fruit is totally outside the pebble's interest. And if the pebble is re-structured in order that it may tend to the fruit, then this re-structuring is conducive not to its perfection but to its destruction.

In much the same way, if creation is seen as purely cosmological, not intrinsically ordained to the incarnation, then the incarnation is totally outside creation. Christ is foreign to this world. It would mean that St. John's words are meaningless when he said: Christ "came unto his own and his own received him not"—which can only mean that this world is Christ's own world. It would mean too that Christ's lordship over the whole of creation mentioned by Paul in

Colossians is purely extrinsic. If the world were purely cosmological to begin with, then there would be no basis for the complaint that Christ is not received by his own. And if the world must be re-structured to tend to the incarnation, then this is not its perfection but its destruction. Should not all these uncomfortable conclusions lead us to suspect the basic aristotelian premise we started with—that creation is purely cosmological? As long as we hold on to the dualistic world-view, then Blondel's observation holds true that our Christology is a feeble and limited one in which Christ appears almost as an accident of history, isolated like a stranger in the universe.

The momentous and fateful event in scholastic theology was the equating of creation with aristotelian cosmology, for it determined the whole formulation of supernatural revelation as definitively extrinsic in character. But I suppose this was what was desired, for truth in scholastic thought was in the eternal and unchanging. Instead of becoming immanent and intrinsic to this world then, the incarnation became extrinsic. In the aristotelian cosmos governed by justice and exigency, the incarnation cannot but be extrinsic, otherwise its gratuity would be imperilled. The only way to make the incarnation intrinsic is to see creation itself as soteriological, gratuitous. Hence in the context of creation as gratuitous, it is not hard to see that the incarnation as a gratuitous act is intrinsic to such a world. In fact, in such a world, the incarnation is the culmination and definitive fulfillment of the series of God's saving events that began with creation as the first gratuitous and salvific act. The incarnation is the "first fruit" of the seed which was creation. That this is the scriptural view is the contention of David Stanley:

> Because they were accustomed to consider cosmic origins as the beginning of the salvation-history, the later OT writers found it quite natural to express the eschatological salvation

of "the last times," the climax of Yahweh's interventions on behalf of His chosen people, as a second and more marvelous creation. The view of Deutero-Isaias is that Yahweh will work Israel's definitive salvation *as creator* (Is 43:18-19; 48:6ff; cf. also Is 65:17ff.), for the reason that God's creation of the universe is thought of as pertaining to the same theological category as His covenant (Is 52:15-16; cf. also Is 66:22). This conception of the creation as a saving event is, I believe, the basis of the biblical view that the *eschaton* must correspond to the beginning, that eschatology, in other words, is determined by protology or ktisiology.[9]

We cannot hope for a clearer proof than is shown here that biblical logic is the logic of process. From the logic of process it is possible to see the truth of the Israelitic view that the creation event is in the same theological category as the covenant. The new covenant is no other than Christ's incarnation. Hence creation is one with the incarnation in the sense that the seed is one with the fruit. And just as the seed (alpha) corresponds to the fruit (omega) and vice versa, so we can understand the biblical view that the beginning corresponds to the *eschaton*.[10]

From the semantics of process we can also see the appropriateness of the scriptural appellation of the incarnation as a second or new creation and the description of the first creation as a saving event. For just as the fruit is a new "seed" so the incarnation is the "new creation," and just as the seed is said to be fruitful, so creation is seen as salvific. Hence when Paul spoke of the incarnation as a new creation he did not mean to say that it was purely cosmological, nor did the Israelites mean that the first creation was already fully and definitively salvific when they saw it as a saving event, nor were they being merely poetic. If the Israelites

9. *Ibid.*, pp. 179-80.
10. Incidentally, it is from this viewpoint that the Apocalypse is symbolically related to Genesis.

were accustomed to thinking of cosmic origins as salvific it is because they were accustomed to seeing reality as process and not simply because they were accustomed to being metaphorical and poetic.

Creation as soteriological is a view that is continued on into the New Testament, as Father Stanley shows:

> What is true of OT literature holds good also for that of the NT, in which the creation-theme is pressed into the service of soteriology. In fact, it may be asserted that the concept of the "new creation," together with its counterpart, the idea of regeneration or birth anew, forms the most apt expression of the salvation revealed in Jesus. Paul portrays the Chrisian who has, through faith and baptism, found a share in Christ's redemption, as a "new creature" or "a new creation" (Gal 6:15; 2 Cor 5:17), while the notion of "rebirth" is found applied to various aspects of Christian salvation in a series of NT writings (Mt 19:28; Jn 3:3ff; Eph 2:4-6; 1 Jn *passim*; 1 Pt 1:3, 23; 2:2).[11]

If creation was pressed into the service of soteriology by both the Old and New Testaments, it was not due to the subjective and poetic whim of some early Old Testament writer whose view was then handed down by tradition and taken as objective truth. Nor was it due to an effort to force a cosmological idea to do the work of soteriology. Rather, the biblical authors were simply stating the truth that creation was really soteriological.

They were trying to convey what they saw of the greatness and grandness of the scale of the redemptive process as extending all the way back to creation as its first stage. They

11. D. Stanley, *op. cit.*, p. 180. We might note, by way of digression, that the ability of NT writers to see creation as soteriological and to relate the first creation with the new creation or rebirth of the new man in Christ is definitive proof that the basic outlook of the NT writers was Hebraic rather than Greek, in spite of the presence of Greek influence in the New Testament and in inter-testamental literature.

were implicitly saying that redemption did not just come from out of the blue, bouncing into time at a fixed moment in history. It is much grander; it is the work of interminable time and patience, of love and mercy. Hence, if Paul used the term "new creation" it was not the result of a choice from many apt poetic expressions. Rather, he used it because it was the only correct way of describing the salvation accomplished through Jesus. The omega is the new alpha. It is only if creation is intrinsically ordained to the incarnation that we can also understand that other expression of Paul which he used in his epistle to the Romans: that creation itself is groaning until now to be redeemed, or, as it can also be translated, to be delivered or reborn.

Through the category of creation understood biblically, then, we are able to see the continuity of creation and the incarnation—an intrinsic continuity. The incarnation is the fullness of creation. It is the "new creation."

2. *The Covenant.* This category is applied likewise to creation and to the incarnation. As Father Stanley pointed out, creation is in the same theological category as the covenant for the Israelites. The doctrine of creation was incorporated into the Hebrews' accounts of their own origins, where it functioned as a kind of prologue to the story of that people's relations with their covenant-God.[12] Again, this is not merely a poetic view or a metaphorical expression. It is because creation is the first covenant between God and man that to recount the dealings of God with man up to its fullness, one naturally starts with the first stage of that covenant.

As Edmond Jacob notes, "the creation is more than the setting in which the covenant is unfolded; it is already a prefiguring of that covenant."[13] And again he observes: "To

12. *Ibid.*, pp. 179-80.
13. E. Jacob, *op. cit.*, p. 138.

the question: Why had God created the world? the Old Testament would answer: He has created it *for* the covenant, that is to say because of his plan of love and salvation for humanity by means of Israel; in creating the world God already had the covenant in view, and it is this motive which gave to the idea of creation its specific orientation."[14] This linking of creation and the covenant can only be understood in the context of one single process.

Creation is not outside this process. It is within it; it is part of it—the first stage. Creation tends to the new covenant in Christ intrinsically. It is its specific orientation, as Jacob notes. Creation is ontologically structured for the covenant since God has created the world precisely *for* the covenant. Creation is in fact the first covenant. Hence, the incarnation is essential to the intelligibility of the universe. Just as the seed is unintelligible apart from the fruit, so is creation apart from the incarnation. In fact, in St. Paul, according to Joseph Huby, Christ as the new covenant or supreme center of unity gives to the world its sense, its value and therefore its reality. And if one were to view the whole universe, past, present and future, in a single instantaneous glimpse, he would see all beings ontologically suspended from Christ and completely unintelligible apart from him.[15]

On the other hand, it is difficult to see how the incarnation is the essential intelligibility of the universe if, as according to scholastic thought, the universe is essentially intelligible apart from Christ. It is only in the context of process that we can appreciate the New Testament view that Christ is the essential meaning of reality. For the New Testament, the new covenant is the fulfillment of the previous covenants of which creation was the first. Hence, creation as the first covenant tended towards the incarnation as the new cove-

14. *Ibid.,* p. 137.
15. See p. 258 above.

nant for its existence, value and meaning. The New Testament does not start with a cosmological or uncovenanted universe already possessed of essential intelligibility and existence to which it then relates the covenant-love of God— the incarnation—as a secondary perfection and accidental intelligibility. There is only the covenanted universe.

In this context, creation is but the prefiguring of the covenant. According to Edmond Jacob, "this means that the idea of creation is secondary to that of the covenant of which it is both the condition and consequence."[16] Creation is not the whole to which is superadded the incarnation as an ornament, any more than the fruit is superadded to the seed. This is a typically ptolemaic-aristotelian view of things. Nature is not the center, the substantial, essential, subsistent to which the supernatural is related accidentally. Rather, creation as covenanted is but the seed, the peripheral, accidental, the predicate, which must tend to the incarnation as to its fruit, its metaphysical center, its substance and subject.

Again, it is only in the context of process that we can see the possibility of creation as an evolutionary process able to tend to the incarnation as its Omega. Since creation and the incarnation are both in the same category of the covenant, there is no difficulty in creation evolving towards the incarnation. For creation as covenanted does not attain the incarnation by its own powers, precisely because it is covenanted. Essential to the structure of a covenanted being is its other. Hence, creation is a being-towards-its-Other. God is its Other, its Ground. Evolution is not a natural process able to attain its end alone.

3. *Baptism*. This category is again an evolutionary one in Scripture. It is applied to both creation and the incarnation. When the New Testament writers describe the baptismal mystery, they go to the Old Testament to find its prefigura-

16. E. Jacob, *op. cit.*, p. 136.

tions. Why this methodology? Because to the New Testament writers the Old Testament is part of a single sacred evolutionary process in which creation is the beginning of time and Christ, the fullness of time. Thus they go to the Old Testament to see the types that point to Christ, the antitype. As Austin Farrer observes, "since the process is of the rebirth of images, it is to the matrix of images, the Old Testament, that the Spirit continually leads; for here are images awaiting rebirth; all this is Christ, could we but see how and why; the Spirit will teach us."[17]

Again we depend on Father Stanley's excellent article to show us how the New Testament writers linked Christ's redemptive baptism on the cross with the Old Testament events:

> When we turn to a consideration of the OT images exploited by the NT writers in their endeavor to describe the baptismal mystery, we find that in their works they lay under tribute almost all the great *gesta Dei* in Israel's salvation-history: the creation, the deluge, the promise to Abraham with its sign, circumcision, the exodus from Egypt, the wandering in the desert, the covenant established through Moses, together with the poignant presentation of it in the prophetic writings as Yahweh's espousals with His people.[18]

In all these events, baptism, which attains its fullness in Christ, is prefigured. In Christ's baptism at the Jordan and on the cross (Jn 19:34), we find two elements: water and the Spirit. We find the same elements in the creation event as recounted in Genesis. There we have the waters being fecundated by the Spirit. Thus the New Testament saw creation as a baptismal symbol that prefigured Christ's baptism on the cross. Hence it was soteriological rather than cosmological.

It is significant that the New Testament writers in describ-

17. *A Rebirth of Images* (Westminster: Dacre Press, 1949), p. 15.
18. *Op. cit.*, p. 178.

ing the baptismal mystery begin from the first salvific act of God, creation itself, and include almost all the great *gesta Dei*. Their purpose is not so much to provide a purely historical recording of all the acts of God as to show that the whole of time from the beginning of time itself up to Christ's redemptive baptism on the cross was one salvific process leading to Christ as its definitive fulfillment. Creation itself was part of this baptismal or redemptive process.

The early Christian liturgies closely follow the New Testament in showing through the baptismal types that there is but one salvific process. Thus during the night of the Pasch, all the baptismal types were recounted to show the continuity of these redeeming acts of God and their fulfillment in Christ's final baptismal act.[19]

We can summarize the biblical view on the relation between creation and the incarnation by making our own the statements of a renowned biblical scholar: "It was not the fall first and then elevation in Christ, but even the time before Creation is regarded entirely from the position of Christ: it is the time in which, in the counsel of God, Christ is already foreordained as Mediator before the foundation of the world (Jn 17:24; 1 Pet 1:20)."[20] "He is then the Mediator in the Creation itself (Jn 1:1; Heb 1:2; and especially vv. 10 ff.; 1 Cor 8:6; Col 1:16)."[21] Thus "all dualism between creation and Redemption is excluded. In the NT there cannot be, in addition to the Christ-line of redemption, another separate God-line of creation."[22]

Cullmann continues: "In the three decisive stages of the Christ-line of salvation the general process is drawn into the redemptive process. It is so in Creation: everything is cre-

19. Cf. Jean Daniélou, *The Bible and the Liturgy,* Chapter V: "Types of Baptism."

20. Oscar Cullmann, *Christ and Time,* trans. F. V. Filson (Philadelphia: Westminster, 1950), p. 108.

21. *Ibid.,* p. 178.

22. *Loc. cit.*

ated through Christ. It is so in Christ's death and resurrection: everything is reconciled through him. It is so in the eschatological completion: everything is subjected to God, who is all in all."[23]

Cullmann sums up:

> From the beginning indeed, it is a Christ-line, so that it is justified to speak of "Christ and time." This presentation confirms the fact that we should not begin to speak of Christ only at some fixed point part way along the line, as though previously one could speak only of God, without reference to Christ. Such a procedure would destroy the line in its magnificent unity of content. The orientation by reference to the mid-point would thereby be surrendered, and there would enter into the divine plan of salvation a dualistic principle, which would completely obscure the view of salvation that is characteristic of Primitive Christianity.[24]

Thus from our preceding considerations we observe that for the Bible there is no natural or cosmological order distinct from the redemptive or supernatural order. There is just one process—the redemptive process. From the vantage point of the New Testament this process is the Christ-line. There is no parallel line—no natural or cosmological line having a natural end. Creation is the first stage of the Christ-line. Already, creation is a prefiguring of the covenant, already it is a type of Christ's baptism, hence soteriological. Christ's incarnation-redemption is the fullness of creation—it is the new creation.

Now this biblical view is exactly what Teilhard de Chardin has proposed in his book, showing with great insight and skill how the data of modern science confirm the biblical view. Evolution is a process and it corresponds with the biblical notion of creation as a process—a salvific process which gives birth to the promised one, the first fruit, the first born. Evolution, says Teilhard, tends to Christ-Omega.

23. *Ibid.*, p. 179.
24. *Ibid.*, p. 108.

Tresmontant and Nicolas Corte, among others, have noted that Teilhard's thought corresponds to biblical thought. Even from our brief and sketchy presentation of biblical thought this should be apparent.[25]

And yet if one reads the strong criticisms of some Catholic critics of this teilhardian view, one gets the impression that Teilhard's thought is dangerous and heretical. If this is so, then one must be prepared to say also that the biblical view is suspect. To clear the Scriptures from this suspicion, it has been customary to explain biblical expression and semantics as metaphorical and poetic; this is also the way the more benevolent critics have explained Teilhard's expression.

We have tried to use the philosophy of process to explain the scriptural and teilhardian views. Creation is not a single monadic force that proceeds from nature alone. It is a joint cooperative effort of God and created reality. As Tresmontant so well observes in his excellent *Study of Hebrew Thought,* reality for the Hebrews is not an individual substance that once and for all encloses everything that can happen to it, an individual substance or monad launched out into existence by an aristotelian or leibnizian God and afterwards left alone to shift for itself and explicitate its contents.[26] "Biblical metaphysics," notes Tresmontant, "is founded on a dialogue. If we are to understand it we must stop thinking in terms of a single force and try to penetrate the more complex and much richer play of a world engendered by two freedoms."[27]

Thus to the Hebrew mind there is no true achievement of

25. We are not saying that the Hebrews had a notion of evolution. With their primitive cosmology, they could not have been aware of the evolution of species, etc. What they knew was the blueprint, so to speak, of creation as a process. What they did not know was how this revealed plan was to be accomplished. That it is to be accomplished through the evolutionary process is Teilhard's great insight.

26. See p. 37.

27. *Ibid.,* p. 38.

created reality which is not more fundamentally and principally achieved by God, directing, orienting, molding, maturing reality unto its fullness. This fact is presupposed. It is the Hebrews' mental pattern, and so is it with the New Testament writers. Therefore the New Testament and even the primitive Church found it perfectly natural to say that creation tended to the incarnation as its fruit. A view of a natural order completely autonomous, purely cosmological and able to achieve its own end by itself is foreign to their mentality.

If they could have read *The Phenomenon of Man* they would have found as perfectly orthodox the view put forth that evolution tends towards Christ-Omega. Thus Christ-Omega is but the culmination of God's saving acts which began with creation and continued through time, which acts are what the Scriptures are all about. That these acts all prepared the way for the coming of the Christ, we have from his own lips: "But he said to them, 'O foolish ones and slow of heart to believe in all that the prophets have spoken! Did not the Christ have to suffer these things before entering into his glory?' And beginning then with Moses and with all the prophets, he interpreted to them in all the Scriptures the things referring to himself" (Luke 24:25-27).

To answer finally the question we proposed at the beginning: how to make the incarnation immanent in the context of an evolving universe—the answer is that we do not need to, for the incarnation does not come from without; it does not bounce into time. Christ is the Within of this supernaturally evolving universe. Evolution is God's creative action expressed in time.

Let us reconsider the conclusion of our last two sections, namely, that both man and evolution are intrinsically ordained to grace and the incarnation, to test now its validity from the aspect of gratuity. For a comment may be made that in the attempt to show the immanence of grace and the incarnation, their gratuity has not been adequately safeguarded. This is the objection which will occupy us in the rest of this chapter. The treatment of this objection has the added purpose of bringing into greater relief the ultimate difference between the pauline-teilhardian and the aristotelian-thomistic methodological approach to the gratuity of the supernatural. Let us state the objection more precisely:

> Can that person who has *himself created* such an ordination to the personal and intimate communion of love between two persons (in our case man and God), once this has been presupposed still simultaneously refuse this communion without offending against the meaning of this creation and his very creative act itself? . . . Thus if the ordination cannot be detached from the nature, the fulfillment of the ordination, from God's point of view precisely, is exacted.[28]

This objection seemingly differs from the many thomistic objections traditionally brought forth against the intrinsic ordination of reality to the supernatural in that it goes outside the I-It context, accepts the I-Thou context for the sake of argument, and from it draws its objection. Thus the objection states that even in the I-Thou context, once we presuppose the intrinsic ordination of the creature to the supernatural, then, even if the personal finite spirit has to accept grace as unexacted *(ungeschuldet)* if it is not to lose its meaning,[29] yet, from God's point of view, grace is exacted. In other words, in order that grace be totally unexacted, God must be able to refuse it. But for God to be able to refuse it, it must be detached from the meaning of the creature. If one were to ask a thomist why God could not refuse grace unless it were detached from the meaning of

28. Rahner, *Theological Investigations,* I, p. 306.
29. *Loc. cit.*

the creature, the answer would be that anything else would be for God to create a nature in vain, or as Rahner would put it, to offend against the meaning of this creation and his very creative act itself. Hence, the basic thomistic theological position is that to explain and save the gratuity of grace and the incarnation, they must be detached from the essential intelligibility of man and evolution.

As a general comment on the thomistic position, we observe that this may well be one way of explaining the gratuity and total unexactedness of the supernatural, but we would like to ask whether this explanation is not achieved at the expense of scriptural data. For the Scriptures are abundantly clear that man and creation are unintelligible apart from the covenant, or in the New Testament, apart from Christ. We have seen in our scriptural study the Hebrew view that man's being cannot be thought of apart from the covenant, for it is in direct conflict with man's essence to be apart from it; one is born of it and into it.

The feminine-masculine imagery clearly implies that man is intrinsically ordained to grace and Christ, for sex is of the essence of being. We have also seen that according to the New Testament, creation is soteriological, a prefiguring of the covenant, a baptismal symbol prefiguring Christ's baptism, and hence, cannot be thought of apart from Christ. For Paul, Christ is the exemplar of all reality, the principle of intelligibility of all reality. This is also John's view as may be seen in the prologue of his gospel. And even Christ himself traced his history back to creation and all the way back to his pre-existence in the Godhead: "before Abraham was born, I am" (Jn 8:58). Now, how are we to explain these scriptural data if we maintain that man and creation are essentially intelligible apart from grace and the incarnation? In the face of these data, is not the logical thing to do to re-examine one's reasoning?

What is the ultimate basis for the thomistic position that in order to explain gratuity, grace must be detached from the meaning of the creature? The answer to this question is the crucial point in the whole discussion. Juan Alfaro correctly observes that in drawing this conclusion, one is stepping out from the realm of formal revelation into that of theological reasoning.[30] It is the basis of this theological reasoning that is in need of re-examination. But as is often the case, that which is in most need of re-examination is taken for granted as an unquestioned starting point. And it is often the case, too, that one has to go outside one's school or tradition to see things in a new light.

The unquestioned assumption of the thomistic position is that one starts with creation as self-intelligible and autonomous and then relates grace and the incarnation to it. What we would like to ask is why we should not rather start with the incarnation and grace and relate creation and man to them, since the testimony of Scripture is that man and creation are unintelligible apart from them. Are they not the given? Should we not then derive the meaning of the gratuity of the supernatural from them as starting point rather than from a philosophical premise such as the self-intelligibility of nature? The importance of the starting point may not be apparent now, but it is in fact the crucial factor in determining how one is to think of the gratuity of the supernatural.

Let us consider the consequences of the thomistic starting point. In the thomistic view, creation is a distinct act from the incarnation. Creation is created in and for itself and not precisely for the incarnation. From the point of view of God's mind, the first in intention was creation as a purely cosmological order intelligible in itself. In relation to creation, grace and the incarnation are purely secondary, freely given as a higher but detachable end. True, thomists empha-

30. *Op. cit.*, p. 31.

size that the real order is a supernatural order, but they also maintain that in order to think of its gratuity, it is necessary to have a theological concept of nature as a remainder after the supernatural has been removed. I suppose they would have to maintain too that in trying to understand God's point of view it is also necessary that he have a remainder concept of nature. The result of this methodology, however, as we have noted elsewhere in our study, is to make grace and the incarnation peripheral and extrinsic to present reality.

Do we have to detach grace and the incarnation from the intrinsic intelligibility of reality in order to show their total unexactedness? Is there no other way by which we can show their total gratuity without also destroying intrinsic ordination? Rahner's objection, we recall, is that even in the context of I-Thou, once intrinsic ordination is presupposed, grace is precisely exacted, at least from God's point of view as creator. We believe, however, that Rahner's objection is a false one because it proceeds from the false methodology of starting with the cosmological order first and from it deducing the meaning of gratuity.

We believe that it is not necessary to have a remainder concept of nature in order to safeguard gratuity if we start with the incarnation as the principal reality. As far as we can gather from the Scriptures, the incarnation was primary in God's counsel for all eternity. As Jean-François Bonnefoy, O.F.M., notes:

> Our election "in Christ" is the fulfillment of an eternal divine plan, and not the result of a decision made as a consequence of Adam's sin—or the defection of anyone else. Far from presenting Christ as willed on our account, as the means of our salvation, St. Paul teaches that we were willed for Christ "before the foundation of the world." Even more

than this, "God has predestined us to be adopted as his sons, through Jesus Christ."[31]

This is also the view of Emile Mersch and is the basis of his theological synthesis. As he notes:

In the order of intention Christ was willed, not only as regards the substance of the Incarnation but also as regards the circumstances of proximate possibility and as actual Redeemer, prior to the natural order and the order of grace and the permission of sin.[32]

Again, Mersch observes:

The creation of the world was the first beginning of the birth of Christ, the Redeemer, the Risen One. The decision that decreed creation was one of the phases of the single decree that willed the Incarnation. The God-man, the well-beloved and only-begotten Son, was willed, prepared, and predestined in all and through all, and we, together with the entire universe, were chosen and blessed in Him, "that in all things He may hold primacy" (Col 1:18).[33]

Mersch concludes that "to understand grace we have to study it in Christ."[34] For Christ is not only the reason for grace but "considered in its totality, the body of Christ in which Christ lives possesses in Him the totality of grace. No grace is given except what Christ has merited and brought to us by being the union between God and men."[35] From the vantage point of the incarnation, Mersch notes that "grace is gratuitous from the initial gift to the ultimate prolongation . . . a gift that comes without interruption from an ever spontaneous love, and it is all the more gratuitous for

31. Cf. his admirable work, *Christ and Cosmos*, trans. M. D. Meilach, O.F.M. (New Jersey: St. Anthony Guild Press, 1965), pp. 308-310.
32. Cf. his book, *The Theology of the Mystical Body*, trans. C. Vollert, (St. Louis: B. Herder Book Co., 1951), p. 136. This is a quote from P. de Godoy which Mersch makes his own.
33. *Ibid.*, p. 140.
34. *Ibid.*, p. 142.
35. *Ibid.*, p. 626.

the reason that it freely imparts a power to merit it in some degree."[36]

It is from the point of view of Christ, in whom the entire divine plan is recapitulated,[37] that we shall try to reconcile the total unexactedness of grace and the incarnation with the intrinsic ordination of man and creation to the supernatural. It would seem then that God thought of Christ and the grace of union in Christ first as a totally unexacted free gift and that the intrinsic ordination of man and creation proceeded from it as a consequence. But Rahner objects that after the free gratuitous gift to create the communion between God and man, grace then becomes exacted by the intrinsic ordination of man to grace. But why, we ask, does he abstract this particular part of the divine plan from the whole plan which gives a fundamental character to each part? No doubt in the carrying out of a plan, there are necessary steps and connections, but if the initial step was gratuitous to begin with, then the whole series or order is gratuitous. Why assimilate the gratuity of the whole within the exigency of the part? Is this not to revert unconsciously to the aristotelian-thomistic approach of assimilating gratuity within creation as a cosmological order? Is this not to put creation before the incarnation in the intentional order?

It is important to realize that one and the same intrinsic ordination to grace in the creature exacts or does not exact grace (from God's point of view) depending upon the context. The thomists have not realized this fact, I am afraid. For them, intrinsic ordination necessarily exacts grace. The difference between the aristotelian-thomistic and the pauline-teilhardian contexts is that the former starts with man, the latter with grace. Thus in the former, grace is for the sake of man and if man is intrinsically ordained to grace, it is

36. *Loc. cit.*
37. *Ibid.*, p. 140.

man's nature that demands or exacts grace. God could not but fulfill this ordination, otherwise he would be offending against the meaning of this creation and the creative act itself. In the latter, however, man is created for Christ and the grace of union in Christ, hence, it is Christ and his love for Christ that requires from God the creation and the intrinsic ordination of the creature to Christ and grace.

We may illustrate the difference in approach by an example. Thus in the aristotelian-thomistic context, it is as if a camera manufacturer made a leather case in and for itself, and only secondarily made a camera to fit the case. In such a situation, the maker is exacted, so to speak, by the specifications of the leather case, to give it precisely the size of camera that fits it. On the other hand, if the camera was the first objective and only secondarily the case, then it is the camera that exacts the size of the case and demands that the case fit the camera. The leather case does not demand, for its specification is not the reason it is given this size of camera; it is the camera that demands the specifications of the case. Similarly, it is the unexactedness of the decision to give grace that demands that the finite "I" be ordained to grace, not that the "I" demands by its intrinsic ordination that grace be given it with the result that God is no longer free to refuse it.

Let us take another example to show the proper context within which the gratuity of grace and the intrinsic ordination of the creature can be understood and reconciled. Thus, instead of a cosmological edifice to which grace and the incarnation are then related as ornaments, the divine plan calls rather for an edifice with Christ as the cornerstone, so that we may call the building the "Christ building" or the "grace edifice," so to speak. The construction of the building is totally unexacted, totally gratuitous. It is in this sense that we should see the total gratuity of grace and the incarnation. The total gratuity of grace on the part of God is the total gratuity of a creative act, and not of a generous act of giving to something already pre-existing. We do not have creation first to which we then relate grace. Rather, grace is part of one and the same creative act which began with creation. In fact, grace is the culmination of that creative act and creation is its first phase.

Grace and the incarnation are the "new creation," and the first creation was already soteriological and Christian. It is false to consider creation and redemption dualistically and then try to relate one to the other. Rather we should see them as phases of the single process of grace. When grace is given to creation, which is intrinsically ordained to grace the way a seed is ordained to the fruit, it is but grace being given to itself. It is not some other thing demanding grace in such a way as to make it nongratuitous. In this dualistic context, grace has to be detachable to be gratuitous. But then we fail to show the immanence of grace which is demanded by its aspect as highest perfection; and we fail to show its gratuity on the side of the creature, for a gift that does not respond to an essential need is not really that gratuitous since it does not evoke total gratitude in the recipient.

It is false to think of the gratuity of grace, we believe, by setting up the problem in such a way that first in intention is the creature to which is then related grace. If God were to create the intrinsic ordination to grace first, then grace would necessarily be exacted. But our contention is that God does not create the ordination first, as Rahner seems to imply in the objection we cited.

First in intention is Christ and grace in Christ, after which the ordination of the creature to Christ and grace follows as a consequence. If the divine plan is to create a creature unintelligible apart from Christ and grace, then it is metaphysically impossible to have the ordination as first in intention, since the very ordination is determined precisely by Christ and grace. Christ must pre-exist the ordination and the creature itself, and this, incidentally, is what we are given in Scripture. Hence if, in the actual order, we have an intellectual creature intrinsically ordained to grace, God cannot refuse grace to the creature, not because the intrinsic ordination of the creature demands it but because God could not go back on his free decree to subject all things to Christ through the incarnation.

If it is objected that grace is exacted in any case since it is demanded by Christ, and that therefore the gratuity of grace is destroyed, we would then have to conclude also that the giving of grace in the thomistic view, which proceeds from God's free decision to give it and not from the creature's ordination, is exacted in the sense that God could not go back on his free decision to give this higher end. If it is countered that in the thomistic view grace is not exacted because it is not demanded by the creature's ordination, then we answer that in our view, the intrinsic ordination of the creature does not exact grace either. God does not create grace for the intrinsic ordination, but creates the intrinsic ordination for grace.

A thomistic objection at this point may be that the implication of our arguments is that "God cannot create intellectual beings without ordering and calling them to the beatific vision," a contention which is contrary to the warning of *Humani generis* that this claim undermines the gratuity of the supernatural. This objection is another opportunity for us to point out that its premise is that God starts with creation first as an act in and for itself, intelligible apart from the incarnation and grace. Given this set-up of the problem, God must be able to create intellectual creatures without ordering them to the beatific vision if the gratuity of the supernatural is to be safeguarded.

Let us admit that the encyclical in question is written in the aristotelian-thomistic context, and given that context, the statement it makes is valid. But the encyclical has not stated that the aristotelian-thomistic context is the only valid one. It is this context that we question, not the conclusion derivable from it. Hence our contention is that if we set up the problem differently by starting with the incarnation and grace, then in order that creatures may share in these totally unexacted gifts, God has to create precisely for these gifts. It is the nature of Christ that determined the structuring of man and not the structuring of man apart from Christ that determined that his end be the beatific vision.

As long as we are in the covenant context of the incarnation, it is valid to say that God could not create us without structuring us for grace because by his free decision we are unthinkable apart from Christ. What this shows is the all-importance of grace and God's infinite love for his son, and not that we have an exigency for the supernatural. Anything God does, he does for the sake of his son, not for the sake of nature. If he puts intrinsic ordination in man, it is because he wants all reality to be totally subject to his son, an end he could not accomplish if human nature were autonomous and ordained to Christ only by an external decree, leaving the depths of nature free from the sovereignty of Christ.

One has to set man's intrinsic ordination to grace in the wider context of God's gratuitous decision to share his trinitarian life to be able to reconcile intrinsic ordination and the unexactedness of grace. If we abstract from that wider context, then it would seem that God could not refuse grace to the creature. But in the wider context, he is not giving grace because of the intrinsic ordination, but giving an intrinsic ordination because of grace. From God's point of view, grace is totally unexacted because God could refuse it without frustrating any creature since the creature is not prior to grace. In other words, there is no extrinsic source that compels God to give grace because before grace there was no prior order of nature intrinsically ordained to grace.

Grace comes first in the order of intention, not the creature. From the creature's point of view, grace is totally and doubly gratuitous because the creature owes not only its intrinsic ordination to grace but its very existence. Instead of being a threat to the gratuity of grace as it would be in the aristotelian-thomistic context, intrinsic ordination is a sign of God's love for us in Christ. The pauline-teilhardian view reconciles the data of Scripture that man and creation are unintelligible apart from Christ and grace, while at the same time explaining through this very ordination the possibility of the headship of Christ over all creation. Christ is not an accident in the universe, but its center and Omega.

With the incarnation as the methodological starting point for understanding the gratuity of the supernatural, we are able to do away with the remainder concept of pure nature —the stumbling block to Christ's full sovereignty and headship over the universe. As we remarked earlier, the concept of pure nature is a necessity in the thomistic view because there the incarnation and grace are related to creation conceived as an autonomous and self-intelligible order. With this presupposition, the removal of grace and the incarnation must leave creation essentially intact if the meaning of creation is not to be frustrated.

It is significant, however, that, as Alfaro admits, "it is true that revelation does not speak of the intellectual creature as such; it speaks of man the sinner who is actually destined to the beatific vision."[38] Might it not be that the reason revelation does not speak of the intellectual creature as such is because there is no need for such a concept, that there is no natural order or state of pure nature as a remain-

38. *Op. cit.,* p. 30.

der concept, that outside the incarnation as the new covenant there is only an unnatural state of sin? Thus if we start with the incarnation as the whole of which creation is a part, then it is false to say that we can remove the whole while leaving the part intact.

In the presupposition that the divine plan is to create all things in Christ so that no creature is intelligible apart from him, then to remove Christ is not to remove a part from a whole but to remove the whole itself. The parts would be meaningless. To explain the gratuity of the incarnation, it is false to assimilate it to a part which can be removed or replaced without affecting the essential unity of the whole. On the side of creation, the gratuity of the incarnation is total and complete in the sense that if God did not decree it, the whole of creation would not only be meaningless but it would not even exist. On the side of God, the incarnation is totally gratuitous and unexacted because, as we said, there is no prior natural order of creation that exacts the incarnation.

The incarnation is first in the order of intention and execution. Creation itself is the first phase of the incarnation. Thus, if God fulfills the intrinsic ordination of creation, it is but the fulfilling of his free decree of the incarnation. If God removes the incarnation it is tantamount to scrapping the whole divine plan. Hence it is false to explain the gratuity of the incarnation as something removable from the universe or replaceable in it. It is the universe that is removable or replaceable. And in the present order, it is we creatures who are either outside or inside the new covenant of the incarnation, not the new covenant which is outside or inside creation. To be outside the new covenant is to be in an unnatural state, not a natural one. To be is to be *per Ipsum, et cum Ipso, et in Ipso.* Christ's sovereignty is complete and total.

Ultimately the difference between the aristotelian-thomistic and the pauline-teilhardian approach to the gratuity of the incarnation is philosophic—a difference of epistemological and methodological outlook on reality. This has been the implied thesis of our whole study. It is the contention of Gregory Dix that the hellenic outlook and ways of thought are the stumbling block to the proper formulation of the divine message. Gregory Dix first contrasts the hellenic and the scriptural outlooks:

> The "objectivity" of the Greek mind seeking to explain the *kosmos* from within itself developed a sensitiveness to *form*, and so to all kinds of aesthetic and intellectual beauty, which the Syriac genius missed. To the Greek *eidos* ("form"), the right arrangement of parts in a whole, is the *vehicle* of significance and meaning. . . .
>
> The Old Testament, on the other hand, finds the idol (*eidolon*, "a little piece of form") the very *negation* of that "meaning" which it sought to find for things in God, and rejects it sternly in consequence.[39]

Thus Dix shows the fundamental difference in epistemological approach. One sees things as possessing form or essence; the other sees reality as a symbol of what it will be. He further notes that "this contrast between the cultures of 'form' and 'formlessness' extends not only over the arts but over every aspect of human living."[40] Dix then tries to give the methodological basis for the difference in epistemological approach:

> The results of this contrast are almost endless, but always in principle it is the same—the contrast between a culture in which "form," the right arrangement of parts in a whole, is seen as the clue to, or the vehicle of, meaning and significance, and a culture in which form is irrelevant to, if not

39. Cf. his book, *Jew and Greek* (Westminster: Dacre Press, 1955), pp. 12-13.
40. *Ibid.*, p. 13.

actually a barrier to, significance and meaning. And behind that lies the fundamental difference between a thought which starts from the *kosmos* and seeks to understand human life (and God in relation to life) from the *kosmos*; and, on the other hand, a thought which starts from the "Living God" and seeks to understand human life in the *kosmos* from its vision of God.[41]

Dix observes that "the two insights not only produce different cultures, different patterns of living. They reveal a different man, a different world, a different God."[42] Dix goes on to note the dire results of the hellenic approach to the Scriptures:

> It explains much of the profound unhappiness and distraction of our times, that post-Renaissance Western men have, generally speaking, increasingly reverted to being Greeks in their thinking about the *kosmos*. . . . Western man is trying confusedly to save many of these consequences [that is, the Syriac God with all its consequences] in his own soul, while thinking like a Greek, and is facing spiritual schizophrenia in the process.[43]

With regard to our particular problem, the hellenic mind, true to its presuppositions, starts from creation and relates the incarnation to it, instead of starting with the incarnation and relating creation to it. This philosophic position is the ultimate basis, it seems, for the conclusion that intrinsic ordination is incompatible with gratuity and the consequent failure to show the immanence of Christ and grace in the world, all of which conclusions are of no help towards curbing the ever growing secularization of the world.

We have to affirm with all the force of our beings that we are intrinsically ordained to grace if we are to save the

41. *Loc. cit.*
42. *Ibid.*, p. 14.
43. *Loc. cit.*

gratuity of the supernatural. For it is precisely our intrinsic ordination that is a witness, a testimony, a proof of God's *chesed* (covenant love), of his infinite liberality—when he gives, he gives as only he could, for he is love. And if our only meaning as creatures is union with God, to fail to give full value to this union is to fail to appreciate the full meaning of our very creaturehood. It is as if a woman were to deny her womanhood. For if the very creation of the human soul, which is feminine in relation to God, is a call to betrothal, then in a very true sense, for the soul to deny its intrinsic ordination to God is not unlike a woman denying the very essence of her womanhood which is to be wife-mother.

To affirm our intrinsic ordination is to praise God. To deny it is to make of God a poor lover, to underestimate his infinite power and beauty, since in this case, all he could excite in man is a mere velleity, a mere indifference to his call. Is this not the danger we fall into when our formulations fail to explain the testimony of human experience of the desire of the human spirit for God, a desire well expressed by the psalmist when he said: "As the hart panteth after the fountains of water; so my soul panteth after thee, O God. My soul hath thirsted after the strong living God; when shall I come and appear before the face of God?" (Ps 41:2-3). Indeed, the need of the human spirit for God is an abyss as deep as the ontological depth of the being itself, and not just some passing fancy, some superadded need, a velleity. It is this depth that is at once our weakness and our strength: our weakness because we cannot fill it up ourselves; our strength because it is a silent testimony of what God is going to do for us. It is this silent depth that, more loudly than words, calls for the beloved, as the psalmist says: "Deep calleth unto deep" (Ps 41:8).

If we look back now and reflect on the history of the formulation of the supernatural union between God and man, we find that the conjugal imagery offered by the Scriptures is the simplest explanation, one that is understandable by the ordinary man possessed of no philosophical training, and for whom, after all, revelation was meant. And yet the marriage imagery is deep enough to challenge the best minds, for as St. Paul says, it is a great mystery. The supernatural is the heart of the message of salvation, hence it must be brought within the reach of every man, as Christ commanded us to do. And it is precisely the task of theology to make revelation reasonable and more understandable. With regard to the success of scholastic theology in explaining the concept of the supernatural, Jean Rivière has some reservations:

> The whole economy of Christian dogma centers about this notion; all our spiritual life is nourished at this reality. But this notion and this reality are not made very luminous for the mind nor captivating for the heart by the maze of technical precisions and distinctions contributed by the professional theologians, whether in their learned treatises *de ente supernaturali* or in their manuals of more popular character. Yet, this doctrine, more perhaps than any other, belongs to that class of teaching which plunges its roots in the deepest soil of human religion and of divine revelation.[44]

With the help of the philosophy of process it may be possible to go back to the Scriptures and accept the revelation that we are made for God without reservation or qualification, and without any fear that it means other than what it says. It may also be possible to confirm the deep belief of the Christian that Christ is the be all and end all of his life, that he was made for Christ. When we say we make something, everyone understands that we structure the thing for the end we have in mind. What else could it mean? When

44. Cf. his article, "Notre état surnaturel," *Nouvelle revue apologétique,* I (1939), 105.

we make a watch we structure the thing to tell time. It is absurd to say that first we make it for some other end and then gratuitously ordain it to tell time. When we end up explaining things this way, then it is time to suspect the adequacy of our philosophic categories.

With man totally structured for God and grace, the command of God to love him with our whole heart and with our whole soul and with our whole mind sounds reasonable; the teachings of the Church that original sin is internal to man and that punishment in hell touches the very core of his being at least make sense. And we hope, too, that the naturalist, even if he does not accept Christian truths, at least sees that the Christian God is not inhuman after all, that the truths we believe in are reasonable. This is not to say that the attempt made here to show the possibility of man's intrinsic ordination to the supernatural is necessarily the final and most adequate one. All we have shown is a formulation in the context of I-Thou that tries to explain the data of Sacred Scripture.

CHAPTER X

The Semantics for a Christian Universe

If there is only one order, the supernatural order,[1] what happens to the terminology that we used to apply to the natural order? Must it be dropped? But the term "natural" is not only imbedded in our thinking and culture, it is also more basic than the term "supernatural" which, compared to the former, is also more recent. What to do? We shall attempt to answer this problem by a study of the semantics for the Christian universe.[2] We will confine ourselves to two problems: first, the semantics for grace, and second, the semantics of the incarnation.

THE SEMANTICS OF GRACE

Because scholastic philosophy and theology started with man as nature, grace had to be above the powers of nature to show its gratuity and transcendence, hence it was aptly called supra-natural. But if, like the Bible, we view man without grace as being in an unnatural state, then grace

1. Let us not be misunderstood as saying that we deny the reality of the present world. This is how we could possibly be understood by one who considers the supernatural as distinct from the present order which he considers the natural order. What we are saying, however, is that this present world is the supernatural order and there is no other.

2. I would like to re-emphasize what I said in the introduction about the nature of this work, namely, that it was meant to be purely exploratory. In an age of transition and renewal, this is all we can hope for. Perhaps the attempt to go beyond Thomism is a step in the wrong direction. If this should prove to be so, the study will nevertheless have contributed to renewal by its very failure.

would be man's natural state. For Eastern theology, too, what is outside the life of union with God is not natural but unnatural. As Nicholas Berdyaev notes, "the natural as an independent sphere of being does not exist; for it is only a state of sin and separation from God. The true being of man and of the world is rooted in God. That is how Orthodoxy regarded the matter and in this it was nearer the truth than Catholicism."[3]

Thus in biblical and Orthodox terminology, the state of grace or union with God is the natural state of man; the state outside this union is termed unnatural.

Why, we might ask, did not the Western Church stick to this terminology? Part of the reason, it would seem, was apologetical. For in the evangelization of the Greeks, such a terminology would have had heretical implications. What had to be conveyed to the Greeks was the gratuity of God's call to union, that it was a gift undeserved by man though to prepare for it one had to pray and do penance. Now in the context of Greek thought, the supernatural state could not very well be called man's natural state, for "nature" in Greek philosophy attains its end by its own powers. It would mean, then, that grace could be attained by man's own powers, and quite apart from prayer, penance, the act of faith, etc. For the Greeks, consequently, grace had to be termed that which is above this world *(huperkosmos)* or the supernatural. It is this semantics that we have inherited.

The defect in Western terminology has been pointed out especially by those who have had the experience of evangelizing non-Christians. If before grace concrete human nature was in a natural state,[4] then on what basis, incentive and urge can non-Christians be convinced of the need and

3. *Op. cit.,* p. 350.
4. We are not saying here that this state is a state of pure nature, although some scholastics, as a matter of fact, have affirmed it to be so. By natural we mean that it was created perfect, essentially and integrally.

necessity for grace? A need of human nature itself is the only one strong enough to compel them to seek this end, which in fact is their only end. In other words, only a natural need would be sufficiently strong to compel man to tend toward a good. In the context of man understood as his human nature, there is really no supernatural need because nature has no need for it. It has no need for it because nature is created complete and perfect, essentially and integrally. In fact, for any nature, the natural is the norm for what is necessary or unnecessary, for what is good or bad. Any deficiency or excess, as Aristotle himself wisely observes, is a vice, not a virtue. It is unnatural. Hence a supernatural need which is really an excess cannot be a need of nature. It would be the vice of intemperance for nature to seek a good beyond what is natural.

If this is so, how can we explain rationally the Christian belief that grace perfects nature? How can we show that an excess is a perfection? It is only when grace is shown as a natural need that nature can justifiably tend to it; only then can it be shown that grace does actually perfect nature. But for grace to be a natural need there must correspond a prior deficiency in nature. Nature must be in an "unnatural" state for it to tend to some good and for that good to be perfective of it. But according to Scholasticism, nature is not in an unnatural state. Yet if it is not, how can we justify the need for grace to unbelievers?[5] And even for believers, the scholastic formulation just does not make sense if one is to be perfectly honest with reason itself.

A related question here is the problem of original sin. Christians believe that original sin is a wound, a mortal wound of man. Now, if human nature is in a natural state, how is it wounded at all? The traditional scholastic explana-

5. We cannot throw dogma and anathemas at them, obviously. It must be from reason that they be convinced.

tion is that man (as his human nature) is deprived of supernatural and preternatural gifts. Now what is gratuitous in the context of Scholasticism is an excess of nature. How then can it be a deficiency, a wound or a lack of perfection?

But the more basic difficulty with regard to the proper explanation of original sin as a wound is the postulate that after the deprivation of original justice and preternatural gifts, human nature, as remainder, is left essentially and integrally intact. For if this were so, it would be hard to prove that there are any scars or wound in it. As a matter of fact, the scholastics would not dare show any deficiency in nature, for this would be to accuse God of creating a nature imperfect. The scholastics are thus caught between the demands of their philosophy and those of their faith.

Since, according to scholastic philosophy, God brings forth natures substantially finished and complete so as to be able to attain their respective ends, he could not very well leave them imperfect and deficient. They must have everything needed to be able to attain their ends. But having made this philosophic assumption, the scholastics are hard pressed to explain how original sin could be a wound of nature, not to speak of its being a mortal wound. The basis of any defect it would seem (and sin is a defect), is unnaturality to nature. But how could the loss of the supernatural, which is what original sin is, be a loss to the natural? How could it be a loss at all, since what is superfluous cannot be said to be a loss. Besides, how can nature feel it to be a loss, since it does not make nature unnatural? But original sin, the scholastics maintain, does not make nature unnatural. How then can it be sin? If nature is natural, then how does it sin? Where is it wounded mortally? If we cannot show this mortal wound in nature, neither can we show the absolute necessity for grace, the precise purpose of which is to heal this wound.

Thus it would seem that once we start with man as in a natural state, we cannot show either the presence of original sin in him or the necessity for grace. It also seems, however, that the whole dilemma could be solved if we started with man in an unnatural state[6] and then showed grace to be his natural state. The loss of grace would then be an unnatural state, and we would call this state original sin. But immediately the objection comes up: How can we possibly call nature unnatural? Experience shows that it is perfect. It has both physical parts: body and soul; metaphysical parts: animality and rationality; and integral parts: faculties and physical members.

Furthermore, to assert that nature is unnatural is to say in the same breath that God is unwise and improvident in creating a nature imperfect. He would be contradicting his very nature. God just could not create a nature in vain. This objection brings us to the root of the scholastic dilemma— the belief in the existence of a cosmological order populated by aristotelian natures. To answer the objection, then, we ultimately have to deny the view that the original state of man was that of an aristotelian nature.[7]

6. We are speaking now, of course, of the human condition *after* original sin, and not of the *original* state of man. For Scholasticism, man's original state was a supernatural state. After original sin, man descended to a natural state, similar to that of pure nature. Our point, however, is that this state after original sin should not be called a natural state but an unnatural state. The implication then is that the original state of grace was a natural state. In losing grace, man descended to an unnatural state and the recovery of grace would be to ascend again to the natural state. This is the semantics we are proposing.

7. We are all agreed that grace is gratuitous, but not all are agreed that its loss leaves man in an unnatural state. For Scholasticism, the remainder is an aristotelian nature. Thus for it, the removal of the concept of gratuity leaves the remainder concept of exigency, for it defines gratuity as that which is over and above justice. The thought process of Scholasticism is to imagine first (logically) a nature ordained to a natural end to which is then added a gratuitous end. Given this formulation of the problem, no doubt, the removal of the gratuitous end leaves nature in a natural state possessed of its natural end towards which it tends. What we

In contrast, we propose the view that the natural state of being is always to be united. In the case of man, his natural state was to be covenanted. This is what it is to be natural. And when we say that this is his natural state, we do not mean it purely in the sense that this was his original equipment, for with this the scholastics would agree. He was created in a state of grace. We go farther, however, in maintaining that from the beginning man was intrinsically ordained to grace. Hence this is his ontological structure. For the scholastics, on the other hand, man's ontological structure is that of an aristotelian nature, and the covenant is not constitutive of it.

Again, we cannot emphasize often enough that to affirm that man's natural state is that of the covenant in the sense that he is intrinsically structured for it is not to affirm that he has an exigency for that end, that grace as the bond of the covenant ceases to be gratuitous and transcendental. The term "natural end" or "natural state" must be understood in the context of the covenant. It is not to be taken in its aristotelian connotation as an end within the powers of

---

have been saying all along, however, is that God's thought process is not aristotelian. He does not start with a nature whose structure is that of exigency and justice to which is then added (logical posteriority) gratuity. Rather, he starts with a creature whose very essence and structure is that of gratuity. The "I" is essentially structured for gratuity, for love. Hence remove gratuity and you are not left with exigency, an aristotelian nature, but a frustrated "I." The "I" separated from the gratuity of love is in an unnatural state. The hellenic mind is not, however, satisfied with this explanation. For he would offer the objection that if the loss of gratuity to the "I" leaves it in an unnatural state, then it would mean that first (logical priority) God created the "I" in an unnatural state, which is to accuse God of deliberately frustrating the creature in the achievement of its end, hence the use of an evil means to achieve a good. But, again, this is to impose on God the aristotelian way of thinking of gratuity. God does not start with the context of justice and then think of gratuity. To think of gratuity, all that is needed is a context of gratuity. If one has to add gratuity on to something before we can think of it or make it a real act, then God could not have created the world gratuitously. Aristotelian logic and process of thought play tricks on us here.

nature to attain and for which nature has an exigency and therefore an end which is nongratuitous.[8] In the context of the covenant, which is a framework of love, the natural end is a necessary condition for gratuity.

Given the covenant as the natural state of man, it follows that the state of separation from the covenant would be unnatural. In this semantic context, the event by which man deliberately broke the covenant is called original sin. The state of separation from the covenant is called the state of original sin. It is an unnatural state. Thus, the original situation was not a dualistic one in which there was a cosmological and a supernatural order. God did not create a natural order but a covenanted universe. This is the natural state of things. Hence to be outside the covenant is to be unnatural.

Let us now try to apply the terms unnatural and natural in the context of the theology of grace to see how the Christian truths about grace and original sin are explained. Let us first try to see how original sin could be a wound, a mortal wound. We said that in the context of the covenant, original sin was separation from the covenant. Now how could this separation be a mortal wound? This is explained by saying that since life or existence for the "I" is union with the "Thou," this very union being grace, the loss of this union is the loss of none other than life or existence, resulting in spiritual death. Thus original sin and any instance of the loss of grace is aptly called mortal, because it results in death. It is like a seed which, if it is outside the ground, is a being-towards-death.

8. Hence we are not espousing the condemned opinion of Baius who, in saying that the integrity found in the first creation was a natural condition, also meant that it was not a gratuitous elevation (see *The Church Teaches*, 378 or *DB*, 1026). In the context of I-Thou, it is possible to use the term "natural" to apply to the original state without thereby implying that it ceases to be a gratuitous state.

We observe, too, that it is the "I" and not nature that is mortally wounded. Hence, original sin and all other sins are of a personal nature. This may be a possible explanation for the Church's teaching that original sin is of a personal nature. The Church teaches too that original sin is internal to man. This would be explained by saying that since the *within* of the "I" is its very life or existence and since this existence is union, the loss of this union touches the very core of being. To be outside this union is to be outside one-self; to be in the covenant is to be within oneself, to possess oneself. Hence the loss of this union is an internal loss. Thus, it is to the "I" that original sin and grace are related.

Nature is the wrong place to go looking for the wound of original sin. Grace as love and original sin as loss of this love would themselves indicate that the logical place to go looking for the wound of original sin is that part of man which can love and hence would logically lose grace. In terms of love, the wound in the "I" caused by original sin would be explained as the loss of the total ability to love. Again, this loss is mortal because without love the life of union cannot be attained. The original dynamism of love, whose natural tendency is to tend towards the "Thou," is now gone astray. It is off the mark, and this is also what sin is, as we have already noted. Not finding its true object, one and the same dynamism of love, that has the power of melting one's heart in God, so to speak, like the sun's rays that both melt and harden, now turns upon the "I" to harden it, burn it and bedevil it. Love has been turned into pride, and from pride as mother are born the bad fruits of all sorts of sins.

Since this fire of love is at the very core of the "I," the "I" suffers in its very depths. The definitive choice of this state is explained as hell. Its eternal fire is the same fire of love which now becomes an everlasting fire of self-hate. To effect union with the "Thou" and thus attain salvation, revelation is needed as the true way to encounter the "Thou." With commitment to, and belief in, the "Thou" comes grace which effects the restoration of the covenant. The new "I" is reborn into the covenant. It is a regeneration, a "new creation," the "new Adam." The dynamism of love is restored to its true direction so that now love flows between the "I" and the "Thou." Grace is aptly associated with charity. From love flow the good fruits of all sorts of good deeds and virtues. Sanctity is the growth in this love, which means greater and greater intimacy with the "Thou" and a resulting transformation into the "Thou," so that now it is the "Thou" that lives in the "I" and not the "I" living for itself.

With regard to grace, the Church also teaches that it is an absolute necessity for man. This is explained by saying that since grace is precisely the bond of union between the "I" and the "Thou," and since this union is the very life of the "I" than which there is nothing more absolute, then grace is of absolute necessity. It is also traditional teaching that grace is not only of absolute necessity but central to man, around which his life revolves, so to speak. But the aristotelian context cannot seem to explain the centrality of grace since it is made peripheral in the sense of being accidental to nature as substance and center.

In the context of the covenant, the centrality of grace is evident since the center of the "I" is the "Thou." The union with the "Thou" is grace. Hence grace is the center of the "I." Grace does not come to the "I" as an accident; it is the "I" that tends to grace as its center and substance. Outside this union, the "I" is unsubstantial. It is like a seed out of the ground, hence unable to bear fruit, and without fruit it is unsubstantial.

Grace as rebirth is the very substance of the "I." Just because grace can be lost and recovered does not make it accidental. For grace is not like the accidents of nature, like weight, for example, that can come and go. In the case of weight, the accident can be lost but the substance remains. But on the level of I-Thou, if the grace of union is lost, the "I" does not remain; it is also lost. It is eschatologically and spiritually dead. The explanation given here about the centrality of grace seems to conform to the biblical view of grace as the "land," "land" meaning fruitfulness (flowing with milk and honey, watered by rivers, etc.), while the absence of grace is like a barren land unwatered by the rivers of grace.

The covenant context also portrays the "I" as dynamic and active rather than passive. It has the obligation to get up and go in search for the "Thou." Man is a wayfarer. The act of faith is not merely an assent to an idea; it is a personal commitment by which the "I" dies to its security in reason; it is like a seed that must trust that in tending towards the ground it does not lose itself but possesses itself; the act of faith is the rebirth of reason. The stress is in action, in leading a good life. In these actions, the "I" dies to its independence, and it is only in giving itself fully that the "I" is reborn.

In the context of process the unbaptized person is explained as one who has not reached his omega which is grace; the baptized is one who has reached it but, in relation to the life of glory, is still in process towards it. Hence in both cases existence is in the subjunctive mood. The attitude is one of hope mingled with fear, for there is uncertainty. The structure of human existence is likewise that of prayer and humility.

To conclude then, we can say that it would seem possible to show the unbeliever the rationality of the doctrine of grace and original sin by using the terms natural and unnatural. Since grace is man's natural state, it is an absolute necessity to attain it if it is lost; it is demanded by nature itself. And original sin being an unnatural state, one is also obliged by nature to get rid of it.

It is also possible to show the absolute and total value of the incarnation-redemption of Christ. Christ came to heal the very core of man's being and restore to us our very life and existence. But in the aristotelian context, where nature is already possessed of essential meaning and existence, the importance of Christ's role is hard to explain. He comes to heal a wound which cannot be located and to bring grace whose need cannot be shown. Hence, one gets the impression that his very presence is superfluous; that on our side he did not have to come, for we are not in that bad need of him. We are not really mortally wounded; as a matter of fact, our natures are essentially perfect.

EVOLUTION AND THE INCARNATION

In the context of process, a given process is named after its term or omega, just as, for example, a seed is called, say, an apple seed, the seedling an apple seedling, and so on. Since the whole evolutionary process tends to Christ as its term or Omega, Teilhard aptly calls it a Christogenesis. But at this point a question of semantics comes up. Is Christogenesis a natural or a supernatural process? The answer depends on what we shall designate the term which is Christ. Is Christ natural to the world or is he supernatural to it? This question is not a quibbling with words but a problem of tremendous importance. For language and terminology determine to a large extent the way we think and act, especially in this instance when the terms we are dealing with sink their roots deep in Western thought and culture. Furthermore, the choice determines the way Christianity is going to be presented to the world. Thus this question directly affects the problem of Christian renewal.

We believe that the choice of the proper term is governed by the following conditions:

1. The term must be able to show the Christian truth that Christ pertains to this world, that he does not come from without, that, in short, he is immanent to this world.

2. In conjunction with the first condition is the necessary implication that the world is in need of Christ as its salvation or savior, hence that the world is defective, lacking in something that is vital to its perfection. This truth must also be shown by the term.

3. The third truth is that while Christ is immanent to this world, he is also transcendent, and so with the whole order of grace. Hence, the term must show the proper transcendence and gratuity of the incarnation and grace.

4. The last condition is that the term must not contradict the modern awareness that the world is important, hence, that the real job is to be found here in the building of the earth and not by a flight from it.

Let us take the term "supernatural" first. With regard to the first condition, Christ and the order of grace as supernatural convey the impression that they are extrinsic to the world, that they come from without and are grafted on to the world as the principal and central reality. With regard to the second condition, the removal of the prefix "super-" from the term "supernatural" leaves a remainder which is natural. But if the world is natural apart from Christ and the order of grace then it is hard to show where it is defective and in vital need of Christ. It is hard to show Christ's place and role in the world. Thus we have the same difficulties here that we encountered in the case of relating grace and original sin to human nature which is in a natural state.

It is for the third condition that the term is adequate for it is able to convey the transcendence and gratuity of grace. In the aristotelian context of nature, to speak of the incarnation as supernatural truth and event and of grace as a supernatural reality is to imply that they are beyond the powers of nature to attain, hence transcendent and gratuitous. It is this aspect of the incarnation and of Christian truths in general that the term "supernatural" is able to safeguard. This is its strong point.

Concerning the last requirement, the term does not respect the modern awareness; if anything, it preaches the opposite. The result is a dichotomy in man that we mentioned in the beginning of our study: on the one hand, the conviction that the world is important, that temporal activity in the building of the earth is our concern and, on the other, the scholastic formulation of our faith which shows that man's ultimate concern is with that which is above nature, the supernatural, attained by a flight from temporality and the world.

The traditional preference for the term "supernatural," while safeguarding the transcendence of Christian truths, has ignored the other aspects of their immanence, pertinence and centrality to the world. The emphasis on the transcendent aspect of Christian truth has led many to identify Christianity with it and as a consequence dissuaded them from embracing it. For this reason, Tillich's whole effort was to present Christianity as an ecstatic naturalism. In our study we have tried to show how Christ and grace are really immanent to the world, but this achievement, if it can be called one, cannot be brought out properly and have any influence on our thinking and activities without the proper terminology. Is there not a terminology that can explain all four? The danger with Tillich's terminology, it would seem, is that it gives the false impression that we are choosing the natural order over the supernatural. On the other hand, the danger with "supernaturalism" is the equally false impression it creates that this world is not important, that we have to leave it to attain the real. What to do?

The continuing discussion among naturalists and super-naturalists takes its point of departure from a common premise—the dualistic world-view. As long as we hold on to this dualism and derive our terminology from it, we are caught in an insoluble dilemma. The whole difficulty is the same as that which we noted in the case of the semantics of grace, namely, the premise that the world without revelation and the incarnation is a natural order. It is the aristotelian view of nature all over again—a world possessed of its essential intelligibility apart from Christ, endowed with natural powers to attain its natural end.

Our contention is that creation, or the whole evolutionary process, is not purely cosmological but soteriological. The incarnation and the whole of Christianity did not come out of the blue and bounce into a cosmological and natural order. Creation itself is already Christian, redemptive, cove-nanted. Hence Christ is of the essence of the universe and therefore the universe cannot be thought of apart from him. To say that the universe apart from Christ is in a natural state is false in two senses of the term: false if by natural is meant that the universe apart from Christ is in its original state, and false if by it is meant a purely cosmological onto-logical structure of the universe. For the original state of the universe is a covenanted one, and its ontological struc-ture is a being-towards-the-Other.

Reality in its essence is covenanted. Hence to think of the universe apart from Christ, the new covenant, is not to think of a natural order. The remainder can only be unnatural. The basic category of reality is a "We," not an "I." To think of the "I" apart from the "Thou" (if it can be done at all) is not to imagine the "I" in its natural state, but in its unnatural state. Individuality does not come first and union later, but the other way around, for only in union is being differentiated. A state of separation for a being intrinsically ordained towards another is an unnatural state. Hence, traditional naturalism, atheistic communism, and all forms of evolutionism and naturalistic humanism are really built on an unnatural foundation.

If now we start with the universe apart from Christ as in an unnatural state, then Christ is the natural end of this evolving universe. Let us examine this terminology in the light of the four requirements mentioned above. With regard to the first requirement, that Christ be shown to pertain to this world, clearly, to say that Christ is natural to the world is to choose a term that cannot be replaced by a better one. By this term we are able to show that he does not come from without, that he is not extrinsic, that he is king of the world not merely from a purely external juridical decree, but that he is organically one with the world, the world being a Christogenesis.

With regard to the second condition, that the world be shown to be in real need of Christ, to speak of the world as unnatural apart from Christ is again to choose a term which, we believe, cannot be replaced by a better one to express the need of the world. For what is a greater need than the need of nature? As we noted in the section on the semantics of grace, if the world were in a natural state, then it is essentially perfect and cannot be shown to be in great need of anything. Only a natural need can compel the world from within its own being to tend to seek that good. And since for a covenanted being the most important natural need is union with the "other," so for the universe separated from Christ, its most important need is Christ.

Christ is its only way, truth, and life as none other than Christ himself said. Thus Christ is shown to be the center and Omega of the universe. It is also possible to show the relevance of Christianity to the world since the incarnation is the focus and center of history. Christ is the fruit of the universe. Without him, the evolutionary process would be barren, all the billions of years of groping and development would be in vain. Christ is also the new covenant of the universe. Without him, a state of separation and death pervades the whole earth.

Concerning the third requirement, that Christ be shown to be transcendent and beyond the powers of nature to attain, here is where traditionalists offer the strongest disagreement. For it would seem that in making Christ natural to the world, we have endangered the transcendent and gratuitous aspect of his emergence. We hope, however, that this objection has been sufficiently answered. In the I-Thou context, with Christ as the "Thou," the natural end of the "I" is not something within the powers of the "I" to attain alone. In the context of love, the "Thou" gives of himself freely. Again, we repeat that the universe is not an aristotelian nature with Christ as its natural end, but an "I" whose end is the "Thou."

Concerning the last condition, with Christ as the natural end of the world, there is no need to go outside this world to seek for salvation. Where before the Christian dialectic, as formulated by Scholasticism, was from the natural to the supernatural, now it is from the unnatural to the natural. Where before one is reborn from the natural order to a supernatural order by baptism and belief, now it is from the unnatural to the natural state, since grace and the whole Christian economy are the natural state of the world.

The difficulty with the scholastic terminology is the false impression it gives that we are abandoning what is perfectly good, because natural, for the supernatural. In the new terminology, we do not abandon any good. What is abandoned is an unnatural state, an evil. Hence, there is no tension created in man between his allegiance to this world and his so-called allegiance to another world.[9] Our allegiance is to this world only. This does not mean that there is no transcendence, that Christianity is not a transcendent religion or that there is no rebirth, for the transition from the unnatural state to the natural state of grace and union with Christ is a transcendence. The "I" is outside itself, hence it leaves this unnatural state of separation from itself, dies to this state in order to be reborn into another "world" —the way a foetus is born from one world, the womb, into the true world outside.

In the aristotelian context, to remove the supernatural order and leave the natural order alone is to leave no possibility for transcendence. But in the covenant context, the supernatural order has now become the natural state and the so-called natural order is the unnatural state.[10] Hence the dialectic from one level to another is preserved, except that now we do not have two distinct orders requiring that we leave this world to go into another. The dialectic takes place within this world, from the unnatural state to the natural.

Christianity is true naturalism. Fears we may have about this term proceed from a deep manichean strain inherited

9. The Scriptures speak of "world" in at least three senses. The first refers to material creation itself; the second has a bad connotation as referring to what is unnatural—the world of sin, sensuality, pride, deceit, etc.; the third refers to an "other" world, a place where one is reborn and lives the life of grace and union with God. Now Scholasticism, true to its dualism of two orders, has literally taken the "other" world as outside this world. Hence the injunction in Scripture to flee this world is taken literally to mean a withdrawal from this world. But one has to understand the semantics of Scripture in the context of the covenant. Thus the "other" world is the world of union, the life within the covenant; the "world," in the bad and sinful sense, is the state outside the covenant, a state of separation, hence of sin. But the covenant is here with us in this world. Hence, we do not flee this world into some beyond. Thus it is a mistake to interpret the scriptural expression naively in the physical and literal sense of the term.

10. We are not introducing a dualism here in another form because the unnatural state is not an order, that is, an autonomous, self-intelligible entity. It is a being-towards-death, while an order is based on the possession of existence and truth.

from Greek thought that identifies the material and sensible with sin, the ungodly, and the unspiritual. But the material world is sacred, spiritual and divine because it leads to Christ-Omega. It is a Christogenesis. Christ is natural to the world and so is the Church and the Christian. The complaint of Cardinal Döpfner that the Church has isolated itself from the world may be true, and if so, the Church has a great task to renew itself since without the Church the world is in an unnatural state.

The complaint of Teilhard that Christians give the wrong impression to others of being indifferent about the world, merely lending themselves to earthly tasks, can only proceed from a false formulation and understanding of Christianity, for the truth is that the world is a Christogenesis. Hence the Christian does not have to go outside time to find Christ. His so-called natural tasks are intrinsically redemptive and are not made salvific only by an intention.[11]

The ultimate stumbling block to renewal, to making Christ and Christianity immanent in the world is the aristotelian postulate of a cosmological order distinct from the supernatural order. Hence, ultimately, Christian renewal is philo-

11. It is the aristotelian notion of nature that has prevented us from understanding Paul's terminology when he tells us to leave the life of nature (Rom 8:12-13) for the life of the spirit (Rom 8:5,8), the natural self (Rom 7:5,18) for spirit of adoption (Rom 8:15), the way of flesh and blood (Rom 8:4) for the way of the spirit (Rom 8:4), natural wisdom (Rom 8:6-7) and thoughts (1 Cor 3:1) for the wisdom of the spirit (1 Cor 2:11-14) and spiritual thought (Rom 8:6-7, 1 Cor 3:1). Thus in the aristotelian-thomistic context all this is interpreted to mean leaving the present world for a world beyond, for the world is profane, unspiritual, the region of sin, etc. But Paul's use of the term "natural" is synonymous with original, not with cosmological. Hence, the original state of man prior to grace he calls "natural" for he describes this "natural" state as one doomed to death (Rom 7:25), the "natural self" as in a state of separation from God (Rom 7:4,25), as a sinful principle (Rom 7:18, 8:2), a state of slavery (Rom 8:15). The subsequent state of grace he calls a spiritual state (Rom 8:5,8), a state of adoption (Rom 8:15)

sophic renewal. We need the philosophical outlook of a covenanted universe and of reality in process.

---

whose spiritual principle of life has set us free from the principle of sin and death (Rom 8:2). Thus the "natural state" for Paul is an unnatural state and does not correspond to a state of pure nature or to a cosmological order. In terms of modern categories, in which "natural" does not mean so much original as present reality itself, we should translate Paul's terminology so that the "natural" state of original sin is really an unnatural state, and the state of grace the natural state.

Conclusion

By way of a conclusion we may observe that we have dared to enter areas of thought "where angels fear to tread." If we have made errors they can be due only to rashness and ignorance. And if we have left many questions within the area of our study unanswered, it is because we have dared enough already, and too, because of the awareness on our part of our incompetence in these matters.

It is not only within the area of this study that many questions have been left unanswered, but also in related areas. Thus, if we go outside the context of our study, we realize that the thesis we proposed, that there is only one order, the Christian natural order, raises more questions whose answers lie beyond the scope of this study. But it may be helpful to mention some of them in order to show the profound and very broad implications of the elimination of the aristotelian notion of a natural order.[1]

First, if there is no longer any supernatural order alongside the natural, then what happens to the traditional distinctions between science, philosophy and religion? What happens to the distinction between sacred and profane sciences? It would seem that there is no longer any basis for it since all knowledge is redemptive and all reality is sacred. Hence there is need to rethink and perhaps renew our understanding of each of the disciplines and their interrelations.

1. When we speak here of the "natural order" we use it in the traditional sense to avoid confusion, although this term should really be reserved for the Christian natural order. For the latter, we shall refer to it as the Christian order simply, or as a Christogenesis.

326

With regard to science, it would seem that it is not a mere body of natural knowledge for, as Teilhard notes, science leads to adoration. Scientific work, it would seem, has a redemptive dimension. It would seem, too, that a deepening of our scientific knowledge does not contradict our faith but leads to it, and that the ultimate mysteries of science are locked up in Christ-Omega.

In philosophy, the distinction between knowledge by reason and knowledge by faith seems to need re-examination if there is no other sphere of operation for reason except the Christian universe. It would seem, too, that there is no such thing as natural reason, but only reason which is intrinsically ordered to a Christian universe. If there is no natural order but only a Christian order, is there a natural knowledge of God? Is natural theology possible? Or is not the so-called natural knowledge of God already possessed of a Christian dimension, but short of full salvific value?[2] Can one attain to an intelligibility of the universe apart from Christ and faith? Thus the position of rationalism, naturalism, and even of Thomism is brought into question.

If there is no natural order but only a Christogenesis, what is the role of philosophy? What should it be doing? If man is intrinsically Christian, then is there an ethics as distinguished from Christian morality? Is there a natural law based on a human nature that is not intrinsically ordained to Christ, possessing essential intelligibility and moral laws apart from Christ? Or is not the law of man's being ultimately Christian? Is not the so-called natural law derived from the actual universe (and not from a pure order of nature) already possessed of a Christian dimension, but not the full dimension of Christian morality derived from

2. This so-called natural knowledge is really derived from the actual universe, not from a purely cosmological universe, so that it is possessed of a Christian dimension.

the Scriptures? Since the world is a Christogenesis, it would seem also that there is no cosmology based on a natural order. And how valid is the distinction between God as creator and God as redeemer when creation is a redemption and redemption is a creation—when, ultimately, there is no natural order as distinct from a supernatural order? This question brings us to the theological discipline.

What then is theology? What is its method? What is the nature of faith and revelation? Is it a knowledge of the supernatural order, or is it about this world? Should not Christology be also a Christogenesis? And what is the meaning of redemption if it is no longer understood as a flight from the natural to the supernatural? It would seem that it is an immersion and participation in Christian time in order to attain the *pleroma Christi*. And if the Church is no longer in the supernatural order but is in the order of a Christogenesis, where is the Church located in the process? What is its redemptive role?

It would seem that the Church is at the omega point of the process in relation to the world. Its role is to draw the world to the omega point. To do this, we have to know the world, not isolate ourselves from it. The Church is the *within* of the world, hence the world belongs to it and it belongs to the world. To accomplish the redemption of the world, we bring the world into contact with Christian time (liturgical time) by belief in Christ and the use of the sacraments. Through our liturgical life, we dispense Christian time which is salvific. For it is only through a participation in Christian time that the world matures into the fullness of Christ. What is the role of the layman in the world? What is the relation between Church and State if the dualistic premise is removed?

These are some of the questions that arise from the elimination of two orders. They are so formidable and overwhelming that sometimes one gets the feeling that it would have been better to stick to the old ways of thought and traditional formulations rather than to have dared to question them at all. But it would seem, too, that their re-examination is the soil from which the vision of the Scriptures, freshly formulated by Teilhard and so vital to a unified and concerted human effort towards the Omega, is to be reborn, namely, that all reality is the fashioning of an offering. This offering is no other than Christ.

This offering is the everlasting seal and bond by which reality restores the covenant broken by man's sin and concludes once and for all the first covenant made at creation. All reality cooperated through billions of years of groping, pain, suffering and toil to fashion that immaculate and spotless sacrifice. So, in a true sense, reality is a liturgy. It is the Mass. It is a procession, a wedding procession in which we follow Christ; it is a baptism in which we die to sin and evil; it is a creation where, participating in Christian time, we are transformed into the "new man" in Christ. All reality is participating in and moving towards a rebirth, towards a new earth, a "new creation"!

Index

act and potency, dynamism of, 129-39, 220-21, 225
Alfaro, Juan, 51, 62, 300
Alexander, Samuel, 103
alpha, 148, 167, 192, 203-04, 276
Anselm, St., 165
Aristotle, 40-42, 79, 103, 151, 168, 200, 309; logic of, 190-92; teleology in, 168; "universals" of, 41, 80, 159, 169
Augustine, St., 39, 41, 157, 165, 223, 263

Baius, M., 44-45
Balthasar, Hans Urs von, 51
Baptism, 206, 284-86, 329; creation as, 284-86; incarnation as, 284-85
Barth, Karl, 250
being, as covenanted, 127-28; being-and-its-ground, 125, 132, 137-38, 225; being-as-object, 216-19; being-as-subject, 216, 227-29; being-towards-death, 144, 313, 323n; being-towards-life, 125; being-towards-the-other, 125, 241, 257, 284; being-with-another, 125, 131-32, 140, 241; being as a "we," 137
Berdyaev, Nicholas, 266, 308
Bergson, Henri, 159
beta, 203-04
"between," 132 (see "we")
biblical metaphysics, 288
biblical view: dynamism of being, 138-39; existence,

127-29; "future," 50; knowledge, 185-87; process, 121n
biblical typology, 196-97, 247
biogenesis, 25
birth, analysis of, 113-15, 121n
Blondel, Maurice, 16-17, 46
Bonhoeffer, Dietrich, 157
Bonnefoy, Jean-François, O.F.M., 293
Bruch, Richard, 46, 59
Buber, Martin, 227, 250
Burnaby, John, 223

Cephalization, law of, 25, 206
Chauchard, P., 7n, 30
Christ as Alpha, 167; as Center, 8, 17, 26, 46, 66, 283, 291, 321; as fulness of time, 153; as natural end, 321, 324; as Truth, 176-77, 283; as the Word, 206; cosmic, 268; lordship of, 37, 63, 300
Christ-Omega, 6, 8, 25-28, 52, 93, 96, 100-02, 167, 189, 206-07, 267, 289, 300, 317, 321, 324, 327
Christianity as true naturalism, 323
communism, 17-18, 22, 70-71, 168, 321
complexity-consciousness, law of, 23-24
concept, 190-91, 205n, 208-09
Congar, Yves, 21
conversion, meaning of, 105n
Corte, Nicolas, 124, 288
cosmogenesis, 24-25
covenant, 127-28, 250-54, 257-

331

359